'THE FRAGILITY OF HER SEX'?

CW00952563

'The Fragility of Her Sex'?

Medieval Irishwomen
in Their European Context

Christine Meek
& Katharine Simms
EDITORS

FOUR COURTS PRESS

Set in 10.5 on 12.5 Stempel Garamond for
FOUR COURTS PRESS
Kill Lane, Blackrock, Co. Dublin
and in North America
FOUR COURTS PRESS
c/o N.E. Hassalo Street, Portland, OR 97213.

A catalogue record for this title
is available from the British Library.

ISBN 1-85182-172-4 cased
1-85182-206-2 pbk

This book is printed on an acid-free and a wood-free paper.

Printed in Great Britain
by Redwood Books, Trowbridge, Wiltshire.

Contents

Introduction

Christine E. Meek & Katharine Simms

On 4 December 1993 the editors of the present volume organised a conference in Trinity College Dublin under the auspices of the Irish Association for Research in Women's History, and we would like at this point to express our gratitude towards the Faculty of Arts (Humanities) for a generous grant towards the cost of organising the conference, and to the Grace Lawless Lee Fund for a further grant in aid of publication. At that time we had a twofold purpose, which has also been reflected in this resulting collection of essays. On the one hand there was a desire to break away from a perceived tendency to discuss medieval woman predominantly in her biological role as wife and mother, and to direct attention instead towards the wealth, power and literary creativity possessed by some women in the Middle Ages. More fundamental was a need to shake off the image of isolation and idiosyncrasy that clings to many aspects of medieval Irish society, and particularly to the subjects of women and marriage. We felt that the position of Irish women in the Middle Ages was discussed too much in isolation from the situation in other countries and wanted to begin to remedy this by setting the experience of Irish women in a European context. Some of the essays included in this volume were first given as papers at the conference; others are by scholars who attended the conference and were stimulated by the papers they heard and the ensuing discussion to take up once more work they had done in the past and prepare it for publication. Other papers were commissioned by the editors from contributors we knew had worked in relevant fields and could provide material that would illuminate the position of women in the Middle Ages.

As we sought additional papers, and prepared the material for publication, new themes began to emerge, especially the nature and limitations of sources for the history of women in the Middle Ages, predominantly written from a male, and even clerical perspective, and the question of the extent to which women were able in practice to take the initiative and make their wishes and opinions felt. The phrase 'the fragility of her sex' in our title derives from Roman Law as codified under Justinian, which speaks not merely of the fragility, but also the imbecility, irresponsibility and ignorance, of the female sex. This may sound merely contemptuous of women, but in fact had both negative and positive connotations. The

concept of the physical, mental and moral weakness of women might lead
to them being excluded from any kind of role in public life, being pre-
vented from acting as guarantor or pleading in court even on behalf of
their husbands and being placed under the guardianship of a male relative,
but it also provided them with a measure of protection. Roman women
could not be held liable for their husband's debts and there were other
measures that protected their economic and financial interests. Some of
the most specific references to the fragility or infirmity of the female sex
are in the context of excusing women from obligations or protecting their
interests. Women could be allowed to plead ignorance of the law and
were offered protection against men who deceived them into marriages
which were in fact invalid 'because of the fragility of their sex'.[1]

Something of this dual significance of the phrase 'the fragility of her
sex' survived in medieval Europe, at least in those parts of Europe that
came under the influence of Roman law. Despite the misogyny of many
Christian writers, who represented women as the daughters of Eve, a secondary creation intended as a companion to Adam, but the first to yield
to temptation and bring about the fall of man, and characterised subsequently as vain, extravagant, loquacious and a prey to their emotions, the
phrase 'the fragility of her sex' is still found in its dual sense of a physical,
mental and moral weakness which rendered women unfit for public
affairs or legal business, but could also provide them with special protection or even allow them to escape the consequences of their actions. Thus
a wife who stated that she did not know the whereabouts of her absent
husband was allowed to appoint proctors to claim on his property, lest
her fragile sex be forced to suffer want or loss,[2] while a widow who had
been named among the executors of one of her late husband's kinsmen
was able to excuse herself from much tedious business on the grounds of
the fragility of her sex.[3] Bertrande de Rols was able to escape any judicial
consequences for having so easily accepted the imposter Arnaud du Tilh
as her missing husband Martin Guerre, 'because of the weakness of her
sex, easily deceived by the cunning and craftiness of men', while Arnaud
himself was executed.[4]

The phrase 'the fragility of her sex' reflects, of course, the views of
men of the Middle Ages on the role and position of women, views not
always borne out by their encounters with the opposite sex in real life. As
Eileen Power observed many years ago, 'it is a poetic justice that a man,

1   *Digest* XXII, vi, 9; *Codex* V, iii, 20.1. Also *Digest* XVI, 1, 2 and XLIX, xiv, 18.
2   Lucca, Archivio Arcivescovile, Libri Antichi 51, ff. 53r–53v, 10 Dec. 1416.
3   Lucca, Archivio di Stato, Testamenti 3, ff. 99r–100r, 18 Aug. 1348.
4   Davis, *The Return of Martin Guerre*, 109–11.

whose ideal wife was a Patient Griselda, should find himself not infrequently married to a Wife of Bath'.[5] Were women really so fragile, so much in need of protection, so passive, so incapable of acting for themselves? The interrogation mark in our title hints that they were not and this theme is taken up specifically in some of the essays making up this book, notably the case studies of particular women by Cormac Ó Cléirigh and Elizabeth McKenna, and Bernadette Williams's discussion of women portrayed by Marie de France.

However the thrust of the first chapter, a comparison by Bart Jaski of early Irish marriage laws with those on the continent, takes us in the opposite direction, by tending to moderate somewhat exaggerated views expressed at times in the past on the legal independence enjoyed by early medieval Irishwomen. In the late nineteenth and early twentieth centuries scholarly interest in medieval women's studies was unusually advanced in Ireland. The Anglo-Irish literary revival had directed attention towards the many strong-minded heroines of Old, Middle and Early Modern Irish sagas, and it has recently been shown that its romantic perceptions of figures such as Maeve, Deirdre and Gráinne provided role models for female political activists in that revolutionary age.[6] More importantly, the publication between 1865 and 1901 of the extensive corpus of Old Irish lawtracts in text and translation documented in extraordinary detail a barbarian society's customary law in relation to marriage, concubinage, polygyny, divorce, disputed paternity, sexual harassment, rape, seduction, abduction, women's entitlements to land, stock and the profits of labour, their rights and responsibilities in relation to their children's education and much more, inspiring in 1905 Henri D'Arbois de Jubainville's *La famille celtique* and in 1936 the publication of *Studies in Early Irish Law*, collected papers on Old and Middle Irish legal texts relating to women arising from a seminar organised by the great Rudolf Thurneysen. At that time the provisions found therein for polygyny and divorce within the framework of a Christian society were considered peculiarly Irish, and until recently that view continued to shape discussion of medieval Irishwomen within Ireland itself, although as the twentieth century progressed, more detailed studies of barbarian societies elsewhere in Europe were producing some striking parallels. Nowadays the Old Irish law tracts are perceived as a sophisticated adaptation and codification of customary law by seventh and eighth-century clerical scholars, and Donnchadh Ó Corráin has shown how the marriage law they contain is

---

5 Power, *Medieval Women*, 11.
6 Sawyer, *'We are but Women'*, 1–8, 43, 55, 80, 87.

indebted both to early canon law[7] and to Roman civil law.[8] Modern reassessments of barbarian law codes from the rest of western Europe have shown that they too were strongly influenced by Roman civil law and ecclesiastical doctrine, particularly in their legislation on marriage, and Bart Jaski's article now brings out the many parallels between the eighth-century Irish legislation on marriage and the more extensively discussed practice of early medieval Europe in general.

While early Ireland was better provided than many contemporary societies with legislation on marriage and women's property rights, it used to be considered unusually devoid of women scholars – of learned nuns to compare with Hrotswitha or Hildegard of Bingen. However, Thomas Clancy's article in the present volume combines the scanty but positive assertions of Irish scribes and annalists as to the existence of individual women poets in the early period, with the criteria suggested by Janet Nelson and other modern scholars to establish the probability of female authorship in the case of certain anonymous early medieval texts produced among the Franks and Anglo-Saxons. Pointing to the undoubted existence of honoured women poets in the related society of Gaelic-speaking Scotland from the sixteenth to the nineteenth centuries, Clancy makes a cautious, carefully substantiated case for arguing that in the case of a number of well-known and admired early Irish literary creations, including the 'Lament of the Hag of Beare' and 'St Ite's fosterling', 'female authorship should be an initial assumption, although not a proven one', while there are other anonymous love-poems and laments set in the mouth of a female speaker, for which female authorship is a real possibility, no longer to be automatically excluded as was the practice of Celtic scholars hitherto.

One of the symptoms suggesting female authorship in the case of an anonymous text was the presence of a distinctively female viewpoint. In an interesting and thought-provoking study Bernadette Williams takes up the themes of marriage and love in the *Lais* of Marie de France. The undoubted work of a woman writer very conscious of her role, the *Lais* were written in the second half of the twelfth century at a time when the church was increasingly stressing the necessity for the consent of both parties in marriage formation, while in practice marriages were a matter of arrangement by the king, the feudal lord or the spouses' parents, especially in the case of the bride. Bernadette Williams argues that, although they are set in an undefined earlier period, the *Lais* reflect the realities of

---

7 Ó Corráin, 'Marriage in Early Ireland', 1–24
8 Ó Corráin, 'Women and the Law in Early Ireland', 45–57.

marriage in the twelfth century and that they present these realities particularly from the woman's point of view.

The heroines of these tales can find themselves married to a man they have barely met and who might be much older or can find themselves parted from a man they are attached to and with whom they have exchanged vows in order to be married to a stranger. At best marriage involves removal to an unfamiliar environment, surrounded by people whose loyalties are to the husband. At worst the husband may already be involved with a concubine or keep his wife a virtual prisoner in order to be assured of her fidelity.

Some of Marie de France's heroines are submissive, but others are more enterprising and audacious. Several take lovers, either as single women or when already married and in some cases these liaisons are treated sympathetically. While Marie de France condemns women who betray the trust of a good or loving husband, wives who take lovers after being imprisoned or ill-treated by husbands who were imposed upon them are viewed more sympathetically and in a few cases are allowed to find happiness in the love they have freely chosen.

A much less sympathetic view of women was taken by the thirteenth-century exempla, or collections of illustrative anecdotes introduced to underline a moral lesson in Dominican and Franciscan sermons. Grace Neville points to the discussion by Georges Duby and others of the situation in which a celibate cleric harangued a mixed congregation, but addressed his message above all to the males in the audience, attempting to win over the husbands to his essentially clerical view of woman as an alien temptress, a treacherous occasion of sin, Satan's helper, even an incarnation of Satan himself, who must be kept under male control by constant vigilance. She demonstrates the working of this one-sided approach in a wryly comic exemplum of the thirteenth-century French friar Jacques de Vitry, which is found retold in an Irish bardic poem from the early modern period edited in O'Rahilly's collection of *Dánta Grádha*. Significantly, although the anecdote in question, about a hypocritical and tight-fisted widow-to-be, refusing the price of a full-length shroud as her husband lay dying, was widespread and popular in medieval Europe, and although many other thirteenth-century exempla were known and utilised by the medieval bardic poets, this particular misogynistic tale does not appear in Irish literature until the Counter-Reformation period, when a spate of moralistic poems were composed in the bardic metres by Observantine Franciscans at the Irish College in Louvain, and other learned clerics of the late sixteenth and early seventeenth centuries. Although the style and incidental details in the bardic retelling of the anecdote are 'quintessentially Irish', Neville argues that in its underlying attitudes the text 'looks outwards towards the wider horizons of continental literature such as the exempla in its representation of women'. It is also noteworthy, perhaps, that manuscript copies indicate the Irish version continued to be popular among (male) scribes well into the nineteenth century.[9]

In his article 'The Absentee Landlady and the Sturdy Robbers' Cormac Ó Cléirigh concentrates on a single case study which bridges the gap between Ireland and the wider world, that of Agnes de Valence and her attempts to hang on to and exploit the widow's dower of a third of the FitzGerald estates in Co. Kildare and life interest in the whole of the FitzGerald Limerick lands, which she had been guaranteed in the marriage settlement when she married her first husband Maurice FitzMaurice in 1266. She is a striking example of the consequences of the English dower system, under which even a brief childless marriage gave a widow the right to hold a proportion of her late husband's estates for life at the expense of his heirs, whom as in Agnes's case she could keep out of what amounted to nearly half the properties of the Geraldines of Offaly for forty and more years. That she had only a life interest in these properties is reflected in the fact that rumours or claims that she had died were used on two occasions to justify seizing her lands.

As Cormac Ó Cléirigh makes clear, Agnes was herself a European aristocrat with powerful connections. Her father William de Valence was one of the Poitevin half-brothers of the English king Henry III, and she married in turn the FitzGerald baron of Offaly, the Scottish magnate Hugh de Balliol and John d'Avesnes, lord of Beaumont, a member of the comital family of Hainault. She thus had property and interests in these areas as well as in Ireland, and was herself a capable, determined and ruthless woman, ready to exploit her legal rights and royal connections to the full. It is worth noting that other female claimants to the FitzGerald lands, Juliana de Cogan and Amabilia, played much more passive roles.

At first Agnes had little difficulty in maintaining control of these lands with the help of her father, who had obtained the wardship of the heir, Gerald FitzMaurice, but in 1283 Gerald tried to recover the Limerick properties and after his death in 1287 she had to face John FitzThomas, the only surviving male claimant, a ruthless and ambitious man, determined to regain the FitzGerald patrimony. The ensuing property disputes, acts of violence, claims for damages and compensation,

9   In the Library of Dublin's Royal Irish Academy alone, apart from the version in the seventeenth-century Munster manuscript no. 5 (23/D/4), p. 52 which probably formed the basis of O'Rahilly's edition, versions of *Mairg doní cumann le mnáibh* are found in MSS 37/214; 126/137; 257/136; 305/147; 316/159; 579/142 (68) col. 2; 672/118; 751/62; 888/8; 908/103; 925/34; 962/17.

efforts to collect debts and get legal judgements put into effect in the face of resistance and the use of local influence were subsumed into the rivalries and disorders of Ireland in the late thirteenth and early fourteenth centuries. In the face of increasing pressure by the Irish from the 1290s onwards Agnes's claims were not a top priority for the English government in Ireland, but she pursued these claims with vigour and some success, demonstrating that a woman of the nobility with a strong character and the right connections could be, in Cormac Ó Cléirigh's phrase, a player rather than a pawn in the world of property and influence. No 'fragility of her sex' in this case.

In an article that builds on and extends her own recent works *English noblewomen in the later middle ages* and *Women of the English nobility and gentry* 1066–1500, Jennifer Ward attempts to explore the realities of family relationships that lie behind documents whose primary concern is land, wealth and business matters. Marriages were arranged and were rooted in property, but this did not preclude affection between husband and wife. Using letters, wills and household accounts as well as the more formal legal documents, Jennifer Ward is able to discuss relationships within the nuclear family, including children, step-children and grandparents as well as husband and wife. Although people in the Middle Ages are rarely found expressing their feelings, and although husband and wife were often apart, she is able to demonstrate that some women could work in close partnership with their husbands and be friends and companions as well as wives. Affection and concern for the husband's welfare could be expressed in correspondence and some married couples travelled together, wives joining their husbands even in war zones, although there are also cases of unhappy marriages. Some women were able to make their own choice of husband; there are examples of girls making runaway matches and widows in particular sometimes chose to please themselves when they remarried.

Similar documents show a variety of relationships between women and their children. The practice of educating children of both sexes away from home meant that their mothers would often see little of them after the first few years, but the basic assumption was of affection between mother and children and concern on her part for their well being and advancement, although her ideas about their future might not always coincide with theirs. A widow's right to dower or jointure was certainly disadvantageous to the heir and could be a source of tension, but widowed mothers sometimes provided land or funds for their children or were active in promoting marriage alliances for them. Evidence of the relationship of women with their own family also varies. There might be visits, bequests and appointments as executor, but there could also be resentments over property and inheritances. Women, especially heiresses who were the last of their own line, might be conscious of their ancestry and their role as a link between the family into which they were born and that into which they married. The paper demonstrates that the surface formality of much of the evidence conceals a great variety of family relationships and attitudes and that the reality of medieval women's relationships with their husbands, children or kinsmen can occasionally be glimpsed.

In her article 'Women, dowries and the family in late medieval Italian cities'. Christine Meek summarises the conclusions of much recent research on the property rights of women in a society where the importance of families based on patrilineal descent left women in an ambiguous position. The system of provision for women in late medieval Italy was markedly different from that of England and arguably shows similarities at some points with early Ireland. Until the twelfth and thirteenth centuries women in Italy had enjoyed the right to a certain proportion of their husband's property, especially as widows, but in the later Middle Ages the economic position of upper class women came to depend more and more on the dowry paid by their own family at the time of their marriage. Women might have no other claims on the family patrimony, but the sums provided as a dowry were high and tended to increase over time and women's rights were protected even to the extent of permitting legal proceedings against insolvent husbands for the immediate restitution of the dowry. On the death of her husband the dowry was repayable to the widow, giving her legal control of substantial sums of money and some say in her own future, though she was likely to come under conflicting pressures from her own family, her late husband's relatives and heirs and his own posthumous wishes as expressed in his will. While the law with regard to dowries and women's property rights was similar in different north Italian cities, with some local variations, recent research has shown that actual practice could differ considerably. In particular artisan and peasant women, while receiving a dowry on marriage that was repayable to them on widowhood, were also likely to receive contributions from their husbands and even to be named as his heir and guardian of any children. Considerations of lineage apparently weighed less and the marriage bond was more important at a social and economic level at which the contributions of both husband and wife were needed to support the household and a widow would need all the resources that could be mustered to keep it going after her husband's death. These variations of practice within the same legal dispositions are illuminating in themselves and point the way for future research.

Returning to Ireland, Mary McAuliffe depicts for us the day-to-day

life of the Anglo-Irish and indeed Gaelic Irish noblewomen who occupied the numerous tower-houses or fortified residences here between the
fifteenth and early seventeenth-centuries. Not only were they called upon
to exercise authority over a staff of indoor and outdoor servants, to manage the domestic economy and furnish hospitality to companies of guests,
but in that turbulent age some ladies were themselves warlike, and might
lead troops into battle, or have to defend the tower against a siege in their
husbands' absence. Some wives or daughters of chieftains can be shown
to have commissioned the building of tower-houses on their own
account.

Just as Gerald Mór and Gerald Óg FitzGerald, the eighth and ninth
earls of Kildare, were arguably the most powerful men in medieval
Ireland so the two sisters of the ninth earl, Margaret Butler and Eleanor
MacCarthy, were surely among the most powerful of medieval
Irishwomen. Politically arranged marriages were the norm for women of
their class, and they were no exception, but Elizabeth McKenna shows
that such marriages, though seen by the heroines of Marie de France's
Lais as a form of imprisonment, 'could be used to allow women of spirit
and intelligence the opportunity of becoming involved in official political
affairs'. Margaret in the intervals of bearing her husband, Piers Ruadh
Butler, six daughters and three sons found time to civilise his territory and
intrigue on behalf of the Butler family against her own FitzGerald kindred. Still more impressive was the career of her sister Eleanor, whose
marriage settlement with her first husband Domhnall MacCarthaigh
Riabhach entitled her to half the revenues of MacCarthaigh's lordship,
while her second marriage to Maghnus Ó Domhnaill, lord of Tír Conaill,
was only concluded on the understanding that he would support the
cause of her young nephew, Gerald eleventh earl of Kildare, in the
Geraldine league which she was largely responsible for forming against
King Henry VIII. When Ó Domhnaill failed to measure up to her political requirements, she abandoned him and returned to her own lands.
McKenna emphasizes that though Margaret and Eleanor were particularly prominent, they were only two of a number of politically active
women in England, Scotland and Ireland whose names are found recur-
ring in the sixteenth century state papers. Reverting to Cormac Ó
Cléirigh's memorable phrase, these women were not fragile pawns, but
players in the plots and politics of the ruling élite.

Marriage Laws in Ireland and on the Continent in the Early Middle Ages

Bart Jaski

§1: INTRODUCTION

In 1074 Lanfranc, archbishop of Canterbury, wrote a letter to Toirdel-bach ua Briain, the most powerful Irish king at that time, complaining about the loose marriage customs in Ireland:

> In your kingdom a man abandons at his own discretion and with-out any grounds in canon law the wife who is lawfully married to him, not hesitating to form a criminal alliance – by the law of mar-riage or rather by the law of fornication – with any other woman he pleases, either a relative of his own or his deserted wife or a woman whom somebody else has abandoned in an equally dis-graceful way.[1]

His successor in the archbishopric of Canterbury, Anselm, wrote a simi-lar list of complaints to Toirdelbach's son and successor Muirchertach, stating that 'it is said that men exchange wives freely and publicly, just as one exchanges a horse for another'.[2] Lanfranc and Anselm were not alone in condemning the Irish marriage customs, and with the increasing Anglo-Norman interest in Ireland in the twelfth century, both ecclesias-tical and political, more voices joined the chorus of disapproval.[3] Notwithstanding the reform of the Irish ecclesiastical organisation in that period which drew the Irish closer to their Christian brothers on the con-tinent, Irish marriage customs were insufficiently tackled and continued to give its people and their Christian faith a dubious reputation. Among other things, this formed an ideal pretext for extensive Anglo-Norman

---

1 Glover and Gibson, *The letters of Lanfranc*, 71 (no. 10). See also Lanfranc's letter to king Guthric of Dublin, in ibid., 69 (no. 9). For the new rules on marriage, etc., see ibid., 77 (no. 11: Council of London, 1074/5, vi).
2 See Bartlett, *Gerald of Wales*, 43–4.
3 For more examples, see ibid., 43–5.

political intervention, which had already received the stamp of approval from the pope.[4]

It may seem strange that in Ireland, once the torchbearer of Christianity in Europe, such practices as described above were still thriving and condoned. Obviously, Lanfranc and Anselm considered the Irish customs to be out of line with the current teachings of the Church, and it raises the question as to why the Irish had deviated from the norm. To answer this we have to turn to the Irish marriage laws, and discuss whether they are basically a legacy from pre-Christian times, or whether clerical scribes made important contributions to their provisions.[5]

For an appreciation of the degree to which the Irish marriage laws adopted or neglected Christian regulations, we have to compare them with the marriage laws of the rest of Christian Europe at the time they were written down. The majority of the extant Irish law-tracts are usually dated to the eighth century, although certain passages and rules may go back to an earlier date. Prior to this period we do not have any securely datable texts which allow us to trace the developments which led to the final shape of the Irish marriage laws with certainty, and this makes it difficult to determine the Christian influence on these laws, the more so because the material at hand lends itself to different interpretations.

§2: THE LEGAL POSITION OF WOMEN IN SOCIETY

Like Roman and Germanic society, early Irish society was patriarchal, which means that women were ultimately subject to men as regards their social status and their legal rights and protection.[6] As the Irish laws seem to give women a remarkable degree of liberty in matters such as divorce, some historians have connected the position of women as reflected in the laws and in saga-literature with a supposed free and independent position of women among the Celts.[7] However, it is perfectly clear from the legal material that a woman was generally dependent on a man: on her husband or the head of the family (her father, brother, uncle, son, or another close

---

4 For a discussion, see Martin, 'Ireland in the time of St Bernard', especially 12–15.
5 For an earlier discussion of this subject, see Ó Corráin, 'Marriage', who suggests a strong Christian influence in the Irish marriage laws. See also his 'Irish law and canon law', 157–61, and note the different interpretation offered by Mac Niocaill, 'Christian influences'.
6 Ó Corráin, 'Women', 1.
7 Ibid., 1–2, and Kelly, *Guide*, 68–9, for examples. For a general discussion, see Davies, 'Celtic women'. For women in saga-literature, see O'Leary, 'The honour'.

male relative).[8] The main legal tract which deals with the Irish marriage laws and sexual relationships is *Cáin Lánamna* ('Law of Full Pairs'), which is part of the great legal compilation *Senchas Már*.[9] The premise of *Cáin Lánamna* is that a man and his wife form a 'full pair', and their relationship is similar to a lord and his client or vassal, a church and its monastic tenant, a teacher and his pupil, etc.[10] In all cases these 'full pairs' constitute long-term relationships in which the latter is dependent on the former, but within the relationship specific arrangements apply in which both partners have certain rights and duties.[11]

The dependency of the woman in this relationship is exemplified in several early Irish law-tracts, which take as a basic rule that a woman has no independent legal capacity, she belongs to the group of persons who are *báeth* ('foolish', 'senseless', 'incapable'). For example, the early Irish law-tract *Córus Béscnai* warns:

> You should not buy from the 'foolish' persons that exist according to Irish law: from women, from a forfeit person, from a male slave, from a female slave, from a monastic tenant, from the son of a living father, from an outlander, from a thief.
>
> (*Ní criae di báethaib do-choisin la Féniu: di mnaí, di chimbid, di mug, di chumail, di manach, di mac béo-athar, di deorad, di tháid.*)[12]

---

8 This is also expressed in the Indian *Laws of Manu*, see Kelly, *Guide*, 76. Note also in a Lombard law code of 643: 'No free woman ... is permitted to live under her own legal control, that is, to be legally competent, but she ought always to remain under the control of some man or of the king', see Drew, *The Lombard laws*, 92 (*Rothair's Edict* §204).

9 *CIH* 502.79–519.35 (*AL* ii 343–409). It is also edited, with German translation and comments, by Thurneysen, '*Cáin Lánamna*' (references are henceforth to this edition, abbreviated as *CL*). For the style, see Charles-Edwards, 'Review article', 154–5, who refers to it as 'textbook prose', and dates it to *c.*700 – *c.*750. The main articles which deal with early Irish marriage are Ó Corráin, 'Women' and 'Marriage'; see also Kelly, *Guide*, 68–79. The Irish marriage customs in the Anglo-Norman period are discussed in two articles by Simms, 'Women' and 'The legal position'.

10 *CL* §§1–3 (*CIH* 502.7–504.25).

11 *CL* pp. 2–13 for discussion. Thurneysen notes that the later glossators and commentators misunderstood the common basis of the various 'full pairs', and even the one who wrote the text is at times inconsistent and confused. This seems to indicate that by the eighth century this legal principle was already subject to change.

12 *CIH* 536.23–4 (*AL* iii 59). Normalized and translated by McLeod, *Contract law*, 59. Other examples of this kind are at *CIH* 351.24–6 (*Senchas Már, AL* i 51–3; Thurneysen, 'Aus dem irischen Recht iv', 177/181, §12); 443.29–444.6 (*IR* 35–6,*Díre* §38); 491.24–6 (*Cáin Aicillne, AL* ii 289; Thurneysen, 'Unfrei-Lehen', 375 [§38]); 593.35–8 (Thurneysen, *Bürgschaft*, 11 (§37) = Stacey, '*Berrad Airechta*'

These persons are considered *báeth* in the sense that they are incapable of making contracts independently; they cannot do anything without the specific consent or authorization of their 'head' (*cenn*).[13] Most of them are without sufficient property or status to assume legal responsibility or to engage in legal transactions, a principle which is also expressed in the early eighth century collection of Irish canon law, the *Collectio Canonum Hibernensis*, which enumerates those who are not allowed to act as (paying) surety (the Irish terms are between brackets):

> *Non est dignus fideiussor fieri: seruus [mug] nec peregrinus [deorad] nec brutus [drúth] nec monachus [manach], nisi imperante abbate, nec filius [mac], nisi imperante patre, nec femina [ben], nisi domina, virgo sancta.*[14]
>
> (Not worthy to act as surety is: a slave, nor an outlander, nor a fool, nor a monastic tenant, unless by the authority of his abbot, nor a son, unless by the authority of his father, nor a woman, unless she is the head of a household, or a holy virgin)

The *domina*, who forms the exception to the rule here (apart from the *virgo sancta*), can be equated with the *bé cuitchernsa* and *cétmuinter* in *Cáin Lánamna* and other Irish legal texts, who are also capable of independent legal action within their marriage.[15] Their exceptional position is related to their control over the property they had contributed to the common household in the marriage. This will be discussed in detail in §4.

---

215); Meyer, *Triads*, §§150–2. In the glosses 'woman' is usually glossed as '*adaltrach* (concubine) without sons', for which see §7 below. For the basic invalidity of a woman's oath and the limited value of female evidence (cf. *CCH* xvi, §3; xxv, §5), see Kelly, *Guide*, 202 and 207–8.

13 For further discussion, see Binchy, 'The legal capacity', and McLeod, *Contract law*, 58–62 and 71–80. McLeod argues at 77–80 that the examples which take women to be *báeth* give the general rule, which is not necessarily the older rule as Binchy proposes; linguistically, they are not older than texts which give exceptions to the rule. We can take this to be the case for the eighth century, but it does not exclude the possibility that a development took place which gave women more contractual freedom.

14 *CCH* xxxiv, §3 (cf. xxv, §5). It is given as in my quotation by Thurneysen, 'Aus dem irischen Recht v', 368. For discussion on the *Hibernensis*, see Sheehy 'The Bible' and 'The *Collectio*'. In the latter Sheehy argues that the influence of the *Hibernensis* on continental canon law was negligible, but Reynolds, 'Unity', thinks that it was substantial, if often indirect. See Pryce, 'Early Irish canons', for the influence of the *Hibernensis* on Welsh law.

15 Ó Corráin, 'Marriage', 7.

§3: TYPES OF MARRIAGE

Cáin Lánamna distinguishes three main types of valid relationships or marriages: by betrothal (*airnaidm*), by acceptance or acknowledgement (*aititiu*), and by abduction (*foxal*).[16] The first is subdivided in *lánamnas comthinchuir* ('union on mutual contribution'), *lánamnas mná for ferthinchur* ('union of a woman on man-contribution') and *lánamnas fir for bantinchur co fognam* ('union of a man on woman-contribution with service').[17] The difference between them is based on the amount of property each partner contributed to the marriage fund, which determined his or her respective rights within the marriage.

The same applies to the two types of marriage on *aititiu*, *lánamnas airite for urail* ('union of acceptance by inducement') and *lánamnas fir thathigthe cen urgnam, cen urail, cen tarcud, cen tinól* ('union of a frequenting man without work, without inducement, without performance, without contribution').[18] Apart from the intermediate *lánamnas foxail* ('union of abduction') and the vague *lánamnas amsa for faeniul* ('union of wandering mercenaries'), all other sexual relationships between men and women were illegitimate: *lánamnas tothla* or *lánamnas táide* ('union of secrecy'), *lánamnas éicne* ('union of violence'; rape) and *lánamnas genaige* ('union of foolishness'; relationship with an insane person).[19] The family did not consent to these relationships, and the person responsible for its joining was held liable for all matters which involved compensation or financial burden.

Marriages on *airnaidm* and *aititiu* are both approved of by the families involved, but with the former the bride's family received property in the form of *coibche* from the groom, which made it binding, while with the latter no *coibche* was given, and no betrothal took place (see §4). The 'inducement' to which the marriage on *aititiu* refers consists of property, which seemingly constitutes the payment which the woman receives for

---

16 *CL* §4 (*CIH* 505.19–23) gives ten types of sexual relationships. The threefold distinction is not mentioned, but can be extrapolated from the discussion of the ten types in the rest of the text.

17 Discussed in *CL* §§5–20 (first type), §§21–8 (second type) and §29 (third type).

18 Discussed in *CL* §33 (*lánamnas airite for urail*), §32 (*lánamnas fir thathigthe*). The two are discussed in reverse order, and sometimes mixed up by later glossators and commentators.

19 Discussed in *CL* §34 (*lánamnas tothla/táide*), §35 (*lánamnas éicne*), §36 (*lánamnas genaige*). *Lánamnas amsa for faeniul* is not discussed, but see the remark given in a discussion of all the ten types of unions by Ó Corráin, 'Marriage', 18, who suggests it may be related to a Roman law. Note also Deutr. 24:5 in this respect. The rule that mentally deranged are not allowed to marry is also included in the *Lex Romana Visigothorum*, see Knoch, 'Ehescheidung', 238.

her sexual services, but the man can also visit a woman without any arrangements being made which would create obligations. In marriage on *aititiu* the woman remained partially a member of her paternal family, especially when she did not have any sons (see §7).

Both forms can be compared with proper and informal marriage as they existed in Roman and Germanic society. In Roman marriage *cum manu* ('with hand') the woman was completely subject to her husband, as opposed to marriage *sine manu* ('without hand'), in which the woman still maintained strong legal ties with her paternal family.[20] In early medieval Germanic society a distinction was made between marriage by purchase (*Kaufehe*), by mutual consent (*Friedelehe*) and by capture (*Raubehe*). *Kaufehe* was a proper marriage: the level of the brideprice was established, a betrothal followed, and property was exchanged. The public ceremony showed the consent of both families to the union, and signified the transference of the authority (*mundium*) over the bride by her family to her husband. *Friedelehe* was a looser form of marriage (*Fridila*: 'friend', 'beloved'), in which no betrothal or property exchange took place, and consequently the husband had no full authority over his wife; she remained a member of her paternal family.[21]

Raubehe can be defined as marriage by rape or elopement, which could lead to a forced marriage (normally a sexual relationship constituted a marriage), to which the family consented afterwards, but it could also be a way for a young man without sufficient property to gain his bride without the need to 'purchase' her, to which her family tacitly consented.[22] Without the consent of the family, this marriage was forbidden, and it was discouraged in later law codes, if not severely punished.[23] It can be equated with *lánamnas foxail* in *Cáin Lánamna*, to which the same observations apply.[24]

20 Brundage, *Law, sex and Christian society*, 32–8; Gies and Gies, *Marriage and the family*, 18–29; Wemple, *Women in Frankish society*, 15–19. For marriage on the continent I have based myself mainly on these three secondary works. Brundage has copious references to sources and secondary literature; Gies offers a more general discussion, but some subjects are treated in detail; Wemple is essential for women and marriage in Merovingian society. Amt, *Women's lives*, contains excerpts from the most important sources on women in the Middle Ages.
21 Brundage, *Law*, 127–9; Wemple, *Women*, 10–15, 34.
22 Brundage, *Law*, 129, 133; Gies, *Marriage*, 54–5. In Roman law *raptus* can refer to both elopement and rape, see Brundage, *Law*, 48.
23 Brundage, *Law*, 129, 148; Gies, *Marriage*, 55; Wemple, *Women*, 33–4, but cf. 82; King, *Visigothic*, 232–3.
24 See *CL* §34 (*CIH* 518.22–7), in which it is put on a par with *lánamnas tothla/táide* ('union of secrecy'), and Power, 'Classes of women', 88–90. Note the similarity between *lánamnas foxail* and Deutr. 22:28–9, and between rape as described in *Gúbretha Caratniad* (Thurneysen, 'Caratnia', 350, §39 = *CIH* 2197.25–31) and

In the Germanic kingdoms the first year of the marriage could be considered as a trial period, during which the marriage could be terminated unless a child was conceived.[25] We have references to temporary or trial marriages in the later medieval period in Wales, Ireland and Scotland, and references in the legal material also suggest that it was known in the early period as well.[26]

The threefold distinction of proper, informal and abduction marriage in early medieval Irish and Germanic society can be related to their common Indo-European roots, but for a clear picture we have to discuss other features they shared.

§4: BRIDEPRICE AND DOWRY

Of the marriages on *airnaidm* (betrothal), *lánamnas mná for ferthinchur* is usually held to be the oldest form.[27] As the man makes the largest contribution, he has the freedom to do as he pleases with the marriage-property, except if it touches upon the basic necessities of life. A primary wife who is of equal status with her husband (*cétmuinter*, see §7) can impugn his disadvantageous contracts via her sons.[28] The wife of this type of marriage is essentially *báeth*.

The common form of marriage in *Cáin Lánamna* is *lánamnas comthinchuir*, in which both partners make an equal contribution to the marriage-property in land, cattle, goods for the household, etc.[29] As her

---

Deutr. 22:23–7. For the latter, see Wagner, 'Zu *Gúbretha Caratniad* §39' and Ó Corráin, 'Women and the law', 50–2. For rape, see Kelly, *Guide*, 134–7.

25 Brundage, *Law*, 131; Wemple, *Women*, 94.

26 Giraldus Cambrensis, *Descriptio Kambriae*, in Thorpe, *The Journey*, 263 (Book ii, ch. 6); Thurneysen, 'Heirat', 126–7; Thurneysen, 'Caratnia', 358. Temporary marriages are forbidden in a commentary at *CIH* 144.10–14, partially also at 25.25–7 (*Heptad* 26, *AL* v 217) and 247.22–3 (*Do Tuaslucud Rudradh*, *AL* v 511).

27 Binchy, 'Legal capacity', 210; Ó Corráin, 'Women', 3.

28 *CL* §§21–2 (*CIH* 512.22–513.6). One can read '*a meic*' in the text as referring to her sons or her enforcing sureties. The glossator is uncertain, but considering the importance of sons for a married woman (see below) and the ability of a 'son of a living father' to impugn his father's disadvantageous contracts (Kelly, *Guide*, 80–1; *CIH* 443.21–4 (*IR* 34, *Díre* §37); Thurneysen, 'Caratnia', 311–12, §7 = *CIH* 2193.5–11, 1582.5–9), it seems that the text refers to the wife's sons (cf. *CL* pp. 48–9). The basic dependent position of the 'son of a living father' is the same as a woman in Irish law, and to both about the same exceptions apply, related to possession of property.

29 *CL* §§5–20 (*CIH* 505.35–512.21), cf. *CCH* xlvi, §19 (see Ó Corráin, 'Marriage', 14); Thurneysen, 'Caratnia', 321–2, §14 (*CIH* 2194.9–14); Stokes and Strachan, *Thesaurus Palaeohibernicus* ii, 239–40.

contribution remains her own, the wife enjoys almost the same contractual capacity as her husband, and can undertake legal transactions and responsibilities up to her honourprice (half of that of her husband, and related to his status); neither can undertake important legal transactions without the consent of the other.[30] Clearly, the woman of this marriage is no longer *báeth*, and her independent status and prestige are reflected in her position as *bé cuitchernsa* ('woman of condominium'), which is glossed as *ben is comtigerna dó* ('a woman who is co-ruler with him').[31]

If it is correct to regard *lánamnas mná for ferthinchur* as the earlier form, it raises the question as to how the wife was able to secure sufficient property to make an equal contribution to the common household. This property did not come from her own assets. A woman was unable to inherit real estate and become owner; she could only acquire it by work or gift (such as a marriage gift), or inherit it for her lifetime if her father died without leaving any sons.[32] This means that a women would usually obtain property after she had married.

For the woman's property we thus have to look at the share of the brideprice or gift she received. The early Irish sources contain a variety of terms which refer to the dowry, brideprice or a similar marriage-contribution. The most frequently used are *tindscra* and *coibche*; the first appears predominantly in saga-literature, the latter in legal material. It is difficult to establish the exact meaning of either term, as they are often mixed up, and were subject to change later on.[33] *Tindscra* is used on several occasions as a payment for services which are agreed upon beforehand, and seems to have been used as a gift to the woman by the man for her sexual services.[34]

30 For a woman's honourprice, see Binchy, *Críth Gablach*, lines 125–7 (*CIH* 779.7–8), and note the correction by Greene, *Fingal Rónáin*, 13–14 (at note 91); cf. *CIH* 1607.4–7 (*Uraicecht Becc, AL* v 71). A man's loss of status did not affect his wife's status, see *CIH* 427.22–3 (*IR* 65, *Fuidir*-text §5).

31 *CL* §5 (*CIH* 505.36); *CIH* 506.9 (*AL* ii 359).

32 *CCH* xxxii, §§17–19 stipulates that daughters should share equally with sons if land is inherited as a gift, but they cannot become absolute owners. The Irish commentators are in doubt: either the daughters only receive household-goods (*IR* 30), or they share equally with the sons. Both possibilities are given at *CIH* 162.25–31, 736.20–31, etc., see also Kelly, *Guide*, 104–5. For a woman's right to claim land, see *Din Techtugad, CIH* 207.22–210.11 (*AL* iv 9–15); Kelly, ibid., 187–8. Land received as *coibche* or *tindscra* (both marriage gifts, see below) is probably what is meant by *orba sliasta* ('land of thigh'), see Ó Corráin, 'Marriage', 12, with references.

33 A discussion of the various terms is at Thurneysen, 'Caratnia', 356–9, 'Heirat', 109–28, 'Aus dem irischen Recht iv', 227–8, and Ó Corráin, 'Marriage', 15–17.

34 For *tindscra* in a legal context, see Thurneysen, 'Caratnia', 356, §44 (*CIH* 2198.22–6); *CIH* 1235.4–13 (= 1486.14 (*O'Davoren's Glossary* no. 540); 2178.26),

Coibche has a firmer place in the legal vocabulary, and is directly related to *airnaidm* (betrothal), which bound a marriage.[35] The payment of *coibche* was witnessed by sureties, like most formal and binding contracts.[36] If a woman did not fulfil her responsibilities within the marriage, a man could divorce her and the *coibche* had to be returned to him, except land and cattle, which she was allowed to keep.[37] Hence the warning of the lawyers not to give an excessive *coibche* to a women of a bad reputation or of low status, considering the possibility that she would keep most of it herself when it came to a divorce.[38] Later texts treat *coibche* as neutral marriage property which the defaulting party would lose at a divorce or as compensation.[39]

In saga-literature the father often exercises some right over establishing the value of the *coibche*, and is entitled to a share, if not all of it. Hence the legal maxim: 'every father his first *coibche* (*cach athair a cét-choibche*).'[40] Later texts provide for a share to be given the woman, and this would explain how she was able to make a contribution to the marriage-property equal to that of her husband: the *coibche* was no longer given to her father, but – directly or indirectly – to herself.[41] It may

---

see Thurneysen, 'Aus dem irischen Recht iv', 227; 987.12–13 = 1197.17–18 (McLeod, *Contract Law: Di Astud Chor* §47); 1491.36–8 (*O'Davoren's Glossary* no. 691). See also Smith, 'Alphabet' 50 (§18), and '*Senbríathra Fíthail*', 19 (§4.9); Meyer, *Triads*, §149.

35 Thurneysen, 'Heirat', 109–13; Ó Corráin, 'Marriage', 15. In Meyer, *Triads*, §151, *aurnadma* is glossed '*pósta*' (at p. 39); *ben pósta* is the later term for the primary wife (*cétmuinter*; *prímben*).

36 *CIH* 572.9–10 (*Heptad* 81, *AL* v 373).

37 *CIH* 25.13–15 (*Heptad* 26, *AL* v 215, with a misleading translation); 247.21–3 (*Do Tuaslucud Rudradh*, *AL* v 511); *CL* §13 and §30, (*CIH* 508.29–33; 516.9–24), cf. 986.31–3 = 1196.35–7 and 987.12 = 1197.17–18 (McLeod, *Contract Law: Di Astud Chor* §43 and §47).

38 *CIH* 221.18–31 (*AL* iv 57–9); see Power, 'Classes of women', 100.

39 Thurneysen, 'Caratnia', 350, §39 (*CIH* 2197.25–31), with a correction at 368: when a woman did not cry out or give notice after she had been raped, she had to pay her *coibche* and honourprice; *CIH* 4.33–5.32 (*Heptad* 3, *AL* v 133–5); 47.21–48.26 (*Heptad* 52, *AL* v 293–7); 805.2–11; 270.15–271.9 (*Bretha Étgid*, *AL* iii 205–7). The rule that the guilty party forfeited his or her marriage contribution is also present in the continental laws, see Brundage, *Law*, 119 (*Lex Justinianus*); Gies, *Marriage*, 24; Wemple, *Women*, 32, 45.

40 *CIH* 294.40 = 503.22 (*Bretha Étgid*, *AL* iii 315); 1948.9–11 (*Cáin Lánamna*, *AL* ii 347 comm.); 222.8 (*AL* iv 59) = 1471.1 (*O'Davoren's Glossary* no. 126) = 1866.27; Smith, 'Alphabet', 49 (§17).

41 *CIH* 294.40 (see note above), with the commentary at 295.11–19 (*AL* iii 317), which states that the *coibche* has to be returned to the woman's father after the divorce; 1915.1–22 (*IR* 37–8 (*Díre*, Komm. 1)). See also Ó Corráin, 'Marriage', 15–16, who, however, at 13 still regards marriage with equal contribution to be a

also be that the family made this contribution or dowry of their own accord, called *tinchor* or *tinól* in the legal texts.[42]

If this theory is correct, it seems that in Ireland the same trend was followed as in the rest of Christian Europe, where a similar development had taken place in the sixth and seventh centuries: first the wife was more or less bought from her family by the payment of a brideprice, later a bridegift was paid to the bride, supplemented by the *Morgengabe*, a payment made after the wedding night in honour of the bride's surrender of her virginity and the acquisition of sexual rights.[43] The brideprice or *arrha* became a token payment.[44] The bridegift and the *Morgengabe* could be paid in money or land; a woman's dowry from her family usually consisted of goods for the household, or treasures among the nobility and kings, over which she retained full ownership when she divorced (without guilt) or when her husband died. The rights of inheritance for women in default of any living brothers could make them the sole heirs of complete estates and fiefs.[45]

The background of this development is probably related to the assimilation of Roman and Germanic marriage customs. In early Rome the brideprice (*coemptio*) had become a token payment, and had been superseded by the dowry of the bride's family (*dos*). In the third century the bridegift (*donatio*), delivered before the actual wedding took place,

---

common Celtic institution, as it is described by Caesar in ancient Gaul. His equation of this marriage with Roman marriage *sine manu* and German *Friedelehe* is very doubtful, see my discussion at §3.

42 Thurneysen, 'Heirat', 125–8, and *CL* p. 11 (*CIH* 1949.8–12, cf. 1948.7–11). *Tinól* is used in *lánamnas fir thathigthe cen urgnam, cen urail, cen tarcud, cen tinól* as property which the man offers to his partner.

43 Brundage, *Law*, 88, 114, 129 for the dowry in Roman and German marriage; Gies, 55–6; Wemple, 44–5. See also King, *Visigothic*, 224–8, 236–7 and Drew, *The Lombard laws*, 84–6. The 'buying' of a wife is particularly well brought out in Anglo-Saxon and Kentish law, see Lucas, *Women*, 63–5 for some explicit examples. In Irish sources there are also a few references of this kind, see Thurneysen, 'Caratnia', 311, §7 (*CIH* 2193.5–6); Hull, 'Milesian invasion'; Best and Bergin, '*Tochmarc Etaíne*', 151 (§12, §14), 187 (§17, §19). For a discussion of the similarities between Welsh marriage property arrangements and those in Ireland and on the continent, see Walters, 'European context' and *idem, Comparative legal method*.

44 Gies, *Marriage*, 55; Wemple, *Women*, 32, 44; Lucas, *Women*, 62–3. *Arrha* is from Latin *arrhabo*, and was originally a payment made to guarantee the delivery of goods, not unlike the Irish *tindscra*.

45 Wemple, *Women*, 45–7, cf. King, *Visigothic*, 246–9, and Mac Cormack, 'Inheritance'.

became more important, and grew so large that by the mid-fifth century many young men found it impossible to raise it.[46]

As described by Tacitus, the German man still obtained his wife by bride-purchase, the bride made only a gift of arms, but in the early medieval Germanic law codes we see a transition in which the brideprice was partially given to the woman.[47] Suzanne Wemple argues that the important improvement of economic rights of Merovingian women 'can be traced through the evolution of the brideprice into a bridegift and the granting of power to women to hold and inherit landed property.'[48] She connects this with the imitation of Roman custom, combined with a wish to protect the weaker members of society (repudiated women and widows) and weaken the power of the family as a legal unit. In the continental law codes of the seventh and eighth centuries the woman's kin has lost almost all control over the marriage settlement.[49]

It seems that in Ireland these changes followed suit, with the result that the wife could make an equal contribution to the common household, which gave her a relatively independent status. By extension, if a woman made the largest contribution to the marriage fund, her husband became dependent on her. This is the case in *lánamnas fir for bantinchur co fognam*.[50] When a woman's father and his sons had all died, she became the

---

46 Gies, *Marriage*, 21–2.
47 Gies, *Marriage*, 33; Wemple, *Women*, 10–12, 44–5.
48 Wemple, *Women*, 44. For the improving inheritance rights of women, see 45–7. In the earliest medieval law codes and also in later law codes of areas which were largely outside the influence of Roman culture, such as Saxony or Thuringia, the inheritance was still given to the nearest kin of a father who had no male descendants, a system which also prevailed in Ireland.
49 Wemple, *Women*, 44–5. In Ireland clerics also took the initiative to protect women and others who were not allowed to bear arms. In 697 Adomnán, abbot of the influential monastery of Iona, promulgated his *Cáin Adomnáin* (also called *Lex Innocentium*) to this effect. It was guaranteed by all the major and minor Irish kings, and issued severe penalties for those who broke its rules. See Meyer, *Cáin Adamnáin*, for an edition, and Ryan, '*Cáin Adomnáin*', and Ní Donnchadha, 'Guarantor list', for discussion. Note also Bieler, *Irish Penitentials*, 195 (Second synod of St Patrick, xxvii), which advocates that a girl should be free to choose her husband.
50 CL §29 (*CIH* 515.23–516.11). Charles-Edwards, *Kinship*, 465–7, contrasts this type with marriage in which the man made the main contribution, and suggests that the latter was the usual form among commoners, and *lánamnas comthinchuir* among the nobility. He argues that cattle was essential for the status of a young nobleman, to which his wife partially contributed, whereas a young commoner could not expect to receive any cattle from his family or bride. However, CL §24 (*CIH* 513.33, 514.5–8), which refers to *lánamnas mná for ferthinchur*, mentions the noble grades as well (cf. CL §20, 512.14–16), and refers to the taking of a secondary wife (see §7 below), while with *lánamnas comthinchuir* both partners are

sole heir of the family-land. As a *banchomarba* ('female heir') she had to take full responsibility for the land and fulfil the duties attached to it; after her death the land reverted to the next-of-kin of her father, who divided it according to proximity of kinship.[51] A *banchomarba* could only preserve her interest in the land for her children if she married one of her father's close relatives, a rule also given in the Old Testament, on which it may have been based.[52] If she was not able or willing to do so, she could still retain control over the land during her lifetime by marrying a man who did not have sufficient property to match hers, so that she made the major contribution into the marriage. Her husband would be restricted in his contractual capacity, as he had not made a worthwhile contribution to the marriage in the first place.[53]

The inability to inherit land permanently restricted the independence of women, and made marriage to a heiress unattractive as a political move, unlike feudal Europe, where lands and lordships acquired through marriage had a considerable effect on matters such as succession and political developments. In this respect the developments in Europe were not followed in Ireland, where the family remained the centre of the social and legal structure.

§5: PRECONDITIONS TO A MARRIAGE

The early Irish law-tracts stress that a proper marriage has to be between equals. The regulation of *lánamnas comthinchuir* only applies 'if it is (concluded) with land and cattle and household requisites, and when their

allowed to rent land (*fochraic tire*), which seems especially relevant to commoners (*CL* §5, 506.16). For these and other reasons, I favour the 'traditional' view.

51 The main text on a woman's right to inherit land is edited by Dillon, 'The relationship'. For a fresh translation of the first part (135–59: 'The kinship poem' = *CIH* 215.15–218.9), see Charles-Edwards, *Kinship*, 516–19. The second part is at *CIH* 1153.5–1155.22, etc.

52 *CCH* xxxii, §19–§20 (cf. Num 27:1–11, 36:8–13), see Dillon, 'The relationship', 150, 176–8 and Ó Corráin, 'Marriage', 10–12 and 'Women and the law', 52–6. Binchy argues for an Indo-European background in 'Family membership', 183–4.

53 At *CIH* 427.2–4 (*IR* 64, *Fuidir*-text §4) three men whose honourprice depends on their wives are named: 'a man without property, without possessions who has a female heir [as wife] ... a man [from another kingdom] who pursues his wife's arse across the border ... a fugitive outlaw (*cú glas*, lit. grey wolf).' The translation is from McLeod, *Contract law*, 76–7. Note also the position of Medb as *banchomarba* and wealthy queen in O'Rahilly, *Táin Bó Cúalnge*, lines 1–44, see Weisweiler, 'Die Stellung der Frau', 233–5, cf. Kelly, 'The *Táin*', 77–84.

partnership is of equal nobility and equal standing'.[54] Donnchadh Ó
Corráin argues that this rule was influenced by the rule of marriage as
described in a letter which pope Leo the Great wrote to Rusticus, bishop
of Narbonne, in 459. It was later incorporated in canon law, and is cited
in full in the *Collectio Canonum Hibernensis.* Leo states that a marriage
is legally valid if it is concluded between free-born equals, with a dowry
and publicly celebrated. Other texts which refer to the same conditions
appear elsewhere in the *Hibernensis.*[55] We have seen above that *airnaidm*
was a formal contract, connected with the man's marriage contribution,
and secured by witnesses, which can be equated with the public celebration.

However, it would be going too far to consider *lánamnas comthinchuir*
as an innovative product of clerical legal thinking, and highly influenced
by the coming of Christianity, as Ó Corráin maintains. As has been
argued above, *lánamnas comthinchuir* is a social phenomenon strongly
connected with the property the wife was able to control within the marriage, and this is not a development which was brought about by
Christianity or clerical lawyers. We may regard the role canon law played
in defining these laws as significant, but not in shaping the institution
itself. After all, that the partners have to be of equal status is an obvious
rule in an hierarchical society such as the Irish – or the Roman or
Germanic for that matter. Furthermore, *lánamnas mná for ferthinchur,* in
which the bride does not receive a dowry, is also considered to be legally
valid according to Irish law.

Leo's letter does not mention that consummation of the marriage was
necessary to make it binding, and this was in line with the Roman rule
that consent, not intercourse, made a marriage.[56] This rule was followed
by patristic writers, and in general the early Christian theologians did not
feel obliged to stress the importance in a marriage of sexual intercourse,
which they thought should be practised solely for procreation and experienced without pleasure.[57] We have seen that in Irish law consent from
both families was imperative to make any sexual relationship legal; consummation of the marriage did not play a role in secular law to make it
binding.

In early Germanic law cohabitation sufficed to create a bond of marriage, and in an effort to reconcile this rule with Roman law and Christian

---

54 *CL* §5 (*CIH* 505.35–6); my translation.
55 Ó Corráin, 'Marriage', 13–15; *CCH* xlvi, §19, cf. xlvi, §§2–3.
56 Brundage, *Law,* 34. Gies, *Marriage,* 21 quotes the legal formula '*nuptias consensus
    non concubitus facit*'.
57 Brundage, *Law,* 57–76, 89–93.

thinking, Hincmar, archbishop of Reims (845–82), put forward a new theory of marriage in which he based himself on the conditions mentioned by Leo the Great, but added that it had to be followed by sexual intercourse.[58] This compromise was a break from canon law, but it had profound juristical virtues, and helped to relieve the tension between secular and canon law. It was later attacked by the reformists, who returned to Leo's rule, but Gratian in his *Concordia discordantium canonum* (circa 1140) advocated that both consent and consummation were essential to conclude a true marriage.[59]

Hincmar's new theory was written in the context of several marriage disputes among the prime nobility of the Carolingian Empire, and it marks an important step in the Church's increasing involvement in defining the secular laws concerning marriage and sexuality. Among the first problems to be tackled were incestuous marriages. Canon law calculated the degrees of kinship according to the Roman method, and limited its ban on consanguineous marriages usually to four degrees: a person was not allowed to marry any of the children or grandchildren of his grandparents.[60] This rule was flagrantly disregarded by the Merovingian kings in the sixth century, but king Pepin (751–68), Charlemagne's father, included the canonical regulation of consanguineous marriages in secular law to obstruct the close marriage-ties of the Frankish nobility. On the advice of the pope Pepin adopted the new rule by St Boniface, the papal legate for the Frankish kingdom, which extended the forbidden degrees from four to seven degrees, and also included in-laws and spiritual kin (godparents and godchildren).[61] The disallowing of marriages between

---

58 Brundage, *Law*, 134–6; Gies, *Marriage*, 97 (see 89–97 for Hincmar's role in marriage disputes in which the Church was involved).

59 Brundage, *Law*, 188–9, 235–8. The discussion whether consummation was necessary to contract a valid and binding marriage continued after Gratian.

60 Brundage, *Law*, 88–9, 130; Gies, *Marriage*, 49–53.

61 Brundage, *Law*, 140–1; Gies, *Marriage*, 83–7; Wemple, *Women*, 76–8, 80–1. The theory of Jack Goody, *Development*, 42–7, that the Church's extension of exogamy, combined with other restrictions, was a deliberate strategy to limit the chances of offspring among the nobility so that their lands might fall to the Church has not found favour among historians, see Brundage, *Law*, 88 and Gies, *Marriage*, 83–4. Note that the Lombard laws of 643 refer to the seven degrees of kinship in the case of rights to inheritance and succession, and that in 723 the definition of incest was already extended to include in-laws and godparents, see Drew, *The Lombard laws*, 77 (*Rothair's Edict* §153) and 160–1 (*Laws of Liutprand*, §§33–4). St Boniface's interest in marriage rules perhaps dates from his missionary days, during which he was asked about the Christian custom of marriage, and found himself ignorant on the matter, see Wood, 'Pagans and holy men', 358. He also complained about the sexual activities among the clergy, see Brundage, *Law*, 150–1.

close and remoter kin and the power of giving dispensations gave the
Church an influential political position which it did not hesitate to use,
and this paved the way for further intervention in the secular regulation
of marriage.

In Ireland the issue was largely ignored. We have seen that in *lánamnas fir for bantinchur co fognam* parallel cousin marriage was allowed.
One of the early Penitentials – probably from the seventh century – condemns the Irish laxity concerning incestuous relationships: 'Understand
what the Law saith, neither less nor more: but what is observed among us,
that they be separated by four degrees, they say they have never seen nor
read.'[62] Political propaganda regards offspring of an incestuous relationship – for example a father with his daughter – as inferior, but does not
treat the matter in a legal sense.[63] The *Banshenchas*, which records the
marriages of the prime Irish royalty, gives examples of relationships
which would have been regarded as forbidden by the Church in the
eighth century and later, such as a king marrying the wife of his brother,
the wife of his step-father, or his half-sister, but not of marriages between
close kin within the four degrees of consanguinity.[64] In the letter of
Lanfranc quoted above incestuous marriages among the Irish still form a
major concern.

§6: DIVORCE

In the regulations concerning divorce the Christian rules profoundly
clashed with both Roman and Germanic custom. In Ireland the *Collectio
Canonum Hibernensis* expresses some doubt on the matter. It refers to
the letter of divorce in the Old Testament (Deutr. 24:1–4), which mentions several reasons why a man can divorce his wife, which were also
known in late Roman law.[65] In the New Testament the letter of divorce is
repudiated by Jesus, who takes adultery by a woman to be the sole justification for divorce, but a man was only allowed to remarry after his wife
had died; this rule is also followed in the *Hibernensis*.[66]

---

62 Bieler, *Irish Penitentials*, 197 (xxix), in the canons of the alleged second synod of
St Patrick. The historical background is discussed at 255 note 17.
63 For examples, see Charles-Edwards, *Kinship*, 112–15. In saga literature some noteworthy kings are born from incestuous relationships, see McCone, *Pagan past*,
192–3.
64 Dobbs, 'The *Ban-Shenchus*'.
65 *CCH* xlvi, §§8–9; Ó Corráin, 'Marriage', 19–20.
66 Mark 10:2–12; Matt. 5:31–2; *CCH* xlv, §§14–15, 27, 32; xlvi, §§10–12. Knoch,
'Ehescheidung', 259–60.

The Irish law-tracts do not accept the latter rule, and still acknowledge divorce by mutual consent, which in *lánamnas comthinchuir* led to the arrangement that each partner's contribution to the household was taken back again, following a complex set of rules which took into account such matters as who was the owner of the land on which the cattle grazed and who had produced most during the marriage.[67] The reasons to divorce which do not entail any payment or compensation, because the partner cannot be blamed for his or her circumstance, are more or less the same for man and wife: a heavy affliction or wounding (both mentally and physically, including infertility and impotence), and acceptance of an ecclesiastical function (although clerics were allowed to marry). Absence for a long period, for example, to make a pilgrimage or to go on a military campaign, could amount to a 'temporary' divorce, in which the wife probably returned to her family.[68]

The *Heptads* state that a wife could divorce her husband when he had concealed his impotency, if he was so fat that it was impossible to have intercourse, if he mistreated or neglected her, gossiped about her sexual performance to others, took a concubine, or if he turned out to be a homosexual.[69] A man could divorce his wife if she betrayed him (to others), damaged his honour, persisted in adultery, if she forced an abortion on herself, killed her children or neglected her tasks in the household.[70]

The text in *Cáin Lánamna* states that if the wife causes a divorce because of the last reason, the produce of her labour falls to her husband, but she is allowed to keep land and cattle (which she received as *coibche*), which was probably returned to her father.[71] In later glosses to the text which discusses the reasons as to why a man can divorce his wife the penalties are heavier: the whole of (the value of) the *coibche*, together with a supplemental compensation, had to be paid to the guiltless party. This is not so much meant to give a woman a higher compensation and more independence as to discourage the provocation of a divorce by irresponsible behaviour – perhaps a reaction to the complaints of the Church that Irish men divorced their wives at will. Lanfranc's letter indicates that the liberal Irish marriage laws were not in favour of women, but on the contrary gave men almost unlimited opportunities to divorce. For a woman, with her socially inferior position, and her dependence on her father, fam-

---

67 *CL* §§10–18 (*CIH* 507.28–511.9), §§26–8 (*CIH* 514.23–515.16). Ó Corráin, 'Marriage', 8–9.
68 *CIH* 48.27–49.7 (*Heptad* 53, *AL* v 297–9).
69 *CIH* 4.33–5.32 (*Heptad* 3, *AL* v 133–5), cf. 443.21–4 (*IR* 34, *Díre* §37).
70 *CIH* 47.21–48.26 (*Heptad* 52, *AL* v 293–7).
71 *CL* §13 (*CIH* 508.29–30), see §4 above.

ily or husband, it would have been more difficult to obtain her rights as
an individual than a man.

In Roman society divorce had also been possible by mutual consent or
for various reasons, such as adultery, impotence, insanity, or capture or
enslavement of one of the partners.[72] The Christian emperor Constantine
changed the laws on divorce in 331, but it was still allowed for several reasons. A wife could not divorce her husband on the grounds of adultery, a
feature which this law shared with Hebrew and Germanic law, and which
exemplifies the sexual discrimination against women.[73]

Constantine also banned divorce by mutual consent, and stipulated
that a specific reason had to be given, but this rule created so many problems that it was reversed by his successor. Fluctuations remained common in the divorce laws of subsequent emperors. In the *Codex Justinianus*
of 533 and especially in the supplemental Novels of 536, a wide variety of
reasons to terminate a marriage are given, which are remarkably similar to
those given in the Irish laws: inability to have a sexual relationship, capture in battle, adultery, homicide, grave-robbery, sorcery, political con-
spiracy, harbouring and aiding bandits, and activities which endangered
the life of the spouse. Seven years later this list was shortened again, and
criminal behaviour by the partner was scrapped as a reasonable cause to
terminate the marriage, while in supposed unfaithful behaviour the rights
of man and wife were now evened out.[74]

In Justinian's laws the Christian concept that marriage was indissoluble is almost completely lacking. In fact, however disapproved of and
seen as a way to explore sexual opportunities in remarriage, divorce
remained a matter of secular law, into which canonical enactments only
slowly and irregularly spilled over.

In the early medieval Germanic kingdoms a man could repudiate his
wife for reasons such as adultery, barrenness or having contracted an illness which debarred her from having intercourse with her husband.
Divorce by mutual consent was still common in the seventh and eighth
centuries.[75] Church councils in the eighth century gave with persistent
inconsistency changing reasons which made divorce acceptable, and it
was only in the Council of Friuli in 796 that adultery was seen as the sole
justifiable cause to divorce, after which it was forbidden to remarry while
the former partner remained alive. The real breakthrough occurred when
Charlemagne included this rule in a capitulary in 802, which was con-

72 Brundage, *Law*, 38–9.
73 Brundage, *Law*, 53, 94–8, 132.
74 Brundage, *Law*, 114–17.
75 Brundage, *Law*, 143–5; Gies, *Marriage*, 57; Wemple, *Women*, 42–3. See also
    Lapidge, 'Debate poem on divorce', for divorce among the Anglo-Saxons.

firmed by his successors.[76] Regarding sexual impotence the same principle was used: the couple could separate but not marry while both were alive. Henceforth marriage, once concluded, was for life.

These stricter rules which were entered in secular law were soon put into force. Charlemagne's five successive marriages (his divorced wives had not died before he remarried) and six concubines (we know of) were still condoned by the Church, but his great-grandson Lothair II, king of Lorraine (855–69) encountered serious ecclesiastical opposition in his attempts to divorce his wife Teutberga in order to marry his concubine Waldrada. In the course of the proceedings, which lasted twelve years, Lothair accused Teutberga of incest with her brother, who was a cleric, sodomy, procuring an abortion, a previous marriage and sterility, and said that she wanted to enter a convent; he had also been married under duress, without his consent. After initial success, pope Nicholas nullified his efforts, and forbade a divorce with Teutberga under pain of excommunication. The case touched upon sensitive political interests, and became so central to the whole question of the rule of marriage and the Church's involvement, that archbishop Hincmar (see §5) devoted a whole treatise to it. Other famous divorce cases in the ninth century underlined the influential position of the Church in these matters, and resulted in a standard set of rules concerning marriage and divorce by which the nobility and the people at large had to abide.[77]

§7: POLYGAMY AND CONCUBINAGE

In Hebrew, Roman and Germanic society a concubine was usually of a socially inferior status to her consort, and her relationship was less formal than a proper marriage.[78] In ancient Rome a woman who lived with a male consort for a long time without any marital affection (*maritalis affectio*) was legally speaking a concubine. As polygamy was not allowed, a married man could not take a concubine (in the legal sense). Once concubinage became tolerated, the laws began to define it and treat it as an inferior type of marriage, in which the concubine had fewer rights and less protection than a legitimate wife. Offspring from the relationship belonged to the woman, who had to take almost full responsibility for

---

76 Brundage, *Law*, 144; Gies, *Marriage*, 88; Wemple, *Women*, 77–81. Byzantine law regarded an adulterer to be morally dead, and thus permitted the innocent spouse to remarry, see Brundage, 143–4, note 75.

77 Brundage *Law*, 144–5; Wemple, *Women*, 84–7; Gies, *Marriage*, 88–97 gives a detailed account of Lothair's troubles.

78 Brundage, *Law*, 24, 54, 129–30.

them. In due course the distinction between a married wife and concubine diminished.[79]

As civil law forbade marriages between persons of different social classes, the early Church accepted concubinage as such, and as an alternative to marriage and non-marital sex. However, some ruled that a man had to marry his concubine if this was possible, and otherwise repudiate her. Strongest advocate of this opinion was Augustine, who, drawing upon his experiences in his younger days, considered concubinage to be nothing more than legalized fornication. Despite the writings of Augustine, Jerome and others who condemned the Roman institution of concubinage, the first Council of Toledo (c.397–400) decided that men who kept only one concubine had a right to receive communion. Men such as Caesarius of Arles and pope Leo the Great also conceded that it would be impractical to ban concubinage altogether. In short, the Church made her disapproval known, but was not yet in a position to punish.[80]

In the fourth and fifth centuries the legal position of the concubine was further upgraded, which brought her even closer to the position of a legally wedded wife. As courts began to distinguish between a dowry given to a wedded wife and 'loans' or 'gifts' given to concubines, this led to the recognition of the inheritance rights of a concubine's children, who were now entitled to a small portion of their father's estates. Further legislation culminated in concubinage being put on a par with marriage in the *Codex Justinianus*, which gave virtually the same property rights for all natural offspring born from both relationships – a situation which resembles the position of the Irish concubine. In accordance with ecclesiastical rulings concubinage had to create a permanent bond, and men were not allowed to have more than one concubine at a time, but for the rest Justinian did not adopt Christian teachings in his laws on concubinage.[81]

We have seen that in early Germanic society besides a proper marriage (*Kaufehe*) a looser relationship without a betrothal or dowry argreement existed (*Friedelehe*). This is not the equivalent of concubinage, which was usually a relationship which a man maintained with a socially inferior woman, without or beside marriage, and which was not by definition a long term relationship. Children from a concubine had no inheritance rights.[82]

A man could also have a number of legally wedded wives, but by the end of the sixth century polygamy had become uncommon in the

79 Brundage, *Law*, 40–4; Gies, *Marriage*, 21.
80 Brundage, *Law*, 79–80, 98–103; Gies, *Marriage*, 57–8.
81 Brundage, *Law*, 102, 117–18.
82 Brundage, *Law*, 130.

Germanic kingdoms, even among the Merovingians, who had carried it to excess.[83] As an alternative, the Carolingian kings kept several concubines, before or during their marriage. Ecclesiastical censure concerning concubinage and informal marriages did not amount to measures forbidding it in secular law, even in and after the period of papal reform in the eleventh century.[84]

At around the eighth century polygamy was a matter of controversy in Ireland, as appears from the legal tract *Bretha Crólige*:

> Everyone is paid honourprice for his union according to the custom of the island of Ireland, whether it be manifold or single. For there is a dispute in Irish law as to which is more proper, whether to have many sexual unions or a single one: for the chosen [people] of God lived in plurality of unions, so that it is not easier to condemn it than to praise it.[85]

The manner in which the Irish lawyers discuss the problem and find a solution for it can be said to typify the Irish approach to legal disagreements: a compromise was preferred above one particular ruling. We have already discussed the difference between *lánamnas comthinchuir* and *lánamnas mná for ferthinchur*. The wife in the former was called a *bé cuitchernsa*, in the description of the latter we meet two other titles, in a passage discussing the fact that a man has total freedom of contract, 'except for the sale of clothes and of food and the sale of cows and of sheep if she be a betrothed wife who is not a primary wife (*mad ben airnadma nabe cétmuinter*).'[86]

Cétmuinter means literally 'head of the household', and is usually translated as 'primary wife'.[87] The text states that a *cétmuinter* is 'equally good and of equal birth (*commaith 7 comcheníuil*) – that is, every equally-good person is of equal birth – she disturbs all his contracts if they be

---

83 Brundage, *Law*, 145; Gies, *Marriage*, 52–3; Wemple, *Women*, 58–70, discusses the influential Merovingian queens.

84 Brundage, *Law*, 145, 183, 206–7, 225; Gies *Marriage*, 87–8; Wemple 78–9, 82–3. For concubinage in Anglo-Saxon society, see Ross, 'Concubinage'.

85 Binchy, 'Bretha Crólige', 45–6, §57 (*CIH* 2301.35–8). The gloss gives the many wives of Solomon, David and Jacob as examples. In O'Donoghue, 'Advice to a prince', 50/54 (§35) it is said: 'Adultery (*adaltras*) ruins every good name – it is not proper for anyone provided [or: except] he be a king'. *Adaltras* can also refer to sexual intercourse on forbidden days, see Breatnach, *Uraicecht na Ríar*, 124 (note to §6).

86 *CL* §21 (*CIH* 512.22–4). Translation by McLeod, *Contract law*, 74.

87 *Cétmuinter* can apply to either spouse, but in this context I use the above translation, to distinguish her from the concubine.

made in ignorance [of their defects].'[88] The difference between a primary wife (*cétmuinter*) and a betrothed wife (*ben airnadma*) is one of descent, similar to that of a wife and a concubine in Roman and Germanic law, but this distinction seems to be slight. It appears that the *ben airnadma* refers to a secondary wife, as the text continues:

> When he [the husband] has given *coibche* to a[nother] wife, be it even out of his own property, then this *coibche* is due to the *cétmuinter*, when she fulfills her matrimonial duties in the union. Every concubine (*adaltrach*) who comes despite a *cétmuinter* (for *cend cetmuintire*) is liable to penalty, she pays the honourprice of the *cétmuinter*.[89]

The giving of *coibche* makes clear that this is a betrothed concubine who is married despite (against the wishes of) the primary wife. As this clause is mentioned under *lánamnas mná for ferthinchur*, it suggests that this type of marriage was also relevant to concubines, as the rule that a betrothed concubine has to hand over her *coibche* to the primary wife results in leaving her without any property to bring into the marriage.

We have seen that marriage on *aititiu* did not involve the giving of *coibche* and a betrothal (*airnaidm*), and this applies to both *lánamnas airite for urail* ('union of acceptance by inducement') and *lánamnas fir thathigthe cen urgnam, cen urail, cen tarcud, cen tinól* ('union of a frequenting man without work, without inducement, without performance, without contribution').[90] The woman of the first relationship on acknowledgement is called *ben for airitin n-urala* ('accepted woman on inducement').[91] We do not find this title elsewhere, but we can safely equate her with the *ben aititen* ('acknowledged woman'), who appears in

---

88 *CL* §22 (*CIH* 512.29–31). Translated by Mc Leod, *Contract law*, 75. He points out that a *díupart*, a contract of which her husband did not know its disadvantage, is meant here.

89 *CL* §23 (*CIH* 513.7–8, 14–15). The translation is based on Thurneysen's, who takes *for cend* to mean 'in the place of', but it appears that the *cétmuinter* keeps her position. See *CIH* 7.29–30 (*Heptad 6, AL* v 143) for the same expression (see §7), Ó Corráin, 'Women and the law', 49, takes this rule to be borrowed from the Lex Romana Visigothorum.

90 *CL* §33 and §32 respectively (*CIH* 517.33–5; 517.18–21). The commentators to the text in *Cáin Lánamna* take it that the woman of the first type (*airech*: 'concubine') was given goods by way of inducement, which were not given to the woman of second type (*carthach*: 'paramour'; 'lover'), see *CIH* 517.36–518.1 (*AL* ii 399). The commentators are sometimes confused between the two relationships, and use the two terms in both cases.

91 *CL* §4 (*CIH* 505.21).

the law-tracts *Gúbretha Caratniad* and the so-called *Díre*-text.[92] The account of the latter is especially interesting, as two types of acknowledged women are mentioned in a section which deals with the question who is entitled to the payment of wergeld (*éraic*) if a woman is killed, to the share of her property (*díbad*) when she dies, and who has to pay for her crimes (*cin*). The text names five categories of women, the first one having the closest ties to her husband, the next being to a larger extent still attached to their parental families.

1   *cétmuinter* with sons.
2   *cétmuinter* without sons.
3   the acknowledged woman betrothed by her family (*ben aititen aranaiscc fine*).
4   the acknowledged woman who has not been betrothed, who has not been sanctioned [to enter the relationship] (*ben aititen nad-aurnascar nad-forngarar*).
5   the woman who has been abducted in defiance of her father or her kindred (*ben bis for foxul dar apud n-athur no fine*).

1   two-thirds of *éraic*, *díbad* and *cin* fall on her sons, one-third on her family.
2   one-half of *éraic*, *díbad* and *cin* falls on her husband, one-half on her family.
3   one-half of *éraic*, *díbad* and *cin* falls on her sons, one-half on her family.
4   two-thirds of *éraic*, *díbad* and *cin* fall on her family, one-third on her 'belly-kin' (*bronnfine*).
5   all of the *éraic* and *díbad* fall on her family, all of her *cin* and children from the relationship to the abductor.[93]

92   Thurneysen, 'Caratnia', 355, §43 (*CIH* 2198.20). For the *Díre*-text, see my next note, and *CIH* 922.13–14 (*IR* 4, *Díre* §2): '*aititiu* i.e. she is acknowledged in visiting the house [of the man], and she is not a first wife, and she is not betrothed' (*aititiu .i. addaimter in naithig[id] tige, nibi primben 7 ni haurnascar*); my emendation (cf. *CIH* 1811.3–5). Thurneysen reads: 'as mistress of the house' (*in naithig*).

93   *CIH* 440.32–442.9 (*IR* 27–8, *Díre* §§27–32). The translation is based on Powers, 'Classes of women', 81. *Bronnfine* refers to all the sons of this woman (cf. *CIH* 54.31, 35 (*AL* v 319)), whether from her husband or another relationship – an indication of her reputation. The *bé cuitchernsa*, the *cétmuinter* and the *adaltrach* with sons belong to the 'lawful women' (*mná dligthecha*) in later commentaries, see Binchy, 'Legal capacity', 220–1 (*CIH* 974.35–975.21), etc. A *cétmuinter* was always under the rule (*cáin*) of her husband, an *adaltrach* could choose to be under

From this text it emerges that if a marriage produced sons, the ties of the woman with her parental family became looser: her son or sons could take over a part of the responsibility for her, and were thus entitled to a share of the *éraic* and *díbad* when she died.[94] Hence the higher status of the *cétmuinter* with sons, she held the ideal situation within the Irish marriage. The importance of a wife's sons is illustrated by the rule that the highest compensation (*díre*) was due to a mother whose son became a king, bishop or master sage, as they had the highest honourprice in the Irish legal system.[95]

The *ben aititen aranaiscc fine* has an intermediate position between a proper marriage with betrothal and an informal relationship, and appears to be synonymous with the *ben for airitin n-urala*, while the woman who is not betrothed nor sanctioned resembles the woman of the second type of a relationship by acknowledgement. Although the evidence is scanty, it may be suggested that even with an informal relationship by acknowledgement a formal betrothal became necessary, and it seems that this refers to the taking of a concubine in particular. Other texts which discuss the relationship of married women with their husbands, sons and families name her as *adaltrach airnadma* ('betrothed concubine'), and this is also how the *ben aititen aranaiscc fine* is glossed in the *Díre*-text itself.[96] Although relationships by acknowledgement are still referred to in the legal commentaries, it emerges that a concubine had to be properly betrothed, and this already appears in *Cáin Lánamna*, as is discussed above.

It may well be that this was propagated by the Church, although there are also similarities with concubinage as treated in late Roman law. As the term *adaltrach* ('adultress', from Latin *adultera*) implies, the Church disapproved of concubinage, but as a compromise they may have promoted the proper betrothal of the concubine, to forestall illegitimate offspring, to favour proper marriages and to force men to take the responsibility for the financial burden of a (secondary) wife. This gave concubines – through their sons – a legal and acceptable status; to have a concubine

---

her son, (paternal) family or husband (*fer a sliasta*: 'man of her thigh'), see *CIH* 443.21–4 (*IR* 34, *Díre* §37).

94 If the sons were still under the authority of their father, he, in his turn, would take over their responsibilities. Mother and son formed a *lánamnas* relationship (*CL* §2, *CIH* 503.26–7).

95 *CIH* 1964.13–17, see also 922.29–30 (*IR* 8–9, *Díre* §9) and Thurneysen, 'Caratnia', 348, §38 (*CIH* 2197.19–24).

96 *CIH* 442.1–2 (*IR* 27, *Díre* §30). Note also *CIH* 240.35–6 (*Di Astud Chirt 7 Dligid, AL* v 481): '*adaltracha iarna hurnaidm no aidite dia finaib fria firu* (concubines after their betrothal or acknowledgement by their kins to their husbands).'

without sons would not only give her a lower status, it would also be more suspect from a proper Christian viewpoint. Without sons an *adaltrach* had only a limited contractual capacity, because she had only her family (and for a small part her husband) to fall back upon – her legal position was still more that of a daughter than of a wife; legally speaking she was still *báeth*.[97]

Perhaps as a justification for this development, the lawyers suggest that it is permissable to take a second wife when the first one is unable to bear children. A commentary to *Heptad* 6 declares that the *cétmuinter crólige*, who was injured to such a degree that she 'was dead in the law of cohabitation', could be sent back (to her parents) by her husband if she did not recover after a certain period; if this was not possible her husband had to maintain her and compensate her in case he took another wife as his *cétmuinter* (called 'a *cétmuinter* on the neck of another').[98] Normally, it would seem that an *adaltrach* was not elevated to the status of *cétmuinter*, unless the first *cétmuinter* chose to divorce her man, to which she was entitled when her husband took another wife.[99] From this it may seem that the main function of the *adaltrach* was to produce sons, but if we meet examples of kings having four, five or six wives with over a dozen sons, it seems that their primary role was to conclude political marriages or that they were held for pleasure.[100]

Although concubines were thus legally acceptable, the lawyers make their disapproval felt by giving them an inferior status as compared with the *cétmuinter*, who is held in high esteem, and who symbolizes monogamy and chastity. The Christian virtues were especially promoted among the poets, who were singled out to practise sexual modesty, rather like the clergy; illicit cohabitation would degrade or disqualify a poet.[101] In more general terms, the *Collectio Canonum Hibernensis* forbids the Irish to take concubines before or during marriage, and one legal passage goes as far as to say that 'lords, poets, commoners are impaired by illicit

---

97 See Binchy, 'Legal capacity', 217–23 (*CIH* 511.29–512.7; 1808.29–1809.5; 974.35–975.21, etc.), and §2 above.
98 *CIH* 7.29–8.20, at 7.37 (*AL* v 145). Repudiation of one's wife because of her infertility is a saga-theme in Knott, *Togail Bruidne Da Derga*, lines 64–7 (§4), and Stokes, *Cóir Anmann*, 343 (§133). In Bieler, *Irish Penitentials*, 88–90 (Penitential of Finnian §41) it is forbidden.
99 *CIH* 48.5 (*Heptad* 52, *AL* v 293).
100 Examples are in Dobbs, '*Ban-Shenchus*'.
101 *CCH* xlvi, §15; Meyer, *Cáin Adamnáin*, 12 (§24); Breatnach, *Uraicecht na Ríar*, 105, §6 (*CIH* 2337.13–18). A detailed discussion is in Ó Corráin, Breatnach and Breen, 'The laws of the Irish', 400–5.

cohabitation'.[102] In *Críth Gablach* the grades of commoners and nobility
are pictured as legally married to a *cétmuinter* of equal rank.[103]

The higher status of the *cétmuinter* is also evident elsewhere. She is
given higher compensation than an *adaltrach* when raped, and better sick-
maintenance.[104] *Heptad* 6 recounts among the seven situations when
blood is shed without entailing liability or sick-maintenance: 'bloodshed
inflicted by a *cétmuinter* through lawful jealousy on an *adaltrach* who has
come despite her (*fora ceand*).' The commentator gives the legal details if
an *adaltrach* was not given a warm welcome in her new home:

> The *cétmuinter* is completely free from liability for anything she
> may do during the first three nights short of killing, and retribution
> is due from her for killing ... the *adaltrach* has the right to inflict
> damage with her finger-nails and to utter insults and scratchings
> and hair-tearings and small injuries in general ...[105]

One may wonder whether these rules would be remembered if it ever
came to blows, but the legal principle in itself is clear enough. The opinion of the Church complies with this, as is expressed in *Córus Bescna*, in
which those who are acceptable as lawful firstlings to be given to the
Church are mentioned. The text specifically stipulates: 'every first-born
of a lawful primary wife (*cétmuinter cóir*)', which the glossator explains:
'lest children of *adaltrach*s or *ben táides* ('secret woman'; harlot) are given
to the Church.'[106] In the matter of succession the son of a *cétmuinter* was
preferred above the son of an *adaltrach*, unless the latter was clearly better qualified.[107]

On the whole, the position of the betrothed concubine can be com-

---

102 *CCH* xlvi, §17–18; *CIH* 725.30–726.2, 1113.40–1, (cf. 1467.15, 1480.5). See Ó
     Corráin, 'Marriage', 18–19 for these and other examples.
103 Binchy, *Críth Gablach*, lines 144–5, 199–200, 346–7, 410–11, 439, cf. *CCH* xxxv,
     §4. See also *CIH* 45.38 (*Heptad* 50, *AL* v 287) and Thurneysen, 'Caratnia', 311,
     §7 (*CIH* 2193.5–11). Not marrying according to rank involved a larger contribu-
     tion from the one with lower status, but less rights, see *CIH* 46.18–22 (*Heptad*
     50, *AL* v 287), and Kelly, *Guide*, 73.
104 *CL* §35 (*CIH* 519.1–4); Binchy, '*Bretha Crólige*', 45, §56 (*CIH* 2301.21–5). For
     further discussion, see Power, 'Classes of women', 98.
105 *CIH* 7.29–30; 8.15–19 (*AL* v 143, 147). The translation is based on Power, ibid.,
     84, 87. For lawful jealousy see also *CIH* 289.31–290.23 = 1645.38–1646.28
     (*Bretha Étgid*, *AL* iii 293–5).
106 *CIH* 531.3–7; 10 (*AL* iii 39), cf. Deutr. 21:15–17.
107 *CIH* 1035.6–13 = 1281.4–9 (Thurneysen, *Cóic Conara Fugaill*, 44, §71 = 16, §3)
     and 1296.32–9; 1300.29–31; 1301.1–8; 1547.2–8, 33–4; 1548.33–40, all glossed
     fragments from the tract *Maccshlechta*.

pared with that of the concubine on the continent, and in both cases we see that their relationships resemble proper marriages. However, whereas in Ireland concubinage could amount to polygamy, and was openly practiced, the nobility and kings on the continent did not go so far, and were not liable to get complaints like Ruaidri Ua Conchobair (†1198) about his six wives. According to an annalist the pope offered him the kingship of Ireland and permitted him to keep his six wives if he renounced adultery henceforth, but Ruaidri preferred sinning above ruling, and thus his descendants lost the kingship.[108]

§8: CONCLUSION

From the above discussion it appears that around the seventh or eighth century the marriage laws and customs of Ireland were quite similar to those on the continent. Certain common elements can be explained by common Indo-European roots, such as the various types of marriage, the position of women in the early period, the purchase of a woman by paying a brideprice to her family. The developments which were taking place on the continent in the early middle ages seem to have been followed in Ireland, and it appears that mutual cultural contacts were to a large extent responsible for the shaping of the Irish marriage customs in this period.

Confronted with these developments, the lawyers, unable to draw upon oral tradition in this matter, seem to have turned to scripture, canon law and continental law for a redefinition and restructuring of their laws. That they did not take over the most extreme opinions in those writings testifies to their practical sense. Furthermore, the large and diverse body of material, so full of contradictory rules and confused regulations, could in no sense be considered as a standardized whole which was readily available to be used for the codification of laws. Indeed, in this period the involvement of the Church in secular legislation and law enforcement on these matters was exceptional rather than a matter of course. Moreover, the Irish lawyers, often belonging to the clergy, reasoned that the traditional law had been inspired by the Holy Spirit, which was complemented by Christian law rather than opposed to it.[109] As certain examples given above suggest, they often adapted those rulings closest to their own legal customs and traditions, a tactic which was also employed on the continent.

108 *Ann. Conn.* s.a. 1233.3.
109 McCone, 'Dubthach Maccu Lugair', 8–13; Ó Corráin, 'Irish vernacular law'; *CIH* 232.32–4 (*Di Astud Chirt 7 Dligid, AL* v 453), 478.8–10 (= Hull, '*Bretha im Gatta*', 218, §2), etc.

The influence of Christianity on these laws was globally the same in Ireland as on the continent, but whereas on the continent the Church's position changed in the ninth and tenth centuries from voicing opinions to actual legislation in cooperation with secular rulers, its position in Ireland remained passive. Although kings could issue laws, their legislative activities were small and they did not produce any new codes or texts for their own kingdom or the whole of Ireland, and ecclesiastical leaders showed no initiative to remedy the situation.[110] As a result, the traditions as encoded in *Senchas Már* and other early texts continued to be the basis for written law, and developments which took place were entered in the existing law-tracts in the form of glosses and commentaries.

The coming of the Vikings may have obstructed contacts between Ireland and the continent in the crucial period of the ninth century, but on the whole it seems that Irish society had already reached its limits to adapt itself to the changing circumstances, and was not able to accept female rights of inheritance and primogeniture which transformed Germanic society so drastically. Irish society remained family based and politically unstable, and did not evolve rapidly enough to deal with the Anglo-Normans, probably the most innovative society at the end of the twelfth century, both politically and militarily. The Anglo-Normans considered the Irish to be backward, their Christian faith suspect, and their marriage customs outrageous. The early Christian culture which the Irish had helped to preserve was now thrown in their faces.

110 For kings issuing laws, see Ó Corráin, 'Nationality', 23–4.

Women Poets in Early Medieval Ireland

STATING THE CASE

Thomas Owen Clancy

Great advances have been made in the last twenty years or so in bringing the role of women in the middle ages to light. The medievalist journal *Speculum* recently celebrated this fact by devoting a special issue to the interface between feminist criticism and medieval studies.[1] Particular areas of study have opened up our understanding of the writings of medieval women: the fact of that women writers existed in sizeable numbers is perhaps only just beginning to really settle into the orthodoxy of medieval studies, and indeed, certain barriers of genre are finally beginning to be broken. Janet Nelson, and others, have recently sought to demonstrate that women historians were more common in the early middle ages than generally thought, as well as trying to develop a generalized description of the difference of their historical perspective.[2] Recent volumes on feminist approaches to both Old English literature and Middle High German literature have appeared, alongside a number of profitable studies of the work of the *trobairitz*.[3] Two important volumes, now a decade old, lay the groundwork for the study of the literature of medieval women: Katharina Wilson's wide-ranging anthology of texts and discussion, *Medieval women writers*; and Peter Dronke's *Women writers of the middle ages*. Dronke's contribution probably remains the most monumental, there and elsewhere, covering as it does a wide range of languages and genres, from the letter-poems of German nuns to the theology of late medieval mystics.

Early medieval Ireland's place in this welter of rediscovery is less certain. Although much has been done to increase our understanding of the legal position of women (indeed, Ireland is probably a better place to

---

1 Partner, *Studying medieval women*. The chapter by Bennett (309–31) provides a good review of recent trends. See also van Houts, 'The state of research'.

2 Nelson, 'Gender and genre', 'Perceptions du pouvoir'; van Houts, 'Women and the writing of history'.

3 Damico and Olsen, *New readings*; Classen, *Women as protagonists and poets*; Paden, *Voice of the Trobairitz*, Bruckner, 'Fictions of the female voice'. The introduction to Classen also contains a valuable review of the whole field.

study this than anywhere else in Europe),[4] and work is continuing on the situation of religious institutions for women in early medieval Ireland,[5] much remains to be done. On the side of literature, such study is perhaps insurmountably hampered by two basic facts about that literature: it is mainly anonymous, and it is also characterized by the frequent use of dramatic *personae* as the speakers of poetry.

The overt use of a *persona* by the poet must always cast into doubt whether a poem spoken by a woman is the creation of a woman. In general, though, the assumption has been that all poems, unless proven otherwise, are created by men. This is based partially on the male-exclusive attitudes of the bardic establishment, and partially on the absence, by and large, of women poets from the period during which our knowledge of poets and poetry becomes more detailed: the classical Irish period, from *c.*1200–1600.[6] The few studies of poems in women's voices in Irish literature to date have been content to present and anthologize poems of all sorts without discrimination or discussion.[7] Statements on the plausibility of women as the authors of some of these poems have been left to asides of a generalized nature. Here, as a sample, are two nearly contemporary and seemingly contradictory statements by James Carney on the authorship of one of the longest and finest poems adopting a woman's voice, *Aithbe damsa*, usually called 'The lament of the Caillech Bérre'. In the first he is discussing the author's imagery:

> When he speaks of drinking with kings and receiving presents of chariots, and horses, he is adverting, I would say, to his own experience as a poet. The difficulty I find in accepting the poem as a literary realization of the plight of an old courtesan who has given up the world (or rather, whom the world has given up) has to do with the Irish social scene *c.*750. Little as we know about this, I have some difficulty in imagining a woman (whether courtesan or wife) continually carousing with the men folk. It is my impression that Irish warrior society was the natural ancestor of the society that

4 Ó Corráin, 'Women in early Irish society'; Kelly, *Guide*, 68–81; Binchy, et al., *Studies in early Irish law* and see now Ó Corráin, 'Women and the law' and Ní Dhonnchadha, 'The *Lex Innocentium*'.
5 Hughes, *Early Christian Ireland*, 234–5; Bitel, 'Women's donations', 'Women's monastic enclosures'.
6 On the existence of Irish women poets during this period, see Simms, 'Women in Gaelic society', 33–6; Cunningham, 'Women and Gaelic literature', 148–54; for recent work, see Ní Dhonnchadha, 'Two female lovers', and see also Kuno Meyer, 'Mitteilungen' (b), 18 and Lehmann, 'Woman's songs', 132. I am grateful to Dr Ní Dhonnchadha for sending me a copy of her article in advance of publication.
7 Lehmann, 'Woman's songs'; Henry, *Dánta ban* is particularly disappointing.

survived in Ireland until comparatively recently: the drinking world was the man's world; the women at best got a token sip, and their main function (as in the sagas) was to serve and pour.[8]

It may, however, be preferable to take the poem at its face value, that is, as having been written by a woman. (Outside the monastic milieu poetry in Ireland was written largely by hereditary professional poets. Líadain [of the tale of Líadain and Cuirithir] is presented in the saga ... as a professional woman poet. There is every reason to believe that in the ninth century, an educated or aristocratic lady might make a habit of composing verse.)[9]

For a more general summary of previous views on the question, we may note Ruth Lehmann's rather inverted logic: 'There is, in fact, no reason to assume that any of the Irish woman's songs were not composed by men.'[10]

Such generalized statements are not convincing, and what this paper sets out to do is to try at least to establish the ground-rules by which we can make an intelligent decision on some of this anonymous poetry. Ultimately, it seeks to show that in many cases application of Ockham's razor would cause us to state instead 'There is, in fact, no reason to assume that many of these songs were not composed by women.' And, very occasionally, we can be more positive than this. The paper is split into two parts: in the first, the basic principles are set out on which we can build an argument for Irish women as having been authors of poems in the early medieval period. The second part examines a few items of literature and considers how they measure up. The time-scale of study is limited to the period up to 1200, since the classical period has come under some scrutiny already in recent years,[11] but material from the Gaelic world in the centuries after 1200 is used later on for purposes of comparison.

In many ways this is a simplistic paper with a rather naive aim. More interesting approaches can and must be taken in regard to this literature. Searching questions about the role of gender in early Irish literature, about the relationship between fictive speaker and author, and about the ways in which poets, whether male or female, engender their speakers by use of language and imagery – all these must be asked. But to do so with-

---

8 Carney, 'Lament of Créidhe', 239.
9 Carney, *Medieval Irish lyrics*, xxv and n.16.
10 Lehmann, 'Woman's songs', 129.
11 See note 6 above.

out some confidence in the existence of women poets in early medieval Ireland is to do so on an uneven playing field, and so the basic questions must be asked first. Hence the ground-level title of this paper: 'stating the case'.

The first thing to be said is that women poets clearly did exist in early medieval Ireland. They are mentioned occasionally in law-texts, although these are prone to covering hypothetical as well as actual situations.[12] However, we know the name of at least one historical woman poet, Úallach ingen Mui(m)necháin, who died in either 934 or 932.[13] The annals call her *banfile hÉrend*, 'the female poet of Ireland'; an accomplished poet no doubt, since this sort of 'poet of Ireland' terminology tends to be complimentary as well as descriptive. Whether any of the poems we have preserved are her work we will never be able to tell, but there are none extant which are attributed to her. However, she is probably not the only poet whose name we know.

The names of four of them may well be contained in a prose preface to the poem *Aithbe damsa*, usually titled *The Lament of the caillech Bérre*. This preface describes the speaker of the poem as having being called Dígde, a woman of the Corcu Duibne of West Munster. More specifically she was of the Uí Maic Íair Chonchinn. The writer then goes on to name three more famous *caillich*, old women or nuns, of that family, two of whom we know to have been poets: Líadain, and Úallach.

> *Sentane Berre, Digdi a ainm, di Chorco Dubne di .i. di Uaib maic Iair Conchinn. Is dib dano Brigit ingen Iustain. Is diib dono Liadain ben Chuirithir. Is dib dono Uallach ingen Muineghain. Foracaib Finan Cam doib ni biad cen caillig n-amra n-ain dib ...*

> [The Old Woman of Beare, whose name was Digde, was of the Corcu Duibne, that is to say of the Uí Maic Íair Chonchinn. Brigit daughter of Iustán belonged to them also, and Líadain wife of Cuirithir, and Úallach daughter of Muimnechán. Fínán Cam has bequeathed to them that they shall never be without some wonderful glorious nun/old woman among them.][14]

Úallach we have already met. Líadain is the heroine of the tale *Comrac Líadaine ocus Cuirithir*, to which we shall return.[15] Although a fictional

---

12 See Kelly, *Guide*, 49.
13 AI 934, AFM 932.
14 Murphy, 'The lament', 83; Ó hAodha, 'The lament', 309; this preface is only found in TCD MS H.3.18, 42 col. 2.
15 Meyer, *Líadain and Cuirithir*.

character, it seems likely that she had a real historical existence, and certainly the author of that tale, who calls her *banéces*, a female poet or scholar, had no difficulty in conceiving of a female professional poet.[16] By force of association it is likely that the third member of this trio, Brigit daughter of Iustán, was also a poet, though nothing further is known of her.

In addition, Professor Máirín Ní Dhonnchadha has argued that the speaker of the poem, Dígde, is not the mythical figure the Caillech Bérre, but is rather an historical woman. Whether this historical woman is the author of the poem or simply the persona adopted by the author, the mythical resonances in the poem are likely to be literary conceits and no more, and may even be meant ironically.[17] We have in that case, not three poets and one legend, but four women whom the author of this preface, at least, thought were poets.

The family to which these women belonged is stated to have been granted by St Fínán Cam always to have a glorious *caillech* among them. We should not be misled by the old age of the speaker of the poem for which this is the preface: here this ambiguous word means nuns, not old women. There was a women's monastery within the territory of the Uí Maic Íair Chonchinn, called Cell Aiched Conchinn, now Killagh, Co. Kerry. This is the monastery which Líadain, in the tale of which she is the heroine, protesting against her being accused with the male poet Cuirithir, says she is from: *messe féin ó Chill Conchinn*.[18] We know that this monastery considered itself under the patronage of Fínán Cam: so says the late Life of St Abban, at any rate.[19] It would later become the Augustinian abbey at Killagh, near Milltown, Co. Kerry.[20] We need to remember also that in general women's monasteries remained related to the family which founded them, usually on their territory, and women generally only entered enclosures on family territory.[21] What this preface seems to tell us then, is that the local women's monastery of the Uí Maic

---

16 Ibid., 12.
17 Summary of 1992 Tionól lecture 'Reading the so-called *Caillech Bérri* poem', *School of Celtic Studies Newsletter*, 1993, 15. She has also argued tentatively that Dígde may perhaps be datable to the ninth century and may have been the mother of a member of the Múscraige Treithirne – a sept of the Múscraige Bregoin in Co. Tipperary – though she would not now support all of these arguments (personal communication, October, 1994).
18 Meyer, *Líadain and Cuirithir*, 18.
19 Plummer, *Vitae*, i.17; *Bethada*, i.8. In the Irish texts the foundation is originally called Cell Aithfe.
20 In 1216, Gwynn and Hadcock, *Medieval religious houses*, 155, see also 391.
21 Hughes, *Early Christian Ireland*, 235; Bitel, 'Women's monastic enclosures', 17–21.

Íair Chonchinn produced three, perhaps four famous nuns who were poets.

It is unsurprising if this were where we should look, in the first instance, for women writers. Certainly it is religious women elsewhere in the early middle ages who produce the most and most easily identifiable works of literature – one thinks of Berthgyth, Lioba, Hrotswitha, Hildegard and many others.[22] Our expectations of Irish poets has also undergone a sea-change in recent years. In the past, too firm a divide was drawn between the 'native', vernacular professional poets, and the monastic writers. Expectations of the early medieval period would now be that most or many poets had some sort of clerical involvement or monastic training, and any assessment of potential women poets should probably incorporate the same expectations.[23]

This is certainly where we know of literate women. The lives of a number of saints contain references which indicate that learning among women was not unexpected.[24] In the hagiographical literature, the monasteries of Íte and Monenna exchange books, Monenna herself is praised for her learning, Daig mac Cairill teaches women letters (*literarum scientiam*, to the daughters of Colum), as does Finnian (to St Lassar), and Íte herself teaches her nephew. One of Monenna's nuns is sent to Britain where she stayed, 'in a certain little lodging in which she read the Psalms and other necessary books'.[25] Admittedly these are later lives about nearly legendary figures, but their expectations, especially in the case of the lives of Íte and Monenna, which were written in still functioning women's monasteries, tell us a great deal about the milieu in which they were written, much the same milieu as some of the texts we will look at later. Of course, the composition of poetry does not in any way depend on literacy, nor does literacy necessarily imply literary creation. Nonetheless, when we turn our attention to the anonymous poetry, it may be well to note Rosamond McKitterick's view that if a manuscript tradition of a text, particularly a hagiographical one, is focused exclusively on female monasteries then it is very likely that we are dealing with a case of female authorship.[26] Although the manuscript tradition is less relevant to the

22 For Berthgyth, Lioba and other Anglo-Saxon letter-writers, see Sims-Williams, *Religion and literature*, 211–42; for Hrotswitha, see Wilson, *Medieval women writers*, 30–63, Dronke, *Women writers*, 55–83; Hildegard, Wilson, 109–30, Dronke, 144–201.
23 McCone, *Pagan past*, 17–28.
24 Bitel, 'Women's monastic enclosures', 20, 25.
25 Heist, *Vitae*, 91, §25; de Paor, *St Patrick's world*, 289.
26 McKitterick, 'Frauen und Schriftlichkeit', cited in van Houts, 'The state of research', 286.

Irish situation, it may be that texts which focus internally on women's monasteries, or which are associated in tradition with them, can also be counted as likely or at least potential cases of female authorship.[27]

As mentioned above, our ability to identify any of the literature composed by women, lettered or unlettered, is undermined by the anonymity of much of the poetry, and by the poets' use of fictive speakers. We are in a position, then, similar to students of Anglo-Saxon poetry.[28] To identify the poetry written by women, we might try to set out expectations of what the poetry would be like, what sort of poetry we would expect women to be composing, based perhaps on comparative evidence or on modern ideas of gendered language. We could perhaps also set some sort of agenda by the sorts of poems which we find being put in the mouths of women: these are predominantly love-poems and laments. In all this, however, we are in danger of circular argumentation, and of placing too much weight on our assumptions about what and how women composed in early medieval Ireland.[29]

Just as an example, in one extraordinary case, the critical approach to laments for dead husbands or lovers which are attributed to women has changed from a view which accepted them at least as the fictive speakers of these poems, to a view which seems to assume that, during the classical period at least, all or at least most such laments written from a female perspective are the product of court poets drawing on a conceit in which they portray themselves, metaphorically, as the widows of the dead man.[30] This analysis has been projected back into early medieval contexts as well. The conceit was indeed in wide use by professional poets in the later middle ages, and perhaps so in the early middle ages as well. But a conceit demands a reality with which to play: it presumes the idea of women composing laments for their husbands and lovers, as we know from different circumstances later in literary history they did.[31] Indeed, we know that women in the early middle ages engaged in keening for dead people: this is implicit in the work of Blathmac, and in prohibitions in the Irish

27 Horner, 'En/Closed subjects', and 'Spiritual truth and sexual violence', focuses on the female monastic milieu implied in two very different Anglo-Saxon poems.

28 Bragg, *Lyric speakers*, esp. 85–111.

29 On the problems and prospects for the study of difference in women's writing generally, see E. Showalter, 'Feminist criticism'. Some discussion of women's language and women's writing in medieval and modern Gaelic literature can be found in Ní Annracháin, ' "Ait liom bean a bheith ina file" '.

30 Carney, *Studies*, 243–75, 'Lament of Créidhe', 227–31; Simms, 'The poet as chieftain's widow'.

31 See, for instance, Ó Tuama, *Caoineadh*.

Penitentials.[32] Though these are not the same as the formal elegies of the classical period, we shall see that at that time in Gaelic Scotland, women were composing laments for their husbands and lovers. It is rash to presume that all such Irish poems are by men, simply because some are, and that none are by lamenting women. It is also perhaps rash to project the literary conceits of classical poetry backwards into the early medieval scene. We will return to this question later, but we should note that Máirín Ní Dhonnchadha has recently argued with reference to both the classical and post-classical period, that poems by male poets in which a female identity is sustained throughout are extremely rare, and among bardic poetry, almost non-existent.[33]

How can one tell, then, whether the voice of a poem, a woman's voice in a poem, has the weight of a real woman poet behind it? One might add, does this matter? In some sense this is a very stodgy sort of pre-occupation, an obsession with the person and personality of the author which is more than a little simplistic.[34] We could produce a very interesting analysis of the gender, and the engendering of the speaker of certain poems in the voice of a woman, but this will not help us to solve the problem at hand. Our assumptions, even if they are neutral, about gender and authorship will necessarily colour our interpretation of what we read, and hence we must address those primary assumptions.

It is dangerous, on the other hand, to assume, as some have done, that women will necessarily write a certain way, that language is gender specific. Medieval scholars have come up with some characteristics within the literature by women which they believe separate it from that written by their male contemporaries. Caroline Walker Bynum, for instance, discussing late medieval mystics, speaks of 'the tendency of women to somatize religious experience and to give positive significance to bodily occurrences' and of 'a more experiential quality in their mystical writings', which she links with stylistic differences, noting 'men's writing often lacks the immediacy of women's; the male voice is impersonal'.[35] Peter Dronke lists some 'general observations' on the women writers he discusses, while noting that these may be 'hardest to analyse in purely literary terms':

32 Carney, *Poem of Blathmac*, 2ff; Bieler, *Irish penitentials*, 162, 230; note the particular injunction against nuns lamenting.
33 Ní Dhonnchadha, 'Two female lovers'.
34 Note again Ní Dhonnchadha, 'it would be rash to claim or imply ... that the sex of the poem's or song's persona indicates the sex of the composer.'
35 Bynum, 'The female body', 168.

The women's motivation for writing at all, for instance, seems rarely to be predominantly literary: it is often more urgently serious than is common among men writers; it is a response springing from inner needs, more than from an artistic, or didactic, inclination. There is, more often than in men's writing, a lack of apriorism, of predetermined postures: again and again we encounter attempts to cope with human problems in their singularity – not imposing rules or categories from without, but seeking solutions that are apt and truthful existentially. Hence the women whose texts are treated here show excellingly a quality (literary, but also 'metaliterary') of immediacy: they look at themselves more concretely and more searchingly than many of the highly accomplished men writers who were their contemporaries. This immediacy can lend women's writing qualities beside which all technical flawlessness is pallid.[36]

This focus on gender difference and language is an interesting and useful way of assessing literature already 'authored' and known to be by women, but much more problematic to use diagnostically, and even more problematic in the case of women of whose language we know little or nothing to begin with, separated as they are from us by vast cultural differences.[37] Applying it to anonymous poetry, the exercise can too easily become either facile in the face of evident personal input and experiential engagement or limiting in the face of artistic technique or authorial distancing.

One scholar has attempted in a fairly rigorous way to take observations on the works of known female authors and apply them to anonymous works in a diagnostic way. Janet Nelson, discussing historical work by women in the early middle ages, synthesized the qualities found in 'authored' texts thus, and used them to ascribe certain anonymous historical works to the hands of women:

> The first trait is one of form: the style is relatively free ... The second and third traits relate to content: a sharp-eyed pre-occupation with the play of power within royal families, and a marked interest in the political roles of royal women.

She stresses that it is the coincidence of these traits which leads her to suspect female authorship, as well as, importantly, more circumstantial fac-

36 Dronke, *Women writers*, x.
37 However, see the attempt by Patricia Belanoff, 'Women's songs, women's language'.

tors, such as a textual tradition centred on nunneries.[38] In the case of early
Irish lyric poetry, however, we have somewhat less in the way of circumstantial detail, and next to nothing by way of comparative material with
already identified female authors. Nonetheless, it should be recognized
that though it is a dangerous route to follow, such diagnosis by literary
quality is feasible under certain circumstances.

For our purposes, literary quality can help in diagnosis really only if
we can swing Ockham's razor far enough over that we can say that it is
best to assume first that a particular poem was written by a woman. Then,
the way in which certain metaphors are employed and certain themes
treated will no doubt be useful in reinforcing our analysis. What we can
almost certainly say is that if a professional woman poet has composed a
poem in precisely the same way as a male poet, a poem of praise perhaps,
or a political poem, and has done so anonymously, we will never know
that it was by a woman.

On the other hand, it might be more profitable to abandon the agenda of this paper altogether, and take heart in Marilynn Desmond's opti-
mism about the anonymous Anglo-Saxon lyric:

> The anonymity of so much medieval literature illustrates just one
> example of these differences: the anonymous medieval lyric comes
> to the modern reader unauthored. Such poetry presents a unique
> set of textual possibilities within the constructs of literary history:
> as 'fatherless' texts these lyrics require no 'serious act of insubordi-
> nation' in order to be adapted to a feminist perspective. For the
> feminist reader, medieval *frauenlieder* provide the opportunity to
> short-circuit issues of historical gender and focus instead on the
> gender of the text.[39]

The anonymity of Irish poetry, and the use of fictive speakers, could like-
wise become an advantage in focusing on the text itself, rather than the
context and authorship of it. However, this would demand a different sort
of study than the one we are engaged in here.

A further sense of both the possible presence of women writers in
Ireland, and at the same time, to cloud the issue, a further dismantling of
assumptions of what they might be writing, can be gained by comparative
evidence from outside Ireland. First, we can turn to the continent, where
significant amounts of writing by women have been re-established in
recent decades. It is fair to say that the social situation, in particular with

38 Nelson, 'Gender and genre', 161.
39 Desmond, 'The voice of exile', 577.

regard to women's learning, is completely different on the continent. The social position of women in Germanic societies, seems to have been much better than in Gaelic society, despite the romantic notions still carried around by some folk about the 'proto-feminist' nature of Celtic societies.[40] Christine Fell notes:

> The statements that are made about the subordination of Saxon women, and the relative freedom of 'British' (i.e. Celtic) ones, are blatant misrepresentations of such evidence as we have. Early Celtic law shows women in a far less favourable position than Anglo-Saxon law.[41]

However, we can point convincingly at least to the existence of a great amount of poetry of many and varying types, from love poetry to religious poetry and narrative, having been composed by European women in the middle ages. The generic and stylistic range of this material, as noted above, militates against attempting to use it diagnostically.

We should touch very briefly here on the situation of Anglo-Saxon poetry, which bears a great similarity to our own problem. There, despite the well-known Latin literary activities of a number of women, primarily female monastics, it has proved impossible to demonstrate beyond doubt that the speakers of the two vernacular poems which appear to be in the voices of women, let alone the authors of them, are indeed women.[42] However, beyond the voice, matters such as the fairly unconventional styles of these two poems, *Wulf and Eadwacer* and *The Wife's Lament*, as well as the nearly unique strophic form of *Wulf*, and the perspective which seems to be represented by them, have all been invoked in trying to establish what may unfortunately be unestablishable: female authorship.[43] The problem here, as in Ireland, is the almost certainly fictive speakers, which create a distance between poet and poem which personality and gender may not bridge. We should, however, bear Fred Robinson's recent dictum in mind:

> We shall never know who composed [various Old English poems]. But we should not pretend to know that women did *not* write them

---

40 For a good corrective to such views, see Márkus, 'Early Irish "feminism"'.
41 Fell, *Women*, 11.
42 Robinson, 'Old English poetry'.
43 Belanoff, 'Women's songs, women's language'; Desmond, 'Voice of exile'. For a good recent discussion of gendered discourse in *The Wife's Lament*, see Horner, 'En/Closed subjects'.

and continue to read these poems with the tacit assumption that they are all the products of male authorship.[44]

Probably the most important comparative evidence for our purposes, however, comes from elsewhere within the Gaelic-speaking world, from late medieval and early modern Scotland. This evidence is important because it comes from within a culture substantially similar to Ireland's, and one which consciously looked to Ireland as its cultural and literary homeland. Indeed, given the later medieval focus of many of the other essays in this collection, we should perhaps be spending more time on this material, but we will concentrate on poetry pre-1200, and use later material only for comparison.

In Scotland there is certainly no resistance to the idea of women as poets, or to ascribing anonymous poems, even ones not certainly in a female voice, to women.[45] There are two main reasons for this: one is that much of the poetry we have was preserved by women, and indeed by their use of many of the poems as work songs, particularly waulking songs, accompanying the fulling of cloth. By this process, many songs have been invested with women's voices even where the original was gender-neutral, and have had stanzas added to them, and other minor alterations, such that we would be justified in terming the female tradition-bearers co-authors of some of the works. By this process also, many anonymous songs, which certainly do appear to have been composed by women, particularly laments, were preserved.[46] It is fair to say that with this poetry or song we are out of the learned milieu of bardic poetry, and so hesitations about training and education need not worry us.

The other reason for the acceptance of the idea of female authorship in Scotland is that from the fifteenth century through to the nineteenth, many of the best and most famous Scottish Gaelic poets in any given century have been women, and their names, lives and works are well-known.[47] Indeed, almost in complete reverse to Ireland, where women poets have had a strong voice only in this century's literary scene, only the twentieth century has not (yet) seen a Scottish Gaelic woman poet whose impact on the poetic tradition has been more than slight, though this may well change soon. The nineteenth sees the work of Màiri Mhór nan Òran, Màiri MacPherson, who was primarily a radical political

44 Robinson, 'Old English poetry', 168.
45 Bateman, 'Gaelic tradition', 12.
46 Ibid., 12–16; Thomson, *Introduction*, 57ff.
47 A selection of poetry from these is in Bateman, 'Gaelic tradition', 53–113.

poet.[48] The turn of the seventeenth and eighteenth centuries sees the work of three important poets: Catríona Nic Gilleain, Mairearad nighean Lachlainn, and Sìleas na Ceapaich, two of them from the Hebridean isles of Coll and Mull, and the other a MacDonald writing in the north-east.[49] Slightly earlier we have the work of Màiri nighean Alasdair Ruaidh, whose patrons were the MacLeods of Dunvegan in Skye.[50] The sixteenth century sees the work of a few anonymous MacGregor poets, and the fifteenth the poetry of Aithbhreac nighean Corcadail and Iseabail countess of Argyll.[51] These are joined by any number of minor and anonymous poets.[52] There are also occasional notices of female poets whose work we do not know, such as the Agnes Carkill, 'barde wife', who performed for king James IV of Scotland on January 3, 1512,[53] and performers who may have been creators of poetry as well, such as the 'twa hieland singing women' who performed for the Countess of Mar in the seventeenth century.[54]

The generic and stylistic range of work suggests that we must approach the whole subject with open minds: formally, this poetry includes both learned verse and vernacular metres. Its subject matter ranges from battle-incitement to love-poetry. The earliest two mentioned poets differ greatly. Aithbhreac, wife of Níall Óg Mac Néill of Gigha, is

48 Ibid., 88–95; Thomson, *Introduction*, 245–8; Meek, *Màiri Mhór*; Mac Gill-eain, 'Màiri Mhór nan Òran' in *Ris a' bhruthaich*, 250–7.

49 Ó Baoill, *Bàrdachd Shìlis na Ceapaich*; Thomson, *Introduction*, 135–45; Thomson, *Companion*, 193, 213; Mac Gill-eain, 'Mairearad Nighean Lachlainn', 'Sìlis of Keppoch', in *Ris a' bhruthaich*, 162–90, 235–49. Note also Diorbhail Nic a' Bhriuthainn of Luing (fl.1645), MacKenzie, *Sar-obair*, 56–7, Thomson, *Companion*, 213; Mòr NicPhàidein, fl.1620–5, in Ó Baoill and Bateman, *Gàir nan clàrsach*, 74–7. Ó Baoill and Bateman edit and translate a number of other seventeenth century poems by women.

50 Watson, *Mary MacLeod*; Thomson, *Introduction*, 132–5.

51 Bateman, 'Gaelic tradition', 52–61, 38–41, 337–40; Watson, *Scottish verse*, 60–5, 234–5, 307–8. Note also that one Máire nighean Néill Stiúbhairt is also credited with poetry in the Book of the Dean of Lismore. See Quiggin, *Poems*, 110.

52 The subject of Scottish Gaelic women poets has been taken up by Anna Frater (herself a poet) in a recent completed doctoral thesis, 'Scottish Gaelic Women's Poetry up to 1750' (unpublished PhD thesis, Glasgow, 1994).

53 *Accounts of the Lord High Treasurer of Scotland*, iv, 402; see also Logan, 'Introduction', xxxvi. The name Carkill is, as far as I know, an Antrim name, derived from MacFheargail (Woulfe, *Sloinne Gaedheal is Gall*, 360), and Agnes Carkill may then have been an Irish woman. The language she performed in could well have been Gaelic, but this is uncertain.

54 In the household book of the Countess of Mar there is also mention of 'ane woman clarshochar', Logan, 'Introduction', xxxvii.

the author of a lament on her husband, *A Phaidrín do dhúisg mo dhéur*,[55] as fine a lament on the death of a chieftain as one is likely to find, and one which despite its personal elements (she writes: 'For want of only this one man / I am alone, longing for him') maintains both the structure and imagery of aristocratic verse (she calls him: 'Lion of Mull of the white walls / Hawk of Islay of the smooth plains'). The attribution to Níall Óg's widow is certainly genuine, and the style, restraint and professionalism of it should be instructive in looking at laments in the voice of lovers and widows in Ireland in both the early and later middle ages.

Iseabail Ní Mheic Cailéin, the Countess of Argyll, however, is a love-poet who belonged to a witty Clan Campbell court circle; she employs the game-playing of *amour courtois*. Some of her poetry resembles that of the *trobairitz*, in its direct, very bodily approach to the genre:

> Atá fleasgach ar mo thí,
> a Rí na ríogh go rí leis!
> a bheith sínte ré mo bhroinn
> agus a choim ré mo chneis.

> Dá mbeith gach ní mar mo mhian,
> ní bhiadh cian eadrainn go bráth,
> gé beag sin dá chur i gcéill,
> 's nach tuigeann sé féin, mar tá.

> Acht ní éadtrom gan a luing,
> sgéal as truaighe linn 'nar ndís:
> esan soir is mise siar,
> mar nach dtig ar riar a rís.

[There's a young man in pursuit of me, / Oh King of Kings, may he have success! / Would he were stretched out by my side / with his body pressing against my breast!

If everything were as I would wish, / no distance would ever cause us separation, / though that is all too little to say / with him not yet knowing the situation.

But it isn't easy if his ship doesn't come, / for the two of us it's a wretched matter / he is East and I am West, /so what we desire can never again happen.][56]

55 Bateman, 'Gaelic tradition', 52–5.
56 Ibid., 60–1; also Watson, *Scottish verse*, 307–8.

There is another poem in the same vein by her in the Book of the Dean of Lismore.[57] A third poem by her is a fairly obscene boast to the court circle on the size and potency of her household priest's penis. The authenticity of the attribution to Iseabail has been questioned, but without substantial grounds. It has not yet been properly edited, or translated in published form.[58]

Sìleas na Ceapaich is perhaps the poet who gives us the most sense of the range and capabilities of a female poet in a Gaelic-speaking society, though she belongs to the early modern period.[59] Much of her poetry is religious: there are not only meditations and hymns but also an interesting dialogue poem between herself and death, describing her conversion.[60] There are laments, but these must cause some rethinking of any idea that women's poetry is necessarily more immediate or less artistically motivated. We have from her three different laments for her husband and daughter, who both died in the same week, three laments in different forms and styles, employing different metaphors and perspectives, which show the experimentation, emotional distancing and stylistic adventure of a professional.[61] There is political poetry too: if we did not know she had written it, what analysis of language and gender could possibly hint to us that a woman had written the lines:

> *Ach Alba éiribh còmhla,*
> *Mun geàrr Sasunnaich ur sgòrnan,*
> *Nuair thug iad air son òir uaibh*
> *Ur creideas is ur stòras*
> *S nach eil e'n diugh 'n ur pòca.*

[Scotland, rise as one body, / before the English cut your throttles, / since your credit and resources / they bought off you with coinage / that's no longer in your pockets.][62]

---

57 Watson, *Scottish verse*, 234–5; Bateman, 'Gaelic tradition', 60–1.
58 Quiggin, *Poems*, gives a diplomatic edition, 78 and see Frater, *Women's Poetry*, 354. For some discussion of Iseabail and her identity, see Watson, *Scottish Verse*, 307. On the bawdy poem, *Éistidh a lucht an tighe-se*, its authenticity and parallels, see Gillies, 'Courtly and satiric poems', 42, 'Gaelic poems of Sir Duncan Campbell', 72.
59 Ó Baoill, *Sìleas na Ceapaich*, lviii–lxv discusses the corpus and range of her poetry. There are some 23 of her poems which survive.
60 Ó Baoill, *Sìleas na Ceapaich*, XX, XXIII, III.
61 Ibid., XI–XIII.
62 Bateman, 'Gaelic tradition', 80–1.

And there is more: she is the author of two poems of advice to young women, adjuring them not to set too much store by men, and above all to listen to the voice of her experience and not be misled into sex by men who will love you and leave you.[63] She is also the author of the justly famous 'Lament for Alasdair of Glengarry', in which all her poetic resources are employed in the cause of a formal lament.[64]

This rather long – it perhaps ought to be longer – detour into Gaelic Scotland has mainly had the purpose of suggesting what is possible in a Gaelic context. We do not really understand why female poets are so prevalent in Scottish Gaelic's literary history, and the questions are really only beginning to be asked, and the poetry to be properly investigated. But if one is approaching the subject of female authorship of poetry in a Gaelic context from the viewpoint of the Scottish Gaelic tradition, one is likely to be more favourably disposed to accept women as authors even in tenuous cases, and more open-minded about what the content of poetry by women might be. Certainly it is possible, then, at least in localized circumstances, for women to write even the 'masculine' verse of the classical period, and in Ireland before 1200 it may also have been more possible than a perspective from afterwards would suggest. To that we may add that one area of Ireland, Munster, in the period after 1600, does show signs of active literary women, not only the composers of personal laments like Eibhlín Dubh Ní Chonaill, author of the lament for Art Ó Laoghaire, but also the seventeenth century poet of the O'Brien's, Caitlín Dubh.[65]

It is time now to turn briefly to the material in the early medieval period which I believe would repay examination both in light of the principles I have been suggesting (that women in early medieval Ireland were composing poetry, were literate, might have a wide range of style and subject matter) and in light of their own particular contents. The first thing to note is that among the bits and pieces of poetry we have in margins and metrical tracts and elsewhere, are some poems obviously in the voices of women, and for which female authorship might well be a possibility.

These include the poem in the margins of the Book of Leinster which comments on the activities of young men who come courting:

63 Ó Baoill, *Sìleas na Ceapaich*, II, XV.
64 Ibid., XIV; Bateman, 'Gaelic tradition', 76–9; 72–5.
65 Simms, 'Women in Gaelic society', 36; Ó Tuama, *Caoineadh*; Walsh and Ó Fiannachta, *Catalogue* iii, 26.

Gel cech nua – sásad nglé
utmall álcha ócduine,
áilli bretha bíte im sheirc,
millsi bríathra fir thochmairc.

[Everything new is neat – cheers! / A young man is changeable in
his desires, / lovely are decisions about love, / sweet the words of a
man who comes wooing.][66]

They also include the following quatrain from *Auraicept na nÉces*, reminiscent of medieval debate poetry about the relative merits of students
and warriors:

Díambad messe in banmaccán
no-cechrainn cach felmaccán,
fer nád fintar co cluinter,
slánchéill chéin dúib, a muinter.

[If I were the young woman / I would love every student, / a man
you can't know until you hear him talk, / a long farewell to you,
my folk.][67]

Many of these poems recall poetry from elsewhere in Europe by
women or in the voice of women. Compare, for instance, this example,
from a Middle Irish metrical tract:

Cride é,	He's a heart,
daire cnó	a grove of nuts;
ócán é,	he's a lad,
pócán dó.	a kiss for him.[68]

with the German coda of a letter by a learned monastic woman of the
twelfth century:

Dû bist mîn, ich bin dîn:	You are mine, I am yours,
des solt dû gewis sîn.	of this you must be sure.

66 LL f.121a; ed. and trans. Greene and O'Connor, *A golden treasury*, 203–4.
67 Calder, *Auraicept*, ll. 533–6; ed. Greene and O'Connor, *A golden treasury*, 112–14,
    trans. slightly adapted.
68 Thurneysen, 'Mittelirische Verslehren', 100 §177; edited by Greene and
    O'Connor, *A golden treasury*, 112–14, trans. mine and see now R. Baumgarten,
    ' "*Cr(a)ide hé* ..." and the early Irish copula sentence'.

Dû bist beslozzen	You are locked
in mînem herzen:	within my heart
verlorn ist daz slüzzelîn:	the little key is lost:
dû muost immer drinne sîn.	there you must rest forever.[69]

Peter Dronke, commenting on these lines, asks, 'Did the learned lady improvise these, or was she quoting a popular *winileod*?' With the Irish example we seem to be faced with a similar possibility, that the authors of the metrical tracts may occasionally quote from popular, as well as learned verse.

Most of these poems seem fairly personal: even in the poem attributed in manuscripts to Gráinne, the heroine of the romantic tale from the Finn cycle, the fictive element is far from explicit, and it may well be that the poem existed prior to its ascription to her.

> *Fil duine*
> *frismbad buide lemm díuterc,*
> *ara tabrainn in mbith mbuide*
> *uile, uile, cid díupert.*

[There's a man / on whom I would be glad to gaze, / for whom I would give the golden world / all, all, though it were a deception.][70]

Although these poems in women's voices seem both popular and personal, it may well be that they are indeed only poems in the voices of women. One may note that the *winileodas* and *frauenlieder* discussed by Dronke, which often have the same tone as our Irish stanzas, were used as the basis of a tradition of 'women's songs' among professional male poets in Germany and elsewhere.[71] It should then be cautioned that we may in fact be dealing with a similar phenomenon in the Irish quatrains, of male poets using the themes and emotions of women's poetry to fashion a new artistic work. Such poems may indeed be found included within narratives, or as speeches presumably extracted from a narrative context, such as the love-lullaby Gráinne sings to Diarmaid, or the lines spoken by Eorann to Suibne in *Buile Shuibne*.[72] Nonetheless, there seems to

69 Dronke, *Medieval lyric*, 94.
70 LU ll.514–17; edited by Greene and O'Connor, *A golden treasury*, 112–14, trans. mine.
71 Dronke, *Medieval lyric*, 94–102.
72 Greene and O'Connor, *A golden treasury*, 184–8; O'Keeffe, *Buile Shuibhne*, §32.

be a contrast between at least some of the stray quatrains mentioned and the more worked lyric compositions, and some of them – *Cride é*, for example – may well derive from popular women's songs.[73]

More important, however, are three of the finest and most out-of-the ordinary pieces of literature from the 8th to the 10th centuries, all of which employ a woman's voice or use a female character as their protagonist. They are familiar to most students of early Irish literature, having been anthologized in nearly every book containing medieval Gaelic poetry. There has been much critical discussion of one of them, but very little of the other two.

The first is the well-known poem *Ísucán*.[74] It has been famous mostly for its 'charm', and for its curious use of diminutives, in a very untranslatable way. Less famous is its use of legal metaphor and its theological aims. These are brought out clearly in E.G. Quin's edition and translation, and though his emphasis loses some of the more aesthetic aspects of the work,[75] it is a great palliative to some of the more cloying sentimental interpretations available. The manuscripts in which it is found attribute it to St Íte, a sixth-century founder of a women's monastery in Co. Limerick, and though we need not assume her necessarily to be the intended speaker, let alone the author (the poem is from *c*.900), it may well originate from her monastery of Killeedy, formerly Cluain Credail.

A cursory examination of the poem shows – though it has not, to my knowledge, been stressed before – that the poem is intended to be performed, or recited, or sung, by women, specifically by the *ingena*, the 'maidens' of a female monastery, who are to sing to Christ 'a fitting harmony/fittingly', or perhaps a 'choral song', which must refer reflexively to the poem itself.

Canaid cóir a ingena	Sing a fitting harmony, maidens,
d'fiur dliges for císucán	to the legal recipient of your tribute.
attá na purt túasacán	Ísucán is at home on high
cía beith im ucht Ísucán.	even though he be in my bosom.[76]

This last verse contextualizes the poem immediately, and provides the

---

73 Note also the tradition of the *síanán* alluded to in a number of Irish tales, such as *Scéla Muicce Meic Da Thó* and *Immram Snédgusa ocus Meic Riagla*, as peculiar to women. See references in *DIL*, 540, *síanán*.

74 Main editions, Murphy, *Early Irish lyrics*, 26–9; Greene and O'Connor, *A golden treasury*, 102–3; Quin, '*Ísucán*'. Quin, p.39, provides a basic bibliography on the poem.

75 As he notes on p.44.

76 Quin, '*Ísucán*', 43, 50. All translations are from Quin. Discussion of *cóir*, 49–50.

basis of an analysis of the poem's purpose and meaning. Designed for the consumption and performance of monastic women, it meditates on a particular aspect of the lives of some of those women: fosterage. We might note that this seems to have been a practice in St Ite's monastery of Cluain Credail. Around the time of the composition of this poem and later, tales which were set in the seventh century certainly depict Cluain Credail as engaging in fosterage, raising abandoned children and others.[77] The poem seeks to invest their mundane task with transcendent meaning: the children they raise, be they of kings or paupers, are Christ. Christ is to be present in their hermitages with them. This theological insight is echoed elsewhere in a story with a similar scenario: 'Eithne and Sodelb ... Christ used to come in the form of a child and was in their bosom and they used to kiss Him, and He baptized them, and even if the apostles were to preach to them, they received more faith from Him than they would have from them.'[78] This is a testimony, then, to the relative power of bodily experience over religious words. It is interesting that the two women in that story were from a smaller religious house, Tech Ingen mBaíti.

The language employed by the poem is, as Quin notes, extremely legal: it is the language of contract and tribute. Interestingly, this is the very sort of language which Lisa Bitel has shown to be prominent in the Lives of Irish women saints, many of whom are shown struggling against their families and social structures to be able to donate their bodies to God, and their lives to a monastery.[79] There is also a similar poem, again attributed to a woman (St Brigit), in which the speaker prays to be a *císaige*, a 'rent-payer', to God.

> *Ropadh maith lem*
> *corbam císaige don flaith;*
> *mad chéss imned*
> *forsa tipredh bendacht maith.*

[I would like / to be a tributary of the Prince; / happily he has suffered care / on whom He would bestow a good blessing.][80]

That poem has been assumed to be by a man, because the speaker is portrayed wanting to provide hospitality for the people of heaven, to be a

77 See, for instance, MacEoin, 'The Life of Cuimine Fota', 201; Bernard and Atkinson, *The Irish Liber Hymnorum*, vol. i, 16; cf. Bitel, 'Women's monastic enclosures', 29–30.
78 Stokes, *Félire Óengusso*, 102–3; Quin, 51.
79 Bitel, 'Women's donations', 11–13; 'Women's monastic enclosures', 22–4.
80 Greene, 'St Brigid's alefeast', 152.

rent-payer to God, to have angels and the apostles at a feast, but again the Lives of female saints depict women in precisely these roles, indeed emphasize them.[81] In the poem, the poet concentrates on investing the act of hospitality with the same sort of pervasive spirituality as *Ísucán* possesses, desiring to serve 'a great alefeast for the king of kings'. Although it takes a somewhat more allegorical tack, imagining the serving vessels of this alefeast to be 'casks of patience', 'beakers of alms', and 'vessels of mercy', it still seems to invest the mundane action of providing food and drink for the stranger with transcendent meaning. More to the point, as in *Ísucán*, the poet prays for Christ and the 'men of heaven' (*fir nime, muintir nime*, vv.1,3,6; cf. *Ísucán*, v.2) to dwell in her house, saying 'I would like the men of heaven in my house ... I would like hospitality to follow them; I would like Jesus to be here continually'.[82]

Both these poems, written in a similar vein, and possibly both emanating from women's monasteries, seek to deepen mundane tasks with spiritual meaning, and use legal and contractual language to do so. Clearly legal language was not thought of as off-limits to women, despite their diminished status in the eyes of Irish law. Indeed, Bitel has pointed to the fact that their selves, their bodies are the principal items of property which women are shown donating in their *vitae*, and that certainly finds its echo in *Ísucán*, and it is apparent in some of the other poems we will examine. In a society in which the dominant form of social interaction and bonding was that of clientship, protection and contract, women were generally excluded from such processes. Within the religious world, however, they could reclaim the language of clientship and service, and participate with God in the lord-client relationship denied them outside it. Alongside the legal language of the poem, however, should be placed the personal and physical language, of nursing and endearment.

Ísucán is a poem firmly set in a woman's monastery, intended for recitation by women, and it employs a woman's voice to meditate on the theological implications of fosterage, as well her 'legal' position between God and man. But is it by a woman? Experiences like this are told of male saints as well, nursing the infant Christ: Adomnán and Moling, for instance.[83] Cluain Credail was a double monastery, and we might suggest that a male abbot, or a *fer léiginn*, a resident scholar, wrote the poem for the nuns. On the whole, though, the most reasonable interpretation would be that this meditation, at once intimate and public, is coming from within the experience of a woman in a monastery and directed towards

81 Bitel, 'Women's monastic enclosures', 26.
82 Greene, 'St Brigid's alefeast', 151–2.
83 Cited in Quin, 51.

investing that experience with greater meaning. Certainly we are not justified in assuming, as all previous editors seem to have, that the author
was a man. The contents seem to argue against such an assumption.

The next major work is the equally famous and much discussed
Aithbe damsa, or 'Lament of the Caillech Bérre', the old woman/nun of
Beare.[84] The very subject matter of the poem gives it an atmosphere at
once aristocratic and monastic. It has received a great deal of critical comment, and many meanings have been ascribed to it, allegorical, personal,
political. There is no reason to discount any of these. It is a complex,
highly wrought poem, which pursues its exploration of change and decay,
of flood and ebb, through the themes of personal fortune as well as the
political fortunes of the Corcu Duibne, the people in West Munster in
whose territory the poem is set, and from whom, according to the later
preface, the speaker/author came. Although it is likely that the common
notion that the speaker is meant to be a mythological personage or a sort
of personalized goddess is misguided, the speaker being drawn distinctly
as a human,[85] there is no reason to reject the notion that the poem also
draws on the female images of sovereignty current at the time to invest its
personal and political levels with added richness.

What evidence is there that the poem is actually written by a woman?
First, the recent suggestion by Máirín Ní Dhonnchadha that the speaker
may be an historical ninth-century figure is promising.[86] It is tempting to
suggest that the woman mentioned in the poem's preface, Dígde, of the
Corcu Duibne, who may have had connections with the Múscraige
Bregoin,[87] is not only the right character to be speaking of the ebb of personal fortune and political fortune, and employing the geographical references of both Corcu Duibne and Múscraige Bregoin to do so, but that
an author in such a set of circumstances is the most likely person to even
consider writing about such things.

Be that as it may, and despite the rich texture of metaphor and allusion
in the poem, it is hard to avoid the sense of a person behind the persona
in this poem: it seems too heartfelt, too much an internalized meditation.
Once one has discarded the legendary figure from the persona in the
poem, it is difficult to see why a man[88] would choose this particular character, choose to locate her in a backwater nunnery, and choose to speak in

84 The most recent edition is D. Ó hAodha, 'The Lament', which reviews the previous literature (308–9) and discusses earlier interpretations in the very thorough
   notes (317–31). All excerpts and translations here are from Ó hAodha.
85 Mooted by Máirín Ní Dhonnchadha, see note 17 above.
86 See note 17 above.
87 Based on tenuous evidence, see note 17 above.
88 One might suggest, for instance, Dubthach Bérre, sapiens, †868 (AI).

the particular language employed: language of cloth and young women's celebrations; of disintegrating beauty and a very bodily former life. It should be said that, like *Ísucán*, this poem speaks of the body as a legal entity: as a deposit, which Christ will reclaim. In verse 7, the poet says:

> *Tocair mo chorp co n-aichri*   Bitterly does my body seek
> *dochum adba díar aichni;*   to go to a dwelling where it is known;
> *tan bas mithig la Mac nDé*   when the Son of God deems it time
> *do-té do breith a aithni*   let Him come to carry off His deposit.

And again at the end, in one of the few optimistic verses in the poem:

> *Mo thuile*
> *is maith con-roiter m'aithne;*
> *ro-sháer Ísu Mac Muire*   *conám toirsech co aithbe.*

[My flood, / has guarded well that which was deposited with me; / Jesus, Son of Mary has redeemed it / so that I am not sad up to the ebb.]

It is this image of the body-contract which seems most clearly to define the speaker's relationship with God. But there are other ways in which the legal situation of women in Ireland sheds light on the poem. There were few things, according to early law, which a woman could alienate personally without the permission of her family, and among these were cloth, food, and household equipment or jewellery.[89] All these find a place in the imagery of the poem, especially cloth. The image of the threadbare cloak becomes a metaphor for the decaying body, and shades into some of the natural and political metaphors within the poem.[90] In particular, the poet contrasts her own state (and in the political subtext, that of her people) with that of Feimen, the plain around Munster's royal centre of Cashel:

> *Nim-geib format fri nach sen*
> *inge nammá fri Femen;*
> *meisse, ro melt forbuid sin,*
> *buide beus barr Femin.*

[I envy no one old, / excepting only Feimen; / while I have worn out an old garment, / Feimen's crop is still yellow.]

---

89 Bitel, 'Women's donations', 8–10; Kelly, *Guide*, 76.
90 §§2, 11–13, 20–1, 25.

Elsewhere she contrasts her own worn cloak with the ever-renewing clothing spread over the landscape – indeed, woven and fulled – by God.

> *Is álainn in brat úaine*
> *ro scar mo Rí tar Drummain;*
> *is sáer in Fer rod-lúaidi,*
> *do-rat loí fair íar lummain.*

[Beautiful is the green cloak / which my King has spread over Drumain; / the One who has fulled it is a craftsman, / He has put a cloak of wool over it after a / cloak of coarse cloth.][91]

The body imagery is sometimes difficult. The extraordinary verses 30 and 31 strike a note which echoes some of the language of the late medieval women mystics, but also of *Ísucán* and 'St Brigid's alefeast'. Here, the speaker makes a generous offer of hospitality to Christ, in terms which seem to deepen the female imagery, whether we interpret the word *cuile* here as simply the larder, or read it with DIL as a sexual metaphor.

> *Tonn tuili,*
> *nicos-toir socht mo chuili;*
> *cid mór mo dám fo-déine,*
> *fo-cres lám forru uili*
>
> *Ma rro-feissed Mac Muire*
> *co mbeth fo chlí mo chuile;*
> *cinco ndernus gart chena,*
> *ni érbart 'nac' fri duine.*

[The flood-wave, / the silence of my larder will not reach it; / although my own company may have been many, / a hand was laid on them all.

If the Son of Mary had known that / he would be under the roof-tree of my larder; / although I have practised liberality in no other way, / I never said 'No' to anyone.][92]

But the bodiliness of the poem relies not just on this one metaphor, but a

91 §§13, 21.
92 §§30–1. See Ó hAodha, 'Lament', 328–9, for discussion of these difficult stanzas, and DIL, p.587, *cuile*, for a meaning as 'bedroom'.

whole panoply of concrete images of the old woman's decaying flesh, hair, and skin.

One may cautiously draw in here the comparative evidence of Scottish Gaelic poetry. Much of the imagery of this poem, both the cloth imagery and the water imagery, is extremely redolent of the language of anonymous laments and love-songs in the Gaelic tradition, particularly ones used as waulking songs. One might also note the imagery of one of Sìleas na Ceapaich's laments on the death of her daughter and husband: she speaks of the year as having levied a double interest on her, and also draws the astounding image of herself after their deaths 'like a boat disintegrating on a beach, with no helm or sail, no oar or bailer'.[93] A reading of Sorley MacLean's discussion of the waulking songs and of the concrete in Gaelic poetry[94] only reinforces the sense of kinship between Gaelic poetry and the lament of the Caillech, though the latter takes that type of imagery and brings it into another dimension, joining it with political and religious metaphor.

Finally, it seems likely that a reading of the language of this poem from a perspective which assumes that a woman was its author would only confirm us in the view that the language and imagery comes out of a female experience of early Christian Ireland, and one which the poetic imagination of a man might not have been able or willing to recreate. One should note here, too, the characteristics which Janet Nelson found conjoined in her anonymous histories: formal oddness (the 'Lament' contains a mix of *rannaigecht* and *deibide*, as well as other stylistic oddities), a heightened awareness of social relationships as well as political ones (and the role of women among them) and an interest in the place of women in political goings-on. Although the histories discussed by Nelson are a far cry from the rich poetry of *Aithbe damsa*, it is still fair to point to these as at least possible indicators of female authorship. Moreover, what circumstantial evidence there is relating to the poem seems to point to an origin in a female monastery (see above), and indeed the internal setting of the poem only reinforces this. As with *Ísucán*, then, context and imagery both combine to suggest strongly that female authorship should be an initial assumption, although not a proven one.

The last of the three main works to be considered is much longer, and is different in its being in narrative prose, with a great deal of interwoven lyric poetry. This is the tale *Comrac Líadaine ocus Cuirithir*, 'The

93 Ó Baoill, *Sìleas na Ceapaich*, XII, §1.
94 Mac Gill-eain, 'Realism in Gaelic poetry', 'Notes on sea-imagery in seventeenth century Gaelic poetry', 'Some thoughts about Gaelic poetry', in *Ris a' bhruthaich*, 15–47, 83–105, 120–33.

Meeting of Líadain and Cuirithir'.[95] The poem which concludes the work is well known, much anthologized,[96] and highly praised for its psychological maturity, its vision of a woman wrestling between the conflicting desires for God and man.[97] The tale as a whole – which describes the woman-poet's meeting with the man, also a poet, their pledge to unite, and his subsequent discovery of her in a woman's monastery (almost certainly the Cill Aiched Conchinn mentioned above), their placing themselves under the somewhat bizarre spiritual direction of a saint, their being put together one night to test their chastity, the man's exile from the monastery and the woman's grief and ultimate death – is less well known. Unlike previous critics of the text who have dismissed it as a botched job or a storyteller's notes,[98] I view the text as a finely wrought, integrated work, with both poetry and prose employing similar language and ideas, the whole bound together by two dominant themes: that of madness and folly, and that of the meeting or tryst of the title, a meeting hinted at, but never realized.[99] The text is peppered with language play, especially with sexual-religious puns, like that in Cuirithir's chat-up line: *Cid ná dénaim-ni óentad?* 'Why don't the two of us unite/make a union', a line customarily spoken from saint to saint in hagiographical tales, as well as containing the more obvious sexual meaning.[100] Much has been made of its supposed confusion, obscurity and patchiness as a text, but these obscurities are no more than are found elsewhere in the terse prose of early Irish literature, and much of the confusion can be ironed out by intelligent and informed reading.

One of the most intriguing aspects of the work is its protagonist, a woman poet (we could even translate the term 'woman scholar'), and her dual position as both desired, and a desirer in conflict. Even more interesting is the way in which the basic paradigm of the Tristan tale (in which

---

95 Edited in full by Meyer, *Líadain and Cuirithir*.
96 See for instance Murphy, *Early Irish lyrics*, 82–5, and 208–11 for earlier editions and discussions; Greene and O'Connor, *A golden treasury*, 72–4. They also edit and translate two other poems from the tale, 75–7.
97 For instance, O'Connor, *Backward look*, 60, 63.
98 These include Robin Flower, who calls the prose 'brief and obscure' (Flower, *Catalogue* ii, 305), O'Connor, who calls them 'the fragmentary notes of a professional storyteller' (Greene and O'Connor, *A golden treasury*, 72), and James Carney, who calls the tale 'confused and improbable' and 'utterly unlikely' (Carney, *Studies,* 220–1).
99 I hope to publish soon a thorough reconsideration of the text. For some comments on the role of folly in the tale, see Clancy, 'Fools and adultery', 120–2, and for more general discussion, 'Saint and fool', 195–210.
100 Meyer, *Líadain and Cuirithir*, 12, l.4; Meyer, 'Mitteilungen' (a), 302, *Betha Colmáin maic Lúacháin*, 92 for saints using this expression.

a woman promised to an older man falls in love with a younger man, makes him elope with her, they spend a period in exile, and their deaths are eventually contrived by the older man) is so thoroughly subverted in this monastic version.[101] Not only is the woman here the desired and the man the propositioner, but her possessor – the older man – is here played by God and his surrogate the saint Cummíne Fota. Unlike other tales of the sort where the man postpones sexual union for his career, it is the woman who does so here, and continues to postpone it for her new-found religious career. Unlike tales where the sexually unstable woman ruins a man's career, the woman is here portrayed as the stable one, despite the assumptions of the men in the story. The tone of the work also runs counter to the ethos of the time, best portrayed in Daniél úa Líathaide's advice to a woman, telling her to give over her natural pre-occupation of thinking about sex,[102] and the misogynist leanings of the Céli Dé, for whom woman was man's 'guardian devil'. One may note also the story-based origins of these attitudes in the so-called 'Rule of the Grey Monks', which counsels monks to avoid women, pointing to the examples of Adam, Samson and Solomon.[103]

The tale seems also to echo many aspects of *Longes mac nUislenn*,[104] and Líadain seems to be in some ways a parallel to Deirdriu: farmyard language is employed, as in the story of Deirdriu, to express sex, but here it describes the lack of it (Cuirithir is to have no cow, nor the bulling of a heifer).[105] Verses from the last poem in *Líadain and Cuirithir* echo the wilderness time of Deirdriu and Noisiu,[106] and the stone on which Líadain finally dies, praying, echoes in a passive way Deirdriu's suicide stone.

The critique of female stereotypes in the tale can also be found among the language of folly and madness. Women and their sexuality were closely associated in early medieval Ireland with madness.[107] Note the words of Daniél úa Líathaide to the woman courting him: *Im-ráidi baís cen bríg*

101 Carney, *Studies*, 220–2 discusses its relationship to the Tristan paradigm.
102 Murphy, *Early Irish lyrics*, 6–9.
103 Strachan, 'Two monastic rules', 229. For Irish narrative realisations of this theme, see Kelly, 'The *Táin* as literature', 77–85.
104 Hull, *Longes Mac nUislenn*.
105 Ibid.,[ll.]109–15, 314–15; Meyer, *Líadain and Cuirithir*, 18, ll.5–8, and see Greene and O'Connor, 75–6, for alternative translation. Their emendation is excessive, however. Read *ná dairt i[n]na dartado* for MS *ná dairti na dartado*. On 'farmyard language' generally, see Kelly, 'The *Táin* as literature', 76–7.
106 See especially Meyer, *Líadain and Cuirithir*, 24, ll.13–15, and Hull, *Longes Mac nUislenn*, ll.232–3.
107 On the general association between sexuality and folly, see Clancy, 'Fools and adultery', 106–8.

mbaí, 'Thy mind is set on profitless folly'; and the words Eve speaks in her lyric monologue, regretting her plucking of the apple: *in céin marat-sam re lá / de ní scarat mná re baís.* 'for that, women will not cease from folly as long as they live in the light of day'.[108] In this tale, however, it is Líadain, the woman, who is sane and Cuirithir who is depicted as mad.[109] It is her sanity and stability which lead Cuirithir, eventually, to holiness.

It is true to say that elsewhere we find desired women leading men to salvation, particularly in otherworld tales.[110] Here, however, the woman is real flesh and blood, depicted from the inside. Her place in society fuels the tale: why does she end up in a monastery after postponing sex with Cuirithir? As a poet, she might well lose all independence once married to a man. Her poems are the ones that carry weight in this tale, none more so than the last, which is a sensitive exploration of the conflict of human and religious love. It does not resolve the problem, but we are assured that Líadain's struggle gains her heaven, however much her human desire continues.

As with the two poems examined above, the choice of character and of voice is unusual, even more so perhaps in this case. As with those poems, there is a certain amount of circumstantial evidence which points towards the composition of the text in a woman's monastery: the brief mention of Cell Conchinn, for instance, and the content which as we have seen emphasizes the woman's wisdom and independence. It shares language with them: like *Aithbe damsa* it blends sexual and religious language; like that poem, it shares insight into the psychology of the human and a mature approach to emotional pain and human sexuality; like *Ísucán*, it juxtaposes human and divine relationships.[111]

I would suggest, following the clues in the tale and the preface to the *Aithbe damsa*, that we might think of this tale as having been composed in Cill Aiched Conchinn, the monastery Líadain says she is from, and the nunnery on the territory of her family, according to my interpretation of the Lament's preface. In any case it seems likely that the personality behind this text is a woman's, insofar as we can discern one. One might even hazard a guess that either of the names mentioned alongside Líadain's as being a 'wonderful glorious nun' of the Uí Maic Íair Conchinn, Brigit daughter of Iustán or Úallach daughter of Muimnechán, the *banfile* of Ireland, was the author of this work, investing the charac-

---

108 Murphy, *Early Irish lyrics*, 8–9, 50–1.
109 Clancy, 'Fools and adultery', 121–2.
110 See McCone, *Pagan past and Christian present*, 79–82.
111 Frank O'Connor has alluded to the common elements in *Aithbe damsa, Líadain and Cuirithir*, and a third poem, *It é saigte gona súain*, in *Backward look*, 57–61.

ter of their predecessor with the conflicts and trials of their own monastic lives.

Briefly, we should note that although the poems we have so far dealt with offer a fairly positive view of women and their place in the Christian world, it is just as plausible that a poem like *Mé Éba*[112] was composed by a woman. It embodies a misogynist notion of both salvation history and the role of women; nonetheless, it seems possible that a woman might choose just this aspect of the contemporary world-view when composing a poem of repentance and sorrow. She might well enter into the original sin of Eve in the way late medieval German Christians entered into the crucifixion when they sang 'Ah holy Jesus, how have I offended? ... I crucified thee.' This is not to suggest that *Mé Éba* is indeed a product of female authorship: there is no evidence either way. It is merely to caution that the search for poetry by medieval Irish women might well lead to poems which present us with less than positive views of women.

Finally we should turn briefly to laments. This paper has attempted to encourage a healthy and optimistic attitude towards the possibility of female authorship in medieval Ireland, and has suggested some poems for which the case for female authorship is credible. Having done so, and having noted the presence in late medieval and early modern Gaelic Scotland of laments for lovers and husbands which are in fact by women, it might be good to consider in passing some of those early laments which have been explained by recourse to the conceit of the poet as the chief's wife or lover. Is this always the most appropriate, or the most obvious explanation? Is it ever the case, as it is perhaps in the poem *Géisid cúan*,[113] that a female author as well as a female speaker best suits the imagery involved? James Carney was quite right to strip the prose legends in which they were embedded from that poem and from the ninth-century lament attributed to Créd.[114] But having set them free, was the poet as chief's wife the right explanation to yoke them to? And, as noted above, does not the very conceit of the poet as the lamenting wife presuppose the composition of laments by wives? *Géisid cúan*, in particular, identified by Carney as originally a lament from around 1100 for a drowned warrior from south Kerry called Cael mac Crimthainn, and only later included in the growing dossier of material for the Fionn cycle, deserves reconsideration. The imagery of the poetry is more redolent of Scottish Gaelic laments for drowned chiefs[115] than of the examples cited by Carney. The

112 Murphy, *Early Irish lyrics*, 50–3.
113 Ibid., 148–51.
114 Carney, 'Two poems', 22–6; 'Lament of Créidhe'.
115 See, for instance, Mac Gill-eain, *Ris a' bhruthaich*, 97–9.

perspective of the speaker is in a few places explicitly feminine. There is no real reason not to take this as a lament by Cael's wife or lover. *It é saigte gona súain*,[116] on the other hand, is a more difficult matter, since whatever we decide about its authorship, it clearly draws on the situation of an earlier, legendary love-affair. It is impossible that it is contemporary with the events it describes, and given that the poem must then be a lyric monologue like *Aithbe damsa* or *Mé Éba*, again this poem would bear re-examination with regard to its depiction of gender, sexuality and religion.

Much remains to be done. All the poems examined here, which range in date from as early as the eighth century to as late as the early twelfth, deserve to be closely studied individually along the lines suggested. A proper consideration of the situation and work of the Scottish Gaelic poets for comparison is a necessity. We also need – and this is an area I have not touched on – to establish more generally the ways in which the voices of women were used in early Irish poetry, even where female authorship is highly unlikely, again for purposes of comparison. Some of the lives of women saints should be re-examined with a view to the genders of their authors. And a scholarly discussion about gender and its depiction in early medieval Ireland which goes deeper than accepted orthodoxies is clearly desirable as well. Finally, we need to go into later medieval Ireland with a more open mind about the literary potential of women in the Gaelic world.

This paper has suggested that women were composing poetry in early medieval Ireland, and that their voices may well have been speaking to us from our bookshelf anthologies for decades. I hope that at least this will give scholars pause to consider, when faced with anonymous poetry, whether the gender of the author is not as open to question as is his or her identity.[117]

---

116 Murphy, *Early Irish lyrics*, 86–9; Greene and O'Connor, *A golden treasury*, 78–80.

117 I wish to acknowledge my gratitude for the helpful comments and discussions of Máirín Ní Dhonnchadha, Christopher Shields, Rob Mullally, Timmie Vitz, and the members of the New York University Orality and Literature Colloquium. I am particularly indebted to Gilbert Márkus for having read a number of drafts of the paper, and for valuable debate and criticism. Finally, I am grateful to the British Academy for a post-doctoral research fellowship which has supported me during the writing of this paper.

'Cursed Be My Parents':

A VIEW OF MARRIAGE FROM THE LAIS OF MARIE DE FRANCE[1]

Bernadette Williams

In the *Lais of Marie de France*, written c.1155–1170, women are the central characters and permit the reader an opportunity to explore the female world in a period dominated by male comment. Medieval women writers are few and far between; writing was a male occupation. The fact that Eve's words had persuaded Adam to eat the apple, and thus caused the woes of the world, was used to justify requiring women to be silent in church and not attempt to preach. It therefore followed that women should not presume to write. Eve's part in the creation story was constantly retold to remind mankind that woman was responsible for the unhappy state of the world. Refreshingly, from Marie de France we get a different view of the story of the creation and fall; one of her heroes on being asked if he believes in God replies, 'I do believe in the Creator who set us free from the sorrow in which our ancestor Adam put us by biting the bitter apple'.[2] There is no mention of Eve here. Needless to say, this viewpoint was not the common one.

We do not know, and might never know, the identity of the historical person known as Marie de France. Her name comes to us from her collection of animal fables, derived from Aesop, which she had translated from English into French where she declared, 'I shall name myself so that it will be remembered; Marie is my name, I am of France'.[3] The convenient habit of combining the words Marie with France to give the author's name as Marie de France dates from 1581. As the name Marie is a common one several possibilities have been advanced in an effort to identify

---

1 Lais are short stories in verse which may have been recited or even sung; in one of Marie de France's Lais we are informed that it was performed on harp and rote, Burgess and Busby, *Lais*, 55 (hereafter *Lais*).
2 *Lais*, 88.
3 She was determined to be acknowledged as the author of all her writings and so she also declared her authorship at the end of another translation, from Latin into French, of the moral and supernatural tale, *St Patrick's Purgatory*, see Hanning and Ferrante, *The Lais*, 6.

her.[4] These suggestions include Marie, abbess of Shaftesbury; Mary, abbess of Reading; Marie, daughter of Waleran de Meulan and the final suggestion is that she was Marie, the daughter of Stephen of Blois (king of England 1135–54) and Matilda, countess of Boulogne.[5] We know this last-mentioned Marie was educated in a convent and became abbess of Romsey in Hampshire. However, she was removed from the convent by Henry II for political reasons and married off to Matthew of Flanders, a marriage to which Thomas à Becket publicly objected as she was a professed nun. She eventually returned to convent life.[6] Marie de Boulogne was well educated, had a knowledge of courtly society, was given in marriage for political reasons and was an abbess. All of these elements are evident in the Lais.

Marie de France was well educated. She knew classical Latin, French, English and possibly some Breton and spoke of long hours spent studying texts. Her level of education is clearly reflected in her heroines, who, apart from the statutory obligation of being beautiful and noble, are declared to be intelligent and well educated.[7] Reading proficiency on the part of the heroine is never questioned and remarks such as, 'when she had read what was written from start to finish',[8] abound in the Lais. It is quite clear that the ability of the heroine to read was considered to be in no way exceptional. What is really interesting is that Marie's heroines can also write. We are told of one heroine about to answer a letter, 'She got hold of ink and parchment'.[9] The ability to write whatever and whenever necessary must clearly have been essential in an illicit love affair. In the Lais, love affairs often arise in the milieu of arranged marriages, marriages such as that experienced by Marie de Boulogne before she returned to her abbey. There are many references to abbeys in the Lais and all are portrayed as exceptionally wealthy and well endowed – in effect the type of

4 Hanning and Ferrante, *The Lais*, 7. In common with other medieval writers, Marie de France dedicated her works to important contemporary figures. Her fables she dedicated to a count William and her Lais she dedicated to a noble king. These dedications are central to the problem of identifying the historical person who calls herself Marie.

5 In this case the noble king would have been the young Henry and her count could have been William de Mandeville. Sidney Painter made a persuasive case for the identity of count William as William de Mandeville, earl of Essex. He examined nine Pipe Rolls between 1167 and 1175 where there were 27 references to the 'earl William' without qualifying name and proved that in 21 instances 'earl William' was understood to refer to William de Mandeville (Painter, 'To whom').

6 *Lais*, 19.

7 *Lais*, 64, 105.

8 *Lais*, 83, 100, 109–10.

9 *Lais*, 100.

abbey to which a high ranking noblewoman would belong.[10] Such an abbess could enjoy a considerable amount of power and the convent could be a very desirable place for the medieval woman. There she would find a safe haven from the turmoil of a dangerous and often violent world. An abbess of such an institution would also find free time to study and to write. Identification of Marie de France with Marie de Boulogne is therefore an attractive proposition.

Marie de France was a strong and very resolute woman determined to pursue her writing career despite opposition. Virtually all medieval women writers felt a need to justify their writing.[11] The great twelfth-century nun and mystic, Hildegard of Bingen justified her presumption by stating that God had ordered her to write.[12] In a similar manner, Marie defended her boldness by calling on God as her inspiration by declaring, 'Anyone who has received from God the gift of knowledge and true eloquence has a duty not to remain silent'.[13] She added weight to this claim by referring to the Parable of the Talents with the words, 'Hear my lords, the words of Marie, who, when she has the opportunity, does not squander her talents'.[14] While Hildegard laid great stress on the fact that she was merely God's instrument, Marie de France did not display such humility and was far more forthright as she claimed her work as her own.

Not only was Marie de France determined to write but she was also determined to ensure that her work would not be interfered with and that no man would claim her work as his own. At the conclusion of the *Fables*, where she identified herself, she added the rider, 'It may be that many clerks will take my labour upon themselves. I don't want any of them to claim it'.[15] She frequently identified herself as the author in the Lais, espe-

---

10 When Eliduc's wife decided to retire to the religious life we are told, 'She had her church and houses built ... and everything endowed with much land and great possessions – it would have everything it needed. When it was all done she took the veil and so did thirty with her then she established her way of life and the rule of her order', *Lais*, 125. An example of such a noble abbey would be Fontevrault, patronised by Henry II and Eleanor of Aquitaine.

11 It has been said of the early thirteenth-century female troubairitz, Castelloza, who defended the right of women to sing love songs, that 'her lyrics depict a woman driven as much by exasperation as by *joi* to justify her breach of silence against the charge that she should not, in conscience, sing', Van Vleck, '*Tost me troubaretz*', 95.

12 Hart and Bishop, *Hildegard*, 59.

13 *Lais*, 41.

14 *Lais*, 43.

15 Hanning and Ferrante, *The Lais*, 6. Marie was justified in attempting to safeguard her writing. In the nineteenth century the theory was advanced that the works of Marie de France could only have been written by a man but this was so patently untenable that it was quickly dismissed.

cially in the prologue and at the beginning of the first of her Lais, *Guigemar*. She encountered criticism in her own lifetime which stiffened her resolve to persevere as she declared, 'Just because spiteful tittle-tattlers attempt to find fault with me I do not intend to give up ... I shall not cease my efforts'.[16] In fact Marie's Lais were popular and well received; a contemporary writer Denis Piramus mentions her Lais in his *Life of St Edmund the King* saying that they were popular among counts, barons, knights and ladies.[17]

Popular literature can be of value to the historian, when used with caution, as a source for the period in which it was written (but not for the period about which it was written). When the environment of the Lais – and not the Breton plots[18] – is explored then a unique aspect of the twelfth-century young noblewoman lies revealed. The central issues in each of the twelve Lais are love and marriage and within the tales a variety of love situations is explored. These Lais reflect the personal situations encountered by young noblewomen in the twelfth century and reveal the concern and anxieties felt by these women. Apart from Marie de France, we have very little real evidence on which to draw for information about the emotional life of the medieval woman. In other twelfth-century romances, such as the Arthurian romances of Chrétien de Troyes (c.1135–83), the woman is present only in a supportive role, where her purpose is to be a source of inspiration for the knight and to allow him opportunities to demonstrate his knightly skills and chivalric ideals. These chivalric ideals were not as favourable to women as is sometimes assumed. The eminent French historian, Georges Duby, has recently declared that, in his opinion, courtly love was a male game with woman as a lure, the counterpart of the tournament, and he does not hesitate in contradicting those who saw courtly love as a female invention. Duby does not see any particular promotion of woman resulting from the idea of courtly love; women remained at once feared, despised and strictly subjugated.[19] A passage from Chrétien's romance *The Knight of the Cart* (Lancelot) illustrates this point. 'If a knight encountered a damsel or girl alone – be she lady or maidservant – he would as soon cut his throat as treat her dishonourably, if he prized his good name. And should he assault her, he would be forever disgraced at every court'. This would appear to be an admirable attitude, however, the passage continues, 'But

---

16 *Lais*, 43.
17 Denis Piramus wrote these words between the years 1170–80 therefore the Lais were written prior to these dates, see Hanning and Ferrante, *The Lais*, 7–8. Jean Renart also cited Marie de France's *Lanval*, see Baldwin, 'Five discourses', 815.
18 *Lais*, 43, 56.
19 Duby, *Love and marriage*, 57–9.

if she were being escorted by another, and the knight chose to battle with her defender and defeated him at arms, then he might do with her as he pleased without incurring dishonour or disgrace'.[20] Clearly such chivalry was superficial. In the *Lais of Marie de France* the heroines emerge as women who struggle for their chance at happiness despite the odds weighed against them in the male-dominated society of medieval France.

Courtly love was the great prevailing topic when Marie de France wrote her Lais.[21] She displays her awareness of the topic but makes it clear that, although the idea of courtly love might be explored in the courts, it had little or nothing to do with the reality of life. In every instance where Marie de France depicts courtly love she reveals it as dangerous and leading to disaster.[22] She does not approve of it as she considers love to be too serious an emotion to be treated in the cavalier manner of courtly love. Love, she states, 'is an invisible wound within the body and since it has its source in nature, it is a long-lasting ill. For many it is the butt of jokes, as for those ignoble courtiers who philander around the world and then boast of their deeds. This is not love, but rather foolishness, wickedness and debauchery',[23] and she believes that 'no one under its sway can retain command over reason'.[24] Love is dangerous, especially for women, and should not be viewed through rose-coloured spectacles. A girl betrayed by the man with whom she has eloped declares, 'She who trusts a man is extremely foolish'.[25] Another heroine astutely remarks, 'If you had your way with me, I know well and am in no doubt that you would soon abandon me and I should be very much worse off'.[26] Also, lovers might not be constant, 'If you leave you will find another love and I shall remain here griefstricken'.[27]

Marie de France was also writing at a time when the church was becoming deeply involved in marriage. During the twelfth century the church was asked the question, 'Can a daughter be given in marriage against her will?' and, after much and careful deliberation, the answer was that she could not.[28] The church wisely considered that 'unwilling mar-

20 Kibler, *Chrétien*, 223.
21 Andreas Capellanus is believed to have written *The art of courtly love* at the court of Marie de Champagne c.1185 see Parry, *The art*; Jackson, 'The De Amore'; Jaeger, *The Origins*; Kelly, 'Eleanor of Aquitaine'.
22 Duby, *Love and marriage*, 58–9.
23 *Lais*, 49.
24 *Lais*, 56.
25 *Lais*, 125.
26 *Lais*, 58.
27 *Lais*, 50.
28 Noonan, 'Power'.

riages usually have bad results'.[29] Furthermore, the church also stated the principle that if there were no impediment between a couple and they had consented to each other, no one, not even her family, could prevent them from marrying. These new deliberations by the church were included by the jurist Gratian in the textbook of canon law, *Concordia Discordantium Canonum*.[30] This work was a massive compilation of excerpts from Christian writers and church council decisions illustrating every aspect of Christian life including the canon law on marriage. It was in the climate of Gratian's work that Marie de France wrote her Lais. Needless to say the family did not fully concur with the new church ideals and the reality of the situation was that the woman of noble class was not free to love. She was an object to be disposed in marriage, at the discretion of her nearest male relative, for the benefit of her family and the survival of her future husband's family. The situation for the medieval noblewoman continued as before and did not encompass freedom of choice in marriage. However, when neither love nor affection are a part of the marriage contract then clearly love outside marriage becomes a strong possibility. Indeed, Andreas Capellanus, author of *The Art of courtly love*, declared that love was impossible within marriage: 'Everybody knows that love can have no place between husband and wife'. He reiterated the sentiment again later with the words, 'We declare and hold as firmly established that love cannot exert its powers between two people who are married to each other'.[31] Love implies freedom of choice.

Marie de France in her Lais describes the dilemma which could occur when women fall in love. Certain themes are evident in her Lais; in four, *Guigemar, Yonec, Laustic* and *Milun*, the woman is trapped in an unhappy marriage to a man she has not chosen and falls in love with another. Marie has sympathy with these women whom she perceives as being, in essence, free to love because their consent was not sought for in the marriage. She allows these adulterous wives a noble love as she explores the theory of marriage of free consent in the reality of her medieval world. In two Lais, *Equitan* and *Bisclavret,* the woman is married to a good husband but betrays him. Marie is a realist and rebukes women who are fortunate enough to have kind husbands and yet cheat them as, 'A loyal partner, once discovered, should be served loved and obeyed'.[32] When love is offered to a woman by her husband it is inestimable and should not be abused. In another two Lais, *Le Fresne* and *Eliduc,* the woman loves her husband or lover but is abandoned by him.

29 Noonan, 'Power', 419.   31 Parry, *The art,* 100, 106.
30 Brundage, *Law,* 229–55.   32 *Lais,* 49.

Although Marie's heroines can be found in court and can meet handsome young men and, indeed, fall in love, this does not lead to marriage. In the Lai *Milun,* the heroine, the daughter of a nobleman, fell in love with the hero, a landless knight, in her father's court. The couple never even attempt to suggest the possibility of a marriage between them. A young girl had no authority to speak of marriage on her own behalf. Marriage was a privately negotiated transaction between the male members of two families with the advice of the kin and when the assent of all parties is given (which does not include the woman) then the marriage can go ahead; the woman was not entitled to question her eventual fate. If the woman had no family then her marriage was at the disposal of the king or her feudal lord. We have the example of the Roll that Henry II had drawn up in 1185 listing the women and children, male and female, under his control who were his to give in marriage. Fiction mirrors fact and in the Lai *Laval* we are told that king Arthur apportioned wives and lands to all who served him.[33]

Girls did sometimes try to rebel against their fate. There are some references to rebellious girls in medieval documents but their defiance is described as reprehensible.[34] In her Lais Marie de France presents so poignant a view of the emotions experienced by young girls trapped in this situation that it appears to be almost autobiographical. Of one girl we are told, 'the girl was plunged in the deepest grief',[35] and another young girl, married to a man she hates, cries, 'cursed be my parents and all those who gave me to this jealous man and married me to his person. I pull and tug on a strong rope. He will never die'.[36] Despite the church's newly voiced ideal of freedom of choice in marriage, this was the reality of life for many young noblewomen. It cannot be mere coincidence that so many of Marie's Lais, written at this period are concerned with marriages which did not embrace the concept of consent and thereby opened the way to love found outside that marriage. It could be claimed that Marie was affirming that where there was no free consent then there was no true marriage. In the Lai *Guigemar,* the marriage between the very old man and the heroine is depicted as flawed. He imprisoned her and ill-treated her, a lover came to her, they exchanged tokens and vowed true love. After many trials and tribulations when the lover's constancy had been proven they were united. This, in effect, was the true marriage, the marriage of consent – the earlier official marriage was not a true marriage.

In the Lai *Yonec,* again there is a marriage between a very old man who wants heirs and a young maiden. The purpose of the marriage was to ful-

33 *Lais,* 73.
34 Duby, *Love and marriage,* 25.

35 *Lais,* 98.
36 *Lais,* 87.

fil a woman's primary function and provide her husband and his family
with the sons and heirs they required. In the Lai Marie tells us, 'in Britain
there once lived a rich old man who was very old and because his inheritance would be large, he took a wife in order to have children who would
be his heirs'. Marie then continues with the words, 'the maiden who was
given to the rich man'.[37] We are told that the young wife lamented tear-
fully, 'My destiny is hard indeed ... death alone will free me'.[38] Such marriages must have been full of despair for the twelfth-century girl. The girl,
we are told, was locked in her husband's tower for seven years and her
husband refused to allow her to go to church or hear God's service. It is
important to note here that no child results from the marriage. As the
purpose of marriage, in the eyes of both the family and the church, is procreation – then the marriage is flawed. A lover appears magically. The
heroine questions him to assure herself that he is not from the devil and
he is able, by magic, to take communion thereby proving that he is not
evil. This, in effect, implies that they have God's approval and they
become lovers and she loves him faithfully. Significantly, she has a child
by her lover symbolising that it is their liaison that is blessed and is not
flawed. This was the true marriage, the marriage of consent that the
church was advocating.

In the Lai *Milun* the young lovers meet, fall in love and exchange
tokens. According to the new promulgated laws of the church, as there
was no impediment between the couple and they had consented to each
other, they could be married and no one, not even her family, could prevent this. The validity of this secret union, which was a marriage in all but
name, was duly confirmed by the birth of a son. Again the implication
present is that the true marriage of free consent had in fact taken place
although her family had no knowledge of it. Subsequently the girl was
given in an arranged marriage by her father to a rich man, a stranger to
her. The years pass and the son eventually meets his true father and discovers the story of his parents' love. His mother's husband is now dead
and therefore he, the son, is now the male who has authority over his
mother. It is the son who now arranges the marriage of his parents; the
contrast between the two marriages is illustrated by the words, 'They
summoned no kinsmen and without the advice of anyone else their son
united them and gave his mother to his father'.[39]

The girl given in marriage should be a virgin. In her role as the mother, and therefore the channel through which the property devolved, it was
vital that the woman was chaste. Despite this love affairs did occur and in

37 *Lais*, 86.   39 *Lais*, 104.
38 *Lais*, 87.

the Lais it is quite clear that the love affairs are fully sexual. 'She promised him her love and gave him her body they exchanged rings and took possession of each other'[40] and 'May the final act ... give them pleasure'.[41] Here it is interesting to compare Chrétien's romances with Marie's Lais. In Marie's Lais the love affairs are realistic and result in pregnancies; in Chrétien's romances, the love affairs are concerned only with the male viewpoint and no pregnancies occur to distract the knight. This is most important. Marie was most acutely aware of the reproductive consequence of a sexual love affair. In four of the twelve Lais children are the result of extra marital as well as marital activity. In the Lai *Milun* the young girl finds that she is pregnant and reacts very authentically bewailing that, 'She had forfeited her honour and good name by allowing such a thing to befall her. She would be severely punished: tortured or sold as a slave in another country'. Marie then interjects saying, 'Such was the custom of our ancestors still observed at that time'.[42] Even if being sold as slave was no longer practised, there can be no doubt about the severe punishment the girl would receive if her pregnancy was discovered.[43] It is not surprising to find the girl in *Milun* concealing her pregnancy with the help of an old woman so that, 'neither by word or outward sign was her condition discovered'.[44] When the child was born it was sent away secretly to her lover's married sister with a letter of explanation written by the girl herself. That this kind of situation did exist in reality is evidenced by the famous twelfth-century lovers, Abelard and Héloise, who conducted an illicit affair which led to a pregnancy. Abelard took Héloise to his home in Brittany where their child was born.[45] The problem for Marie's heroine was not over with the birth of her child. Subsequently she was told that her father had betrothed her to a nobleman, 'a very wealthy man ... of great power and reputation'. Marie tells us that, 'she was plunged into the deepest grief', and often thought of her absent lover who had gone to seek fame as a mercenary. The problem now confronting the girl is that her husband would find out soon that she was no longer a virgin.

40 *Lais*, 58.
41 *Lais*, 50.
42 *Lais*, 98.
43 We only have to recall the abuse suffered by the young Paston girls, Elizabeth and Margery for their rebellions against their family. In a Paston letter we are informed, 'since Easter she [Elizabeth] has been mostly beaten once or twice a week and sometimes twice in one day, and her head broken in two or three places.' The person who administered the beating was her mother Agnes. Virgoe, *Illustrated letters*, 58.
44 *Lais*, 98.
45 Radice, *The letters*, 69.

Even Marie cannot resolve this problem and apart from saying, 'When the time came for her to be given in marriage her husband took her away',[46] she leaves us in the dark as to whether or not the husband discovered that his wife was not a virgin. Her lover eventually contacted her by letter and when she recognised his writing she feared discovery. The words used, conveying the fear under which many medieval women must have lived, are very revealing. We are simply told that her blood ran cold.[47]

Perhaps it is this ever present element of fear that accounts for the number of times that we are told that a heroine swoons. If women frequently lived in a state of anxiety then fainting may well have been occasioned by sudden fear. In the Lai *Eliduc* a good and faithful wife worries when her husband is silent and pensive. We are told, 'He behaved most secretively and his wife was sad in her heart because of this, not knowing what it meant. She lamented to herself and often asked him whether someone had told him that she had misbehaved or done wrong while he had been out of the country for she would willingly defend herself in front of his people if he wished'.[48] Even where a good marriage existed there was an ever present sense of anxiety on the part of the woman. In *Le Fresne* a wife has not conceived while her neighbouring lord's wife has produced not only one but two sons, twins. She has fulfilled her function to provide sons for her husband's family. The unfruitful wife, beset by jealousy, accused the other woman of infidelity saying, 'it has never occurred that a woman gave birth to two sons at once – nor ever will – unless two men are the cause of it'.[49] This bitter remark was carried to the father of the twins with the result, we are told, that the husband hated his wife and mother of his sons and was highly mistrustful of her, keeping her in close custody without her having deserved it.

There was an automatic assumption that if anything had gone amiss it was the fault of a woman. In the Lai *Eliduc* the young girl, Guilliadun, eloped with Eliduc, unaware that he was already married, and fled with him by ship to his country. A storm blew up and one of the sailors in fear of their safety cried out to Eliduc, 'Lord you have with you the woman who will cause us to perish ... You have a loyal wife and now with this other woman you offend God and his law, righteousness and faith. Let us cast her into the sea and we shall soon arrive safely'.[50] It was the innocent woman who was blamed not Eliduc. When Guilliadun, who had placed her faith in her lover and left all her security behind her and eloped, heard that Eliduc already had a wife in the place to which he was bringing her

46 *Lais*, 98–9.   49 *Lais*, 61.
47 *Lais*, 100.   50 *Lais*, 121.
48 *Lais*, 120.

she swooned. It should be recognised that these heroines never swoon for trivial reasons. Another heroine, after recovering from a swoon occasioned by fear pleaded saying, 'Beloved, I should rather die together with you than suffer with my husband. If I go back to him he will kill me'.[51] It is also possible that fainting may have been used as a ploy to gain time and enable the woman to marshall her defence. In one instance we are told, 'The lady was very afraid and pretended to faint';[52] so fainting may also have functioned as a defence mechanism.

Tension must have been ever present, at least in the early days, within a medieval marriage when the girl passed from the guardianship of her father to the guardianship of her husband and his family. In an alien house she might always be regarded as a stranger and would be constantly under scrutiny until she fulfilled her function and presented her husband's house with an heir. This situation is frequently depicted in the Lais. Husbands were frequently old and as Marie puts it, 'all old men are jealous and hate to be cuckolded. Such is the perversity of age'.[53] Marriages could be breeding grounds for resentment and indeed they result in both spite and hate in the Lais, for example, in the Lai Laustic.[54] Hate was present in such a marriage as the vehement declaration, 'may God grant he be consumed by hell fire',[55] attests. We are continually presented with a picture of the young girl living a life of virtual imprisonment in an unfriendly environment and surrounded by her husband's people who are all too eager to betray her. Only when her own children had survived past the age of infant deaths would she receive eventual recognition but that could take many years. Husbands, we are told, did not take lightly the task of guarding their wives. The fourteenth-century wife of the Goodman of Paris had an older woman, Agnes la Béguine, as chaperonhousekeeper to help and guide her, 'Dame Agnes the Béguine (who is with you to teach you wise and ripe behaviour and to serve and lesson you ...)'.[56] Marie's young brides are constantly guarded, usually by the husband's female relatives or his chamberlain or elderly chaplain. One closely guarded wife cries in despair, 'I could put on a friendly mien for him, even without any desire to do so, if I could talk to people and join

51 Lais, 91.
52 Lais, 88.
53 Lais, 46.
54 The unhappy wife enjoyed the song of the nightingale and frequently got up at night to hear it sing. Her husband became angry and we are told 'with a spiteful and angry laugh' he devised a plan to ensnare the bird which he then killed out of spite. He then threw the body of the bird at the lady so that the front of her tunic was bespattered with blood. Lais, 95.
55 Lais, 47.
56 Power, The goodman, 138.

them in amusements'.[57] Despite this restricted life love could enter even when the woman was closely guarded. In *Yonec* we are told that the husband, 'took good care to watch over her and locked her in his tower in a large paved chamber. He had a sister old and widowed without a husband and he placed her with the lady to keep her from going astray'.[58] Even such diligence could not be foolproof as Marie declares when we are told, 'No one can be so imprisoned or so tightly guarded that he cannot find a way out from time to time'. The thirteenth-century author of *The Romance of the Rose*, Jean de Meun, agrees with this premise. He states, 'No man can keep a woman under guard if for her honour she has no respect, though it were Argus' self who kept the watch and spied upon her with his hundred eyes'.[59] Marie de France deals with the harsh reality of love found in a world of arranged marriages. Marriage generally meant exile and loneliness; 'When the time came for her to be given in marriage her husband took her away',[60] Marriage was, in effect, a form of exile that the male did not have to endure. The young man might go away from home to seek his advancement but he was, in any case, in the company of his peers and comparatively free; he did not find himself placed under conditions of perpetual scrutiny.

Another problem that could be encountered by the young bride was that when she arrived at her husband's home she might easily find another woman already in residence. For men sexuality was not limited to marriage. Giselbert of Mons informs us that the nobles were not in the habit of settling for only one woman and the places reserved for illegitimate offspring in genealogical literature confirms this.[61] In the history of the counts of Guines, written between 1201 and 1206, the purity of the wives that the family received is constantly affirmed, but, by contrast, the sexual prowess of the men of the family is lauded; the twelfth-century Baldwin II of Guines had 33 children out of wedlock.[62] History relates the male viewpoint, Marie de France relates the female. In *Le Fresne* we are given a glimpse of what must have been a situation frequently encountered by new brides in arranged marriages. In this case the husband had a concubine in residence whom he loved dearly but could not marry because of her lack of social rank. He had only agreed to marry at the request of the landed knights who had reproached him for his lack of heir. We are told, 'They brought Gurun's wife to him, but her mother who accompanied her, was afraid of the girl [the concubine] whom he loved so much lest she try to cause ill-will between her daughter and her husband.

---

57 *Lais*, 87.
58 *Lais*, 86.
59 Robbins, *The romance*, 300.

60 *Lais*, 99.
61 Duby, *Love and marriage*, 34–5.
62 Ibid.

She planned to cast her out of her own house and advise her son-in-law to marry her to a worthy man, for in this way she could be rid of her'.[63] A woman in residence could and probably frequently did make life very difficult for a new bride who had been married by her family to a stranger.

When Marie does portray women in a happy marriage or relationship she depicts them as submissive. In *Eliduc* when the wife discovers that her husband loves another she does all to assist him. We are told, 'she asked him for permission to leave and to separate from him, for she wanted to be a nun and serve God. He could then ... marry the girl he loved so much'.[64] In the Lai *Le Fresne* the hero falls in love with a young girl in an abbey. As part of his campaign to seduce her he endows the abbey with lands in order to have a lord's right to a dwelling place and residence in the abbey. He succeeds and she becomes his concubine. When he decides to marry another she submissively prepares his house and bedchamber for his bride, even placing her most treasured possession on the marriage bed. Her meek and submissive behaviour leads to her reward and she is discovered to be of noble birth and can therefore marry her lover.

It is in *Eliduc*, the last Lai, that Marie alludes most frequently to the new ideal of Christian marriage. Eliduc is reproached because, he is told, 'You have a loyal wife and now with this other woman you offend God and his law'.[65] The point is made that God expects fidelity and one heroine declares, 'He sinned when he tricked me for he had a wife and never told me'.[66] An awareness of the obligations in a Christian marriage is emphasised by statements such as, 'If I were to marry my beloved the Christian religion would not accept it' and 'It was neither right nor proper to keep two wives, nor should the law allow it'.[67]

Marie de France in her Lais describes a world where women tragically encounter overwhelming love in a society that does not allow for such a situation. Marriages were arranged for the benefit of the family and women, constrained by their families, had little or no control over their eventual fate. Marie offers to the reader a rare insight into marriage in the twelfth century, rare because it enables the reader to observe marriage from the viewpoint of the medieval noblewoman. Although Marie's women might appear to comply with society's demand for women to be submissive and docile, they are frequently portrayed as taking the initiative and even being audacious. They often achieve their objectives by employing subterfuge and deceit but they have no other option. They are revealed as being in essence stronger than the men under whose control

63 *Lais*, 65.
64 *Lais*, 125.
65 *Lais*, 121.
66 *Lais*, 124.
67 *Lais*, 125.

they live. The men can constrain them physically – and frequently do so – yet it is evident over and over again that the only power that can really hold the woman is the love that she herself has freely chosen. Physical restraints are, in the end, of no real importance because love and freedom are of the mind and therefore unconstrained.

Marie de France is undervalued as a source for the history of the twelfth-century marriage from the perspective of the medieval woman. In the romance genre it is only Marie de France who sees marriage as from the woman's point of view – often repressive and even sinful. Perhaps the whole purpose of the Lais was to give voice to Gratian's decretals and demonstrate the problems that inevitably arose because of unhappy marriages? Marie de France claims the right, already accorded by the church, to a marriage of free consent. The young girl in the Lai *Milun* encapsulates the position of women when she declares passionately, 'I thought that I could marry my beloved ... I would rather die than go on living. But I am not free'.[68]

68 *Lais*, 99.

Short Shrouds and Sharp Shrews

ECHOES OF JACQUES DE VITRY IN THE
DÁNTA GRÁDHA

Grace Neville

Exempla were a constant feature of the literature of medieval Europe, oral and written.[1] For the purposes of this paper, the definition of an exemplum proposed by three scholars at the École des Hautes Études en Sciences Sociales in Paris, Jacques le Goff, Claude Brémond and Jean-Claude Schmitt, will be used:

> A short story presented as true and intended to be inserted into a speech (usually a sermon) in order to win over an audience through a salutary lesson.[2]

Not only did exempla fulfill the function of illustrating and enlivening homiletic texts but they also constituted a pool of anecdotes and motifs upon which writers in other areas could draw.[3] The exempla that figure in the *Dánta Grádha*,[4] an anthology of largely anonymous Irish poems on love from the medieval and early modern period, have already attracted some attention: Liam Ó Caithnia identifies references to exempla in DG 16, 19, 43, 61 (twice), 81, 83, 86.[5] To date, interest has been focussed in particular on the 'maddening rain' motif (indexed by Stith Thompson as D1353.1)[6] which figures in DG 92[7] and on the story of the fox and the heron in DG 81.[8] This essay will compare two versions of an exemplum

---

1 Brémond et al., *L'Exemplum*; Mosher, *The exemplum*; Owst, *Literature and pulpit*; Schmitt, *Prêcheurs d'exemples*; Tubach, *Index Exemplorum*; Welter, *L'Exemplum*.
2 'un récit bref donné comme véridique et destiné à être inséré dans un discours (en général un sermon) pour convaincre un auditoire par une leçon salutaire', Brémond et al., *L'Exemplum*, 37–8.
3 See inter alia MacDonald, 'Proverbs'; Pratt, 'Chaucer'.
4 O'Rahilly, *Dánta Grádha*, henceforward referred to as DG.
5 Ó Caithnia, *Apalóga*.
6 Thompson, *Motif-Index*.
7 Cormier, 'The maddening rain'; Mac Craith, 'Cioth na Baoise'.
8 Neville, 'Fox eats heron'.

widely disseminated throughout medieval Europe, that of the woman
who refuses to provide an adequate shroud for her dying husband, as it
occurs in two texts – one from medieval France and the other from early
modern Ireland – in an attempt to establish what they have to say about
the representation of women. The texts in question are:

- item CVII in the widely disseminated *Sermones Vulgares* of
  Jacques de Vitry (c. 1180–1240), arguably the most famous rendering of this exemplum,[9]
- the early modern DG version of it (DG 18, lines 9–60).

Text 1:

> Audivi de quadam muliere cum de vita mariti sui desperaret et ille
> morti vicinus usum lingue et ceterorum membrorum amisisset,
> vocata ancilla sua, dixit uxor hominis illius qui jam in extremis lab-
> orabat: 'Festina et eme tres ulnas tele de borello ad maritum meum
> sepeliendum'. Que respondit: 'Domina, habetis telam lineam
> habundanter, date illi quatuor ulnas vel amplius ad sudarium'. At
> illa indignans ait: 'Bene sufficiunt ei tres ulne de borello'. Et super
> hoc domina et ancilla diutius inter se discordabant. Quod audiens
> homo ille sicut potuit cum magno conamine respondit: 'Curtum et
> grossum facite mihi sudarium ne luto inquinetur'. Quod est dicere
> secundum vulgare gallicum: ' Cort le me faites pour ne le croter.'

> [Translation]: I have heard of a certain woman who, as she
> despaired of the life of her husband and he being close to death had
> lost the use of his tongue and other members, she called her maid,
> and the wife of the man who was in grave danger said: 'Hurry and
> buy me three ells of coarse woollen cloth to bury my husband'.
> And she replied: 'you have linen cloth in abundance, give him four
> ells or more for his shroud'. But she said indignantly: 'Three ells of
> coarse woollen cloth will suffice'. And at this the mistress and maid
> quarrelled for quite a long time among themselves. The man, hear-
> ing this, answered as best he could with great effort: 'Make it short
> and thick for me that it may not be soiled with mud'. Which in
> common French means: 'Make it short for me lest it be dirtied'.

9 Crane, *The exempla*, 48–9; from BN MSS lat. 17, 509, fo. 84ro, thirteenth-century, parchment. The enormous popularity of the *Sermones Vulgares* is borne out,
   inter alia, by the high number of versions of them extant from as early as the thirteenth century.

Text 2:

[...] Iarla glic do bhí san Róimh
agá mbíodh cuirn fá fhíon;
ar mhnaoi an tighearna mhóir mhaith
12 do chuala sgéal ait, más fíor.

Lá dá rabhadar ar-aon
taobh re taobh ar leabaidh chlúimh,
do leig air go raibh ag éag,
16 dochum bréag do bhrath a rúin.

'Romham dá bhfaghthá-sa bás
badh beag mo chás ionnam féin;
ar bhochtaibh Dé leath ar leath
20 do roinnfinn fá seach mo spréidh.

Do chuirfinn síoda agus sróll
i gcomhrainn fhairsing d'ór dhearg
i dtimcheall do chuirp san uaigh',
24 do ráidh an bhean do smuain cealg.

Do críochnaigheadh leis an bás,
do bhrath mná na malach seang;
gá dtáim acht níor chomhaill sí,
28 tar éis a bháis, ní dár gheall.

Do chuaidh amach ar an sráid,
gur cheannaigh, gé'r chráite an lón,
dá bhannláimh nó trí do shac
32 nách ráinig ar fad a thón.

Tar éis ar gheall dá fear féin,
do rinne bréag ar ndul don chill;
ní thug pinginn d'eaglais Dé,
36 's níor thairg déirc do dhuine thinn.

Ar ndearbhadh intinne a mhná,
an t-iarla glic (fa cás cruaidh)
d'fhiarfaigh créad fá raibh a chorp
40 dá chur nocht aca san uaigh.

Do ghabh sise leisgéal gar,
do nós na mban bhíos re holc,
dá saoradh ar a fear féin,
44 an bhean nár ghaibh géill dá locht.

'Do chumas eisléine ghearr
nách ráinig meall do dhá mhás,
do chuimling re tús an tsluaigh
48 ar Sliabh Síón (cruaidh an cás).

Brailín fá chosaibh gach fir
ní bhia a-nois mar do bhí riamh;
ag rochtain go Rí na ndúl
52 badh leat tús ó dtéid san tSliabh'.

'Tuigim do mhíorún, a bhean –
ní bhfuil tú ach mar gach mnaoi;
dom dheóin ní bhfuighe mé bás
56 romhat, a ghrádh na nglac saor'.

Gá dtáim ach do bhí an bhean –
ó sin amach dá fear féin
is éadána do bhí sí;
60 ag sin agaibh brígh mo sgéil.

[Translation]: A clever earl who was in Rome / who used to have golden goblets of wine; / about the wife of the great, good lord / I heard a strange story, if it is true.

One day when they both were / side by side on a feather bed, / he pretended to be dying, / he devised a lie to test her secret.

'Before me if you should die / I would not mind for myself; / on God's poor half and half / I would share out my dowry.

I would put silk and satin / in a roomy coffin of red gold / around your body in the grave', / said the woman who was plotting treachery.

Death finally came, / testing the woman of the slender eyebrows; / in short she did not fulfill / after his death any of her promises.

Out onto the street with her, / and she bought, though miserable the provision, / two lengths or three of sackcloth / that did not quite cover his bottom.

After what she had promised to her husband, / she committed treachery after he went to the churchyard; / she did not give a penny to God's church, / nor did she give alms to the sick.

Having confirmed his wife's mind, / the clever earl (what a difficult case) / asked why his body / was being put naked by them into the grave.

She made a short excuse, / in the manner of women involved in evil, / to justify herself to her husband, / the woman who did not acknowledge her fault.

'I have made a short shroud / that did not reach your two buttocks, / so that you would be at the front of the crowd / on Mount Sion (a difficult plight).

A sheet under every man's feet / is not now the custom as it once was; / reaching the God of the elements / you will be to the front of those going on the Mountain'.

'I understand your treachery, woman; / you are just like every woman; / if I can help it I will not die / before you, o love of the noble hands.

In short the woman – / from then on to her husband / subservient was what she was; / there you have the meaning of my story.

Apart from the above versions of this exemplum, others survive in the following texts:

- British Library (BL) Royal 7 D. i #248 (a late thirteenth-century Latin manuscript written in England);
- BL Additional 33956, fo. 84b, col. 2 #99 (a fourteenth-century Latin text);
- BL Harley 463, fo. 7b, col. 2 #35 (early fourteenth-century Latin text of Jacques de Vitry's exempla);
- BL Harley 268, fo. 33 #70 (anonymous fourteenth-century Latin manuscript sometimes attributed to the thirteenth-century Étienne

de Besançon or to Arnold de Liège, both Dominicans);
- BL Harley 268, fo. 155b, #126 (a fourteenth-century Latin text);
- BL Royal 7 E. iv., fo. 165vo: from the *Summa Praedicantium* (E. viii., 13) of English Dominican, John Bromyard (d. 1418);
- *Scala Celi*; exempla compiled or composed by Johannes Gobii (Jean Gobi the Younger) at the Dominican house of Saint Maxim in Provence between 1322 and 1330;[10]
- BL Additional 25719, fo. 127b (a fifteenth-century translation into a Northumberland dialect of the *Alphabetum Narrationum* which was a compilation of exempla in alphabetical order for the use of preachers and whose author remains anonymous despite various hypotheses);
- BL Additional 6716, fo. 44b, col. 2 #40 (a fifteenth-century text)
- Bibliothèque Nationale (BN) MSS lat. 9606, fo. 21, v, by the Franciscan, Guibert de Tournai. The French scholar, Barthélémy Haureau, states that Guibert de Tournai had borrowed this story from Jacques de Vitry;[11]
- BN MSS lat. 12402, a thirteenth-century version of the *Alphabetum Narrationum*. According to Haureau, this rendering is very similar to that found in BN MSS lat. 9606 ('presque dans les mêmes termes');[12]

Apart from the Irish, French and Latin sources indicated above, the exemplum would also appear to have existed in medieval Spanish and Portuguese sources.[13]

Whereas this exemplum was widely known in the Continental literature of medieval Europe, the DG version of it[14] (anonymous like most DG texts) is the only one with Irish connections that I have been able to locate from the medieval or early modern period.[15] It is not mentioned in

10 See de Beaulieu, *Edition*.
11 Haureau, *Notices*, XI, 75.
12 Ibid.
13 E.g. the fourteenth-century writer, Frei Hermenegildo de Tancos, *Orto de Sposo*, reprinted in Braga, *Contos*, II, 40–1, 'A Morte dos Avarentos'.
14 As possible sources of the exemplum in DG under discussion, Ó Caithnia (p. 193) simply lists M250, H466 and H156.1: 'false death to test a promise'. He describes such motifs as very widespread.
15 I have located a modern Irish-language poem in the Archives of the Irish Folklore Commission in which the male narrator lambasts a beautiful woman who had promised him a fine funeral with a silver coffin, silk and a nine-day wake, but who reneged on her promise. The moral of this poem is very similar to many of the texts at the conclusion of the DG: 'ná pós bean ...' : 'marry no woman ...' (Archives of the Irish Folklore Commission, MS 202, pp. 75–9, dated 1933, Galway).

the *Liber Exemplorum ad Usum Praedicantium*, compiled by an unnamed late thirteenth-century Franciscan who seems to have been born in England, studied in Paris and lived in Ireland.[16] Nor is it mentioned in Tom Peete Cross' *Motif-Index of Early Irish Literature*.[17] In fact, DG 83 is of particular interest as it contains one of the very few instances in the entire DG anthology in which an exemplum is deemed to warrant a full retelling rather than a mere allusion. (The only other example of a full recounting of an exemplum in the DG is to be found in the story of the fox and the heron, DG 81). DG 83 consists of a total of fifteen quatrains i.e. sixty lines of which fifty-two (lines 9–60) recount a variant of the exemplum under discussion.

Central to all these versions – the common denominator, as it were – is the dialogue between a woman and her husband/servant on the subject of her dying husband's shroud, this shroud ultimately functioning as the 'agent' responsible for unmasking the wife's 'true' nature. In most versions, this conversation takes place between the wife and her maid. In several of them, the dying man requests a short shroud in order to avoid the possibility of its becoming muddied. Code-switching often occurs as this request is recorded in Old French although the body of the text is in a different language (e.g. Latin). It would appear that of the extant medieval versions of this anecdote, Jacques de Vitry's is the fullest and best-known. One could therefore be tempted (as Haureau seems to be) to see his version as a kind of prototype for many of the others.[18]

A comparison specifically between the DG rendering of the narrative in question and that attributed to Jacques de Vitry reveals significant similarities and differences between the two:

- In the Latin/French version, the 'dramatis personae' consist of three people, the husband, wife and maid, the latter acting as the voice of humanity or loyalty, urging her mistress to do 'the decent thing' by the husband whose spokeswoman she thus becomes. In the Irish version, the maid is dispensed with, and the resulting 'tête à tête' between husband and wife becomes all the more intense and dramatic.
- The plot is significantly different: in the Latin/French version, the husband really is dying. In the Irish one, the husband tricks his

16 Little, *Liber exemplorum*. Referring to this text, Robin Flower states: 'Much exemplary material was thus accessible to the Irish Franciscans, and it is from sources of this kind that we must derive the exempla which are so frequent in the later Irish poetry', Flower, 'A Franciscan bard', 223.
17 Cross, *Motif-Index*.
18 Haureau, *Notices* XI, 74–5.

wife by pretending to be dying in order to test her; in other words, a separate motif – the widely-attested motif of feigned death as a truth-testing device – is grafted onto the Irish text.

- The conclusion is different: in the Latin version, the husband presumably dies. In the Irish one, the tables are turned on the trickster wife by her husband's 'return' to life.

The similarities between the two texts, however, are arresting. Despite obvious surface differences (for instance at the level of genre), the overall representation of women which is at the very heart of these two narratives is strikingly similar. In both texts, the space inhabited by females is identical: both wives are seen as narrowly tied to the family home i.e. to inner space, the private sphere. Marriage and social status place these upper-class women under a form of house-arrest (unlike their husbands who share their marital and social status, and unlike the presumably unmarried female servant in the Latin text whose lowly status renders her a 'non-person', consequently allowed wider margins of mobility: she has ready access to the space beyond her employers' front door). In the Latin text, it is significant that the wife orders her servant to go and buy cloth for a shroud: she herself may negotiate with the exterior world only at one remove, ironically through another woman. In the Irish text, similar remarks could be made. Here, the wife's normal habitat is also indoors. Indeed, the opening 'pillow-talk' vignette in DG 83 (line 14) is claustrophobically restricted: the wife is depicted not just indoors but in a smaller 'locus' still, the marital bed. It is highly significant that the first thing this woman does as soon as she thinks that her husband is dead is to erupt into the outside world, into forbidden space, as if to lay physical claim to her newly-won independence: 'do chuaidh amach ar an sráid' (line 29): 'she went out onto the street'. For her, this bursting forth into the public sphere represents her liberation from the place and state of marriage: for the narrator, however, this spacial transgression perfectly replicates the woman's 'moral' transgression for which revenge must be exacted. The conclusion represents a mirror image of this literal outburst: physically and morally put back in her place, the woman is house-bound for the rest of her days.

Women's personality in both texts is remarkably similar. Indeed, the narrators did not see themselves as talking about individual women but about the species, woman. Moving from the particular to the general, we are asked to believe that the anonymous women or rather woman in these texts is a paradigm for all women: She is: DG line 42: 'do nós na mban bhíos re holc' ('like women involved in evil'); DG line 54: 'ní bhfuil tú ach mar gach mnaoi' ('you are just like every woman').

Stripped of the specificities of time and place, ageless and timeless, she becomes Everywoman, spanning past, present and future, just as the messages vehicled through her about women and the institution of marriage are presented as universal and eternal verities.

Central to both versions is the revelation of the wife's 'true' nature. The exterior image of the obedient, caring wife (especially in the Irish text) is quickly dispelled as the little story advances to reveal the 'truth' underneath. Indeed, this follows the pattern in exempla in general, where the entire world is seen as a place where things are never as they appear: loyal, generous wives transpire to be latter-day Eves, 'dead' husbands return to life, widows are not widows since their husbands have not died, their professions of loyalty and generosity are smokescreens hiding yet more lies. Layers of deception are peeled away to reveal yet more deception behind. The world is a series of Chinese boxes: boxes within boxes within boxes, casting doubt upon the very nature of reality. In particular, whatever her surface image, the wife in these texts is seen as a subverter of the 'God-given' order of female subordination to male control. In an illustration of the age-old 'monde-à-l'envers' topos, we are given to understand that her very nature leads her to disobey her superior, her husband, just as Eve defied God. Disorderly, she dares to embark on courses of action sanctioned by no one but herself in an ultimately doomed attempt to seek out space over which she might have some control. However, her ambition to become a 'woman-on-top' is gleefully quashed:[19] male authority, mirroring that of God, must not be challenged. At the end of the DG version, 'natural' order is restored, male authority stamps out female unruliness, stability is assured and the danger of anarchy, ever-lurking just underneath the surface, is averted.

In these anecdotes, the woman's entire spacial and temporal world revolves around herself. Like Eve, her ancestor, she is unashamedly self-centred, her own immediate welfare is her sole concern, not that of those around her, even those close to her like her husband. Her husband is seen as having an understanding of the importance of things, a sense of priorities and a wide vision of time. The woman, by contrast, has no vision, no thought for the future – only for the here and now. In other words, like a child or an idiot, she lives in an eternal present, unlike her husband who is concerned for the future (even if it is for his own future!) and unlike the exempla in general which range over past, present and future, and see this world merely as an antechamber of the next.[20]

19 See Davis, *Society and culture*, Chap. v 'Women on top', 124–51; Owst, *Literature and pulpit*, 389–90.
20 Hence in Brémond et al., *L'Exemplum*, 37, the pithy definition of the exemplum

   The wife's function in both texts is remarkably similar. At a basic level, she is the angel of the house, responsible for the efficient management of her husband's goods. As in the fabliaux (a genre with which exempla present striking similarities), she acts as a kind of watchdog, an unpaid guardian of his wealth. She brazenly sabotages this rôle, however, and deliberately violates the trust placed in her by her superior, going so far as to waste his money on the purchase of more cloth although plenty already exists in the family home. This 'truer' image of the wife as the insider trader, the thief or depleter of her husband's fortune, is a constant motif in the fabliaux and elsewhere in medieval French literature.

   However, in these texts, another – more important – function is attributed to her: that of ensuring the smooth enactment of the rites of passage for her husband's soul between this world and the next. It is she who is charged with the responsibility of providing an appropriate shroud for her husband's body and, in the Irish text (lines 19–20), of distributing his goods to the poor (obviously as a kind of insurance policy designed to find favour for him with higher authorities once he is dead). In fact, women are widely cast in this rôle of attendant to the dead, from the 'pleureuses' of France to the 'mná caointe' of Ireland. This woman, however, is interested mainly in the things of this world: she refuses to clothe her husband's corpse properly just as she refuses to ensure that his wealth is delivered to its intended recipients, presumably intending to spend it instead on herself. In so doing, she deliberately botches the rites of passage for her husband from this world to the next.

   This leads me to what I believe to be the central element in these two texts: the supreme importance they both attach to having a proper burial, and the belief that unspeakable calamity will follow if this is not done. The conviction that a person denied a proper burial will never rest in peace is engrained not just in early Irish literature[21] and in the Irish psyche, ancient and modern,[22] but also across a wider geographical and temporal domain.[23] The refusal to provide a corpse with an appropriate shroud would, in this context, constitute the denial of a proper burial. In his classic study of attitudes to death throughout the ages *L'Homme devant la Mort*, French historian, Philippe Ariès explains how and when

---

   (in unexpectedly 'franglais' terms, it must be admitted!) as 'un gadget eschatologique'.

21 Cross, *Motif-Index*, 214 (E234.2), 222 (E750.0.1).
22 See Ó Súilleabháin, *Irish wake amusements*.
23 The vision of the afterlife in the DG text is a curious hybrid of classical (references to Rome) and Christian elements! Central to both systems of belief here is the insistence on a proper burial.

the practice of covering the entire corpse from head to toe in an ample shroud first arose:

> Around the thirteenth century [...], something happened which might appear insignificant but which, nonetheless, highlights a profound change in attitudes to death: the corpse which used to be seen as a familiar, sleeping figure, was now deemed to possess a power such that the sight of it became unbearable. From now on, and for several centuries, it was kept from view, hidden in a box, under a monument, where it was no longer visible.[24]

This hiding of death or 'occultation de la mort', as Ariès dramatically calls it, which he holds responsible for a profound change in attitudes to death, is ensured by various means such as the use of ample shrouds to hide corpses from head to foot. In an era imbued with symbolism and ritual like the Middle Ages, narrators and audience alike would have understood that by her refusal to give her husband a decent burial i.e. by her refusal to adhere to highly-symbolic, pre-ordained burial rituals, including the provision of an ample shroud, the wife is responsible for condemning her husband to a fate worse than death: she is sentencing his soul to eternal torment, casting it into outer darkness.[25] Just as Eve introduced death to earth, this woman now sends her husband to an endless death. And just as she is credited with powers of generation, she neatly turns this on its head by bringing about her husband's eternal demise. No greater calamity could befall anyone. The belief that, despite their ignoble status, women had power sufficient to wreak havoc in this world and the next, is here propounded by DG and exempla narrators whose own social status was far from lowly. This paradox, consequently, cannot have been easy for them to accept. Ironically though not accidentally, it comes as no surprise to learn that the husband's downfall will have been brought about by his closest companion, the enemy within, his wife. For Brémond et al., the woman portrayed in the exempla is Satan's helper on earth ('Satan et son auxilliaire, la femme').[26] That, however, is not the full story:

24 'Au treizième siècle environ [...], il est arrivé quelque chose qui pourra paraître insignifiant, qui rend cependant manifeste un changement profond de l'homme devant la mort: le corps mort, auparavant objet familier et figure de sommeil, possède désormais un pouvoir tel que sa vue devient insoutenable. Il est, et pour des siècles, enlevé aux regards, dissimulé dans une boîte, sous un monument, où il n'est plus visible', Ariès, *L'homme*, 168.

25 Interestingly the thirteenth-century poet, Rutebeuf, urging his audience to go on the Crusades, threatens that they will have only a short shroud if they refuse to go ('assez auriez d'un pou de toile', *La complainte d'Outre Mer*, line 100).

26 Brémond et al., *L'Exemplum*, 81.

the uncovered corpse in these texts uncovers the true identity of the woman here: she is not just a bad wife, not just Satan's helper: she is Satan himself.[27]

Who is being addressed here? Exempla audiences were mixed, and reference is made in the DG text to women as well as men being in the narrator's vicinity (line 4). However, within the framework of these texts, one is aware of the forging of a kind of male bonding directly between the (undoubtedly male) narrators and the men directly addressed. (e.g. in DG line 5). In other words, an overwhelming sense is conveyed here of men talking to other men:

> Preachers spoke before men and women, drawn up in front of them, in two separate groups. But it was to the men that they directed their remarks, emphasising certain points. One theme came back again and again, dominating the entire discourse: woman is evil, lustful as a viper, unstable as an eel, nosy, indiscreet and bitter too. Husbands love listening to that.[28]

From the beginning of the DG text, the narrator supports the husband whom he identifies as the victim: witness his use of laudatory epithets for the earl: 'glic' (lines 9, 38), 'mór', 'maith' ('clever, great, good') and his damning access to the wife's innermost thoughts: 'an bhean do smuain cealg' (line 24: 'the woman who was contemplating treachery'). His bias is again clear from his lack of comment on the earl's deceitfulness which was at least as great as his wife's. The male protagonists are offered as positive (as in the DG) and negative (as in the exemplum) rôle models for the male listeners. The narrators' concern for these male protagonists and for their male listeners binds all three together (narrator/audience/protagonist) in a trinity from which the woman, the focus of this tripartite male gaze, is excluded. Truly she is 'l'Autre'.

What advice did the narrators of these primarily didactic texts have for their male listeners? The narrators' distaste for and hostility towards women in general and the institution of marriage in particular is clear. Indeed, the closing statement in the DG that the wife was obedient towards her husband for the rest of her days echoes like a cry of glee, the conclusion proving the proposition set out in the introduction: that any-

---

27 Delumeau, *La peur*, Chap. v (ii) 'La diabolisation de la femme', 411–21.
28 'Les prédicateurs [...] parlaient devant des hommes et des femmes, rangés devant eux, en deux groupes distincts. Mais c'est aux hommes qu'ils s'adressaient, marquant l'accent sur quelques points. Un premier thème revient sans cesse, dominant tout le discours: la femme est mauvaise, lubrique autant que la vipère, labile autant

one bestowing affection on a woman will come to rue this.[29] The narrators try to frighten their male listeners out of any inclination towards marriage (a message which is reiterated in other late DG texts): a wife is a liability in this world and a disaster in the next; like Eve, she drags down all who come close to her.

This advice is presented as being based on incontrovertible evidence: the narrators indicate their 'sources' ('do chuala'/'audivi'), their story has the weight of age and authority behind it and must consequently be respected and believed. However, should the men in the audience be so foolish as to disregard this advice and get married (and the signs are not good: in his introduction, the DG narrator recognises that the men in his audience do, indeed, appear to be interested in women!), they must never 'give an inch': for the narrators, living in a state of constant apprehension and threat, the perceived risk seems to be that the whole situation could quickly spin out of control. Constant vigilance towards their wives is thus their prime duty: 'le premier devoir des maris est donc de se montrer vigilants'.[30] This is especially true at vulnerable times such as illness or death. Since women are profoundly amoral and have no scruples about their 'modus operandi', they will use foul means rather than fair, even sacrificing the weak (a dead/dying man) in order to get their way. Hence, having learnt his lesson, the husband in the Irish text vows (lines 55–6) not to predecease his wife! The audience has been warned!

As in so much clerical literature of medieval Europe, legitimised by the authority of the Christian church, aggressive antifeminism is at the heart of both texts. Their tone is dogmatic, their message black and white. In this, DG 83 recalls the 'memento mori' poems towards the end of the anthology rather than the more reflective ones like the haunting love poems attributed to Maghnas Ó Domhnaill (DG 49, 50, 51, 52, 53) or Seathrún Céitinn (DG 100). Ultimately, the two texts under discussion represent a rallying call for male solidarity in the face of 'typical' female unruliness. Woman must be put back in her place. The shrew must be tamed.

It is not possible to establish whether the DG text sprang directly or indirectly from that of Jacques de Vitry or, indeed, from any medieval prototype: it may descend directly from some classical exemplum to

que l'anguille, de surcroît curieuse, indiscrète, accariâtre. Les maris aiment écouter cela'. Duby, *Le chevalier*, 223–4.

29 Strubel, 'Exemple', p. 347: 'le sens est donné en amont de l'anecdote, la conclusion n'en est que la confirmation et l'adaptation plus précise à l'évenement raconté'. [Translation]: 'the meaning is given at the start of the anecdote, the conclusion is just a confirmation and a more precise adaptation to the event narrated'.

30 Duby, *Le chevalier*, 225.

which Renaissance writers had increasing access. At all events, it is interesting to note that, while it is undoubtedly reminiscent of indigenous
bardic poetry in its love of aphorisms and is quintessentially Irish in its
promotion of generosity and in its concern with having 'a decent burial',
the Irish text looks outwards towards the wider horizons of Continental
literature such as the exempla in its representation of women. One is
therefore tempted to conclude that it constitutes further proof that the
DG, far from being 'sui generis' as has been suggested, are indeed part and
parcel of the wider world of European literature.

* * *

An earlier version of this paper, entitled 'More Exempla Echoes in the
Dánta Grádha' was read at the Fifth Irish Conference of Medievalists, St
Patrick's College, Maynooth, on 27 June 1991.

The Absentee Landlady and the Sturdy Robbers

AGNES DE VALENCE

Cormac Ó Cléirigh

In the summer of 1266, the feudal host of England was gathered around Kenilworth castle in Warwickshire. It had assembled to besiege the castle, which was the last major bastion of the defeated supporters of a great baronial revolt against the authority of King Henry III which had racked England since 1258. The siege was a protracted one, lasting until December of that year, which left the assembled royalist magnates with plenty of time to pursue their own business interests.[1] Prominent amongst them was a Frenchman, named William de Valence. He was one of King Henry's half-brothers from Poitou, the de Lusignans, whose grasping behaviour had been partially responsible for the baronial revolution in the first place, and who were now poised to regain their former wealth and influence.[2] Apart from his English estates, William also had a major stake in the lordship of Ireland, being the lord of Wexford by virtue of the fact that his wife Joan was one of the heiresses to the great Marshal inheritance of Leinster.[3] Because of this, it was natural for William to try to make connections with the numerous Irish magnates who were taking part in the siege or in pacifying areas of rebel support.[4] This group included two members of the family known to historians as the Fitzgeralds or Geraldines of Offaly, namely Maurice fitzMaurice, whose main interests lay in Connacht, and his young nephew, Maurice fitzGerald, the third baron of Offaly. The pair had rallied to the royalist side in the English civil war, serving their lord, Edward, eldest son of King Henry, at the decisive battle of Evesham in August 1265 and afterwards.[5] It was to them, and to the recently widowed Maurice fitzGerald in particular, that William turned. Maurice entered into an agreement with William whereby he would marry William's daughter Agnes, having provided for her by giving her joint-possession of his Limerick properties. The advantages for

1 Powicke, *The thirteenth century*, 208–9, 213.
2 Clanchy, *England and her rulers*, 261–2.
3 G E.C., *Peerage*, x, 377; Cosgrove, *New history*, II, 168–9.
4 Frame, 'Ireland and the barons' war', 161.
5 See Frame, 'Ireland and the barons' war', 158–67.

both men were obvious. The maintenance of William's Irish interests would be facilitated by having a local ally. Maurice, by marrying the king's niece would be gaining close access to the ultimate source of patronage and favour. The agreement was confirmed in August 1266, at Kenilworth by an impressive list of magnates, which included the king's sons the lord Edward and the lord Edmund, three earls and Maurice fitzMaurice.[6] And so Agnes was duly dispatched, to what in her eyes must have seemed to be the end of the world.

There is no surviving evidence that can tell us how Agnes found life in Ireland, or indeed life with Maurice. All that can be said is that the marriage was both short and childless, as Maurice was drowned in July 1268, while crossing to Ireland from England.[7] Agnes, who was in Ireland, lost little time in returning home to her father.[8] However, a young widow of such rank was a naturally tempting prospect, and Agnes was rapidly remarried, this time to a Scottish magnate, Hugh de Balliol, who held extensive properties in England. This marriage was also both short-lived and childless, as Hugh died in April 1271. Apart from these bare facts, the only significant point is that Agnes thus acquired some valuable properties in Northumbria as her widow's dower.[9] In any event, William de Valence was granted the rights to her marriage in January 1272, and no doubt began looking for another suitable husband for his daughter.[10] The search appears to have been a surprisingly long one, as Agnes was still using her own surname in December 1276.[11] By October 1277 however, a third match had been made.[12] Again William had looked further afield than one might expect, but on this occasion he chose the heart of Europe, rather than its periphery. Agnes's new husband was John d'Avesnes, lord of Beaumont, a junior member of the comital family of Hainault, a region of the Holy Roman Empire situated in modern Belgium, inland from Flanders, which at that time was falling into the French sphere of influence.[13] This marriage proved to be more enduring and more fertile. By 1279 the couple had settled down in Hainault, and Agnes, styling herself lady of Offaly and of Balliol, could write to her first cousin, now King Edward I, informing him that God had sent her a fine son.[14] In all, Agnes and John had three children, a daughter Felicité, and two sons John and

6 *Cal.doc. Ire.1293–1301*, no. 672.
7 *Ann. Clyn*, 9.
8 *Cal. doc. Ire., 1252–1284*, no. 1106.
9 *Cal. inq. post. mort.*, I, Henry III, no. 773; *Close rolls, 1268–1272*, 345–6.
10 *Calendar of the patent rolls, 1266–72*, 615.
11 *Cal. doc. Ire., 1252–1284*, no. 1308.
12 *Calendar of the patent rolls, 1272–81*, 229.
13 G.E.C. *Peerage*, x, 16; Hallam, *Capetian France*, 50, 216.
14 *Calendar of the patent rolls, 1272–81*, 302; P. R. O , S. C. 1/21, no. 33.

Baldwin. But, in 1283 Agnes became a widow for the third and final time. She returned to England again, bringing her two young sons, her daughter having died a year previously.[15]

From this point onwards, Agnes does not appear to have contemplated remarriage. Instead she concentrated upon safeguarding her children's interests in Hainault, managing her dower lands, and going into the property market in her own right. The connection with Hainault necessitated frequent and lengthy stays on the mainland. For example, Agnes is recorded as having travelled there three times during the 1290s alone.[16] As far as her English dealings went, the picture that emerges is of a capable and rather unscrupulous businesswoman (which is only to be expected of a de Lusignan). By 1290, complaints had surfaced in parliament about her harshness as a landlady, and she showed no hesitation in clapping dishonest bailiffs into the debtor's prison at Fleet.[17] Her property acquisitions are also revealing. Her first major investment was in the manor of Great Shelford in Cambridgeshire. The relatives of the vendor, one Tibbald leMoyne, later testified that Tibbald was in fact insane, but Agnes kept possession of the estate.[18] She showed a good eye for a bargain in her next acquisition, a manor in Dagenham in Essex, which today is still called Valence. It had been held by Sir Thomas de Weyland, the chief justice of common pleas, who was disgraced and exiled in 1289 during Edward I's great campaign against official corruption and after his death Agnes snapped it up from his unfortunate widow.[19] Her most important purchase, that of Hertingfordbury in Hertfordshire, was conducted irregularly, as Agnes neglected to obtain a royal licence for the property transfer. However the king forgave his cousin, and the customary fine was waived.[20] In fact, this epitomizes Agnes's dealings with the administration and with officialdom in general. Repeatedly, the phrases 'the king's beloved niece' and later 'the king's kinswoman', appear to have had a very successful effect upon royal officers.

These details, interesting as they may be, appear to be of little relevance to the paper's title. They have been dwelt upon at some length in order to make three salient points. First, that Agnes was a good example of the kind of aristocrat whose mobility transcended national boundaries, being at home in any location where what was essentially French culture

15 G.E.C., *Peerage*, x, 16; *Calendar of chancery warrants, 1244–1326*, 24.
16 *Calendar of the patent rolls, 1281–92*, 413; *Calendar of the patent rolls, 1292–1301*, 125, 128, 313.
17 *Rotuli parliamentorum* I, 46a, 47b.
18 Wright, *History of Cambridge* , VIII, 210.
19 Powell, *History of Essex*, IV, 268, 278.
20 *Calendar of the close rolls, 1288–1296*, 352.

had been introduced. Secondly, that she could and did exploit her kinship with the English royal family, and lastly that she was a competent businesswoman in her own right. For, as it turned out, this member of the international aristocracy was to require both her connections and her resilience to deal with the problem that came to dominate her public life; namely, the management of her estates in Ireland.

At this point, it might be worthwhile to provide some idea of the extent of Agnes's property in Ireland. In 1266, Maurice fitzGerald had made Agnes the joint-owner of all of his estates in Co. Limerick, an extremely generous settlement. One of the clauses in the agreement specified what should happen if Maurice predeceased his wife and if there were no children – Agnes was to enjoy the properties for the rest of her life, after which they would be recovered by Maurice's heirs.[21] This arrangement meant that Agnes was left with a sizable portion of central Limerick, namely the manors of Adare, Croom, Uregare, Athlacca, Castleroberts and Grean. It is difficult to get an accurate idea of the value of the property. While some explicit valuations were undertaken sixty years later, they appear to have greatly underestimated the properties' true worth.[22] Aside from retaining all of Maurice's lands in Limerick, Agnes also acquired a widow's dower from the Geraldines' heartland in Co. Kildare. Here she gained a third part of the great manor of Maynooth, the manor of Rathmore, and the manor of Geashill.[23] Perhaps the best way of looking at her lands is to note that after her first husband's death, Agnes was in control of nearly half of the territories that made the Geraldines of Offaly, in Professor Frame's words, one of 'the two most powerful settler families', along with the de Burghs.[24]

But, how could an absentee landlady administer such vast estates? The obvious practical solution was to employ agents in Ireland, of whom the first recorded was one Philip de Flury in 1271.[25] Over the next four decades, the English patent rolls provide a list of the men who were empowered to act on Agnes's behalf in Ireland, amongst whom was John de Hothum, who later rose to great prominence in both the Irish and English administrations.[26] Apart from the efforts of her own servants, Agnes's hold on her estates was made easier because of the actions of her father William de Valence. For William had turned the loss of his son-in-law to his own advantage. Maurice fitzGerald had in fact left an heir by

21 *Cal. doc. Ire., 1293–1301*, no. 672.
22 *Red book of the earls of Kildare*, nos. 127, 128, 133, 135.
23 Ibid., nos. 36, 47.
24 Frame, 'Ireland and the barons' wars', 158.
25 *Cal. doc. Ire., 1252–1284*, no. 905.
26 *Cal. doc. Ire., 1293–1301*, no. 111; Phillips, 'John de Hothum', 63–4.

his previous marriage, a son Gerald fitzMaurice who was three and a half
years old when his father was drowned.[27] In 1270 William bought the custody of Gerald's lands, and the right to his marriage for £2,333 13s. 4d. (a
revealing sum when estimating the value of Agnes's manors).[28] And so,
for as long as William had control, Agnes was not likely to face a legal
challenge to her rights to the property on young Gerald's behalf. William
was forced to hand over custody of the manor of Lea to Roger Mortimer,
because of his rights as lord of Laois in 1274, but this had no effect upon
Agnes's interests, and for thirteen years the de Valences, father and
daughter, peacefully enjoyed almost total possession of the estates of the
barons of Offaly.[29] In 1283 however, this situation changed. In order to
maximize his investment, William had to find a wife for Gerald
fitzMaurice before he reached his majority. And so, in December of 1283
de Valence sold the custody of Gerald's lands and his right of marriage to
Geoffrey de Geneville, the French lord of the liberty of Trim for £1,200,
and Geoffrey promptly married Gerald to his daughter Joan.[30] The
sources reveal that within a year of being released from William de
Valence's tutelage, Gerald started court proceedings against Agnes to
recover the Limerick estates. He argued that they rightfully belonged to
him as his father's heir, a claim which apparently ignored Agnes's marriage agreement.[31] By the early summer of 1285 the case had been stalled,
as the king himself was considering it.[32] Whether this was another example of the advantages of being the king's cousin or not is unclear. In any
event, by then the young baron of Offaly had far more serious problems
to face. Most of the land in Kildare that he actually held was in the marches, and the Irish had again become hostile. In 1284 they destroyed his castle at Lea, and in the following year he was taken prisoner and held
captive by what the annalist Friar Clyn calls 'his Irish' of Offaly.[33]
Possibly, this experience broke his health, as he is not recorded as having
taken part in the defence of the marches thereafter. By September of 1287,
Gerald, styled *Capitaneus Geraldinorum* by Clyn, was dead, childless,
leaving an aunt, named Juliana de Cogan as his closest relative and, by
customary law, his heiress.[34] Gerald's death, taken in conjunction with

27 *Chartularies of St Mary's, Dublin*, II, 290; see also Orpen, 'The Fitzgeralds',
    99–113.
28 *Cal. doc. Ire., 1252–1284*, no. 866.
29 Ibid., no. 970.
30 Ibid., no. 2163; *Red book of the earls of Kildare*, no. 33.
31 *Cal. doc. Ire., 1252–1284*, no. 2151; *Cal. doc. Ire., 1285–1292*, no. 29.
32 *Cal. doc. Ire., 1285–1292*, no. 56.
33 *Ann. Clyn*, 9–10.
34 Ibid., 10; Orpen, 'The Fitzgeralds', 110–11; *Cal. doc. Ire., 1285–1292*, no. 459, 207.

that of his great-uncle, the Connacht based Maurice fitzMaurice in the previous year, who also left female heirs, meant that the Geraldines of Offaly were facing extinction.[35] While Gerald's death might have had ramifications for the balance of power within Ireland, from Agnes's perspective it appeared to remove the immediate problem of a legal challenge to her property rights. By way of contrast, her next major problem originated amongst her own officials.

In November 1291, one John de Valle was being held in the debtors's prison of Fleet in England. He had been Agnes's bailiff in Ireland during her marriage to John d'Avesnes and for some time afterwards. An audit of his accounts had revealed that he had received £5,300 from Agnes's estates over this unspecified period, but he was unable to account for it all. The sum of £426 was definitely missing, and he lacked receipts for a further £1,023, which he claimed to have paid to merchants, hence his imprisonment. It was now proposed to release him, so that he could explain himself to the English treasurer and barons of the exchequer, on condition that he found four guarantors, or mainpernors, who would be liable to pay the missing £426 should de Valle fail to appear before the exchequer court. De Valle succeeded in finding quite an impressive set of mainpernors, including Geoffrey de Geneville, a former justiciar or chief governor, William de Oddingeseles, a future justiciar, and fatefully, one John fitzThomas. When the case opened, the English barons of the exchequer rapidly decided that they would need to appoint auditors in Ireland. In April 1292 they selected the Irish treasurer and the Irish chief justice of common pleas for the task. At this point de Valle asked that the case be postponed, to give him time to find the receipts from the merchants, who he claimed were from Lombardy, Hainault and Brabant and so could not be located. Agnes agreed, provided that if de Valle failed to turn up after the postponement, he should be charged with the whole £1,023. De Valle accepted this, and was ordered to appear before the barons again in January 1293. He was also ordered to find a new set of mainpernors to guarantee the £1,023. De Valle's second group of mainpernors again included fitzThomas, and a group of magnates of the second rank, such as Sir Walter l'Enfaunt junior and Sir James Keating. But in January, when the case was reconvened, de Valle defaulted. The barons then ordered the Irish justiciar, William de Vescy to start court proceedings against de Valle's mainpernors.[36] Possibly unwittingly, Agnes had launched herself on a collision course with the man who was her greatest threat in Ireland – John fitzThomas.

35 *Ann. Conn.*, *s.a.* 1286; Orpen, 'The Fitzgeralds', 110.
36 *Cal. doc. Ire., 1285–1292*, no. 993; *Calendar of the justiciary rolls, Ireland, 1295–1303*, 102.

To explain why this was so requires going back a little in time. John fitzThomas came from a junior branch of the Geraldines of Offaly, who held lands in Sligo.[37] In 1287, as he appears to have been Gerald fitzMaurice's only surviving male Geraldine relative, the dying fourth baron decided to make John his heir, and began to transfer his properties over to him, thus permitting fitzThomas to become the fifth baron of Offaly, at the expense of Juliana de Cogan.[38] Starting with the estates which he took over from Gerald (Rathangan, Lea, Offaly and part of Maynooth), John embarked upon a remarkable series of manoeuvres which were designed to unite all the Offaly Geraldines' lands under his own control. One approach which he adopted was to build up a support base from amongst the notables of Kildare like Piers de Bermingham of Carbury.[39] Another was to turn his attentions towards his female relatives. First he persuaded Amabilia, daughter and co-heiress of Maurice fitzMaurice, a childless widow, to grant him her half of the inheritance, by which he gained great estates in Connacht, and to a lesser extent in Co. Limerick.[40] More pertinently, he also expended much effort in attempting to resolve his difficulties with Juliana de Cogan. Gerald fitzMaurice had in fact died before he could finalize the transfer of his properties and rights to John fitzThomas, a situation which left Juliana de Cogan with some rights to both the estates which fitzThomas already had, and to the properties which Agnes de Valence currently held. John therefore tried to induce Juliana to surrender her rights to him.[41] His success with her is rather uncertain, possibly because she had two sons to provide for, but from the agreements made between them that have survived, it is clear that by 1293 John was already casting envious eyes over the Limerick properties, and must have resented Agnes as an obstacle in his path.[42] From this perspective, the outcome of Agnes's case against de Valle, with its consequent burdening of John with the greatest share of de Valle's debts, cannot have endeared her to him. But what made it so damaging was its timing.

For by 1293 fitzThomas was also engaged in two intense power struggles in Ireland, one with the greatest magnate on the island, Richard de Burgh earl of Ulster, and the other with the Irish justiciar, William de Vescy. De Vescy was also the lord of the liberty of Kildare and as such had

37 *Red book of the earls of Kildare*, nos. 30, 74; *Ann. Clonm.*, s.a. 1271; Orpen, 'The Fitzgeralds', 110.
38 Orpen, 'The Fitzgeralds', 110.
39 *Red book of the earls of Kildare*, no. 11.
40 Ibid., nos. 32, 34, 86–94.
41 Ibid., nos. 30, 33, 73, 116, 136, 183.
42 Ibid., nos. 33, 45, 136; *Cal. doc. Ire., 1285–1292*, no. 622.

some judicial rights over fitzThomas's estates there.[43] And now Agnes, while trying to recover the money which de Valle owed, began to harass fitzThomas by seeking judgments against him in de Vescy's liberty court, no doubt with the justiciar's active encouragement.[44] Increasingly, John fitzThomas appears to have viewed Agnes as another enemy. In the English parliament of Michaelmas 1293, amongst a whole bloc of complaints which he made against de Vescy's administration, fitzThomas alleged that Agnes and de Vescy had colluded together to entice Juliana de Cogan into disinheriting him altogether. While there is evidence that Agnes had been in contact with the de Vescy family in August 1293, the justiciar's response that he and Agnes had merely been negotiating about the manor of Geashill, which Agnes herself held, may have been true. Nonetheless, fitzThomas does not seem to have believed it.[45]

The drastic steps which John fitzThomas took in 1294 to resolve his difficulties with de Vescy and the earl of Ulster are both too complex and too well known to go into in any great detail here. Suffice it to say that he had de Vescy recalled through the expedient of calling him a traitor and retailer of slanderous tales about the king; that in December 1294 he imprisoned the earl of Ulster and attacked his supporters in Connacht, Meath and Kildare in an explosion of lawlessness known to contemporaries as 'the time of disturbance'; and that, at the very least, he facilitated the burning of the records of the liberty of Kildare by the Irish warlord Calbhach O Connor Faly.[46] Significantly, he also targeted Agnes. On 6 October 1294, two months before the earl of Ulster was captured, fitzThomas, using the story that Agnes had just died, sent his men into the manors of Adare, Croom, Athlacca and Rathmore, taking possession of them and carrying off Agnes's movable goods.[47] This act of trespass tends to be overlooked because of John's more spectacular activities immediately afterwards. However, it was connected to them, inasmuch as its outcome was directly influenced by the royal response to 'the time of disturbance'. John's attempt to intimidate the earl of Ulster failed completely, casting his own survival into doubt. By August 1295 he had been summoned to England to answer for his misdeeds and had placed himself at the mercy of the king.[48] While he was there, old William de Valence, on his living daughter's behalf, exploited fitzThomas's weak position by extracting an agreement from him whereby John promised to hand back

43 Cosgrove, *New history*, II, 185–7.
44 *Calendar of the justiciary rolls, Ireland, 1295–1303*, 327–8.
45 Richardson and Sayles, *Rotuli* , 34; P. R. O., E. 101/353/18, m. 5d.
46 Cosgrove, *New history*, II, 186–7.
47 *Calendar of the justiciary rolls, Ireland, 1305–07*, 236, 240–1.
48 *Cal. doc. Ire., 1293–1301*, no. 246.

all of the lands which he had seized, to restore all goods which he had taken and to pay for any damages incurred.[49]

However, the evidence from the next two years would suggest that Agnes had not forgiven him. In November of 1296 she granted her manor of Geashill, which was in fitzThomas's barony of Offaly, to his archenemy Richard de Burgh.[50] She also continued to pursue the surviving mainpernors of John de Valle for her money. From the record of a hearing in April of 1297, it becomes apparent that the administration had been ordered to collect the debt by seizing their goods and rents. Ominously, it also becomes clear that figures like de Geneville and l'Enfaunt, who had close connections with the government, were making arrangements to pay up, while the various sheriffs and seneschals were having much less success with characters like Keating and fitzThomas.[51]

Between 1297 and 1303, apart from the fact that in 1299, a copy of the marriage agreement that she had made with Maurice fitzGerald 33 years earlier was drawn up, little is known about Agnes's legal battles against fitzThomas, or indeed about her dealings in Ireland in general.[52] Possibly this is merely due to gaps in the sources. Alternatively, fitzThomas was trying to redeem himself by performing military service in Scotland and Flanders, and was thereby gaining immunity from prosecution and pardons for his transgressions, and it is possible that this deterred Agnes from making an attempt to pursue her claims.[53] But it is more likely that a personal bereavement was the decisive cause. Around July 1297 her elder son John died. By October she had decided that she would have to travel to Hainault personally to ensure that her second son Baldwin's rights to the ancestral land were upheld.[54] And so, despite the fact that England had been teetering on the brink of civil war, and that Flanders was a war zone, Agnes departed from Dover in November with her son, her personal knights, chaplains and damsels, not to return until 1300.[55]

Whatever the reasons were for the lull in Agnes's pursuit of her rights, there was no question of John fitzThomas remaining idle during the same period. Most fundamentally, his standing both within the lordship and with the king began to improve. In Ireland, the most important develop-

49 *Rotuli parliamentorum*, I, 130b–131b.
50 *Red book of the earls of Kildare*, nos. 36–7.
51 *Calendar of the justiciary rolls, Ireland, 1295–1303*, 104–5.
52 *Cal. doc. Ire., 1293–1301*, nos. 671–2.
53 Ibid., nos. 344, 436, 438, 461.
54 G.E.C., *Peerage*, x, p. 17.; *Calendar of the patent rolls, 1292–1301*, 290, 293; *Calendar of the close rolls, 1296–1302*, 66.
55 Powicke, *The thirteenth century*, 678–683; *Calendar of the close rolls, 1296–1302*, 66; *Calendar of the patent rolls, 1292–1301*, 313, 316, 354; *Cal doc. Ire., 1293–1301*, nos. 580, 581.

ment was that fitzThomas's feud with the earl of Ulster was finally resolved. In 1298, a commission set up to examine the issues found in the earl's favour, and fitzThomas was obliged to hand over his Connacht estates to de Burgh, thus removing the main source of friction between the two magnates.[56] John's military service in Scotland and Flanders also began to pay dividends in terms of gaining the king's favour. For example, following the death of his Desmond Geraldine kinsman, Thomas fitzMaurice in 1298, John was awarded the valuable custody of his under-age heir's lands.[57] Similarly, in February 1302 the king awarded him the right to free warren (or hunting) in all of his manors, which, significantly, included the properties which Agnes actually held.[58] However, his better fortune did not lessen his animosity towards Agnes, and he began to plan to challenge her on a legal basis, apparently by setting his lawyers to examining the family archives. During the latter half of the thirteenth century, there is no hint that the manors which Agnes held were anything but Geraldine property. Nonetheless, at some point between 1299 and 1301, a woman named Christiana de Mariscis petitioned the king that Agnes was intruding upon the manors of Rathmore and Athlacca to which Christiana claimed to be the heir.[59] While it is possible that Christiana had some rights dating back to the early thirteenth century, the claim had not been pursued.[60] But an agreement drawn up near Windsor in March 1302 explains Christiana's sudden interest. John fitzThomas undertook to pursue the case for Christiana, bearing all the costs, on condition that she would grant him the properties, and that they would share any damages accruing to Christiana, if the case was successful.[61] By this action fitzThomas acquired a legal weapon against Agnes which the records reveal to have hung over her head for the next decade.[62] However, it seems as though John did not exploit this opportunity fully, preferring instead to use more forceful methods.

The first sign of unusual activity to surface in the official records dates from March 1303, when letters patent were issued in England informing all in Ireland who might be interested that Agnes was alive, and in good health.[63] Subsequent court records allow us to reconstruct what had hap-

56 *Calendar of the justiciary rolls, Ireland, 1295–1303*, 234–6.
57 Ibid., p. 311.
58 *Cal. doc. Ire., 1302–07*, no. 7.
59 Brooks, 'The family of Marisco', 66–7.
60 See Brooks, 'The de Ridelesfords', 54; and Empey, 'The settlement of Limerick' 1–25.
61 *Red book of the earls of Kildare*, no. 59.
62 *Calendar of chancery warrants, 1244–1326*, 242; *Calendar of the close rolls, 1302–07*, 305–6; *Calendar of the patent rolls, 1307–13*, 29, 102.
63 *Cal. doc. Ire., 1302–1307*, nos. 189, 190.

pened. In January 1303, again using the pretext of Agnes's death, John had
seized her properties. When Agnes heard of this, she had the letters patent
sent to Ireland, and by April John had been officially informed that
Agnes was alive.[64] He was slow to relinquish the properties however, and
became embroiled in a lawsuit with John de Cogan, Juliana's heir, as to
which of them had the better title to the estates. FitzThomas won on a
technicality, but the victory was pyrrhic, as by the end of 1303 Agnes had
regained possession anyway.[65] But on this occasion, he did not leave
peacefully. Instead, it was alleged, 'increasing his former trespass ... he
threshed and carried away her corn, drove off her cattle, broke her chests,
took her goods found there ... threw down certain houses and burned the
timber of them, cut the trees of the garden and hedges, caused two iron-
bound carts and four ploughs to be burned ... and imprisoned her
bailiffs'.[66] Conceivably, fitzThomas had initially made a genuine mistake,
but his subsequent actions demanded a response from Agnes. It came in
the form of an all-out effort, using her connections to the utmost to
obtain justice and compensation, both for the trespass and for the de Valle
default. In this article, the two cases will be outlined separately, but as
both actions were being undertaken simultaneously, their impact in
Ireland was all the greater.

In April 1304, King Edward, noting 'the many outrages and despites
which had been committed in Ireland against the king's cousin Agnes de
Valence by Sir John fitzThomas ... in manner of open robbery' and the
fact that she had not yet received redress, ordered the English council to
discuss the problem.[67] Their response was to order the Irish justiciar, John
Wogan, either to resolve the case or to send the parties to appear before
the king at the next parliament in England. Despite this unambiguous
command, the case was not opened until October 1304, when it was postponed until the following May.[68] Clearly, Agnes's grievances were not at
the top of the Irish administration's agenda. She refused to accept this,
and in the English parliament of February 1305, she accused Wogan of
dragging his heels, and succeeded in having him penalized.[69] More English
writs were sent out to speed up the process in April, and the case was
heard, as originally scheduled, in May 1305, before Edmund Butler, with
Agnes claiming £2,200 in losses and damages.[70] At this point however,

64 *Calendar of the justiciary rolls, Ireland 1305–07*, 76.
65 Ibid., 76; *Red book of the earls of Kildare*, no. 105.
66 *Calendar of the justiciary rolls, Ireland, 1305–07*, 75, 236, 240.
67 *Calendar of chancery warrants, 1244–1326*, 212.
68 *Calendar of the justiciary rolls, Ireland, 1305–07*, 76.
69 Maitland, *Records of the Westminster parliament*, 240–3; *Calendar of the close rolls, 1302–07*, 325.
70 *Calendar of the justiciary rolls, Ireland , 1305–07*, 75–6.

Agnes's usage of English influence proved to be her undoing. John's lawyers contended that John could not answer the allegations, as they were contained in a writ out of the English chancery, rather than one from the Irish chancery. Despite Agnes's attorneys' protestations, Butler, who happened to be fitzThomas's son-in-law, postponed the case until Wogan, who was still in England, returned. In July, after Wogan had done so, the case was reopened. But now, a group of Irish magnates including the earl of Ulster, Eustace le Poer and Piers de Bermingham stated that John was indeed correct, and that it would be contrary to the customs of the land to allow the case to proceed. Wogan promptly referred the problem to the king who, in November 1305, faced with a united front of Irish magnates, ruled in fitzThomas's favour.[71] Agnes was going to have to start all over again and she did so in January 1306, this time using Irish writs. The allegations were heard in April and juries from Kildare and Limerick were ordered to testify in July. The Kildare jury met, stated that Agnes had indeed been trespassed against, and assessed her losses at £110 rather than the £300 which she had been claiming. The Limerick jury on the other hand initially failed to appear, but after they had been re-summoned and the sheriff penalized, they turned up, assessing Agnes's losses at £606. Finally, in January 1307, four years after the trespass, Agnes was awarded her money back, with another £70 added for damages.[72] However, it is very doubtful that it was ever actually paid to her. What is certain is that in the last reference to this case in the *Calendar of the Justiciary Rolls*, dating from May 1307, and referring to the damages awarded, Agnes's attorneys had managed to extract the princely sum of £8 from fitzThomas.[73]

So, Agnes's highly powered and tenacious effort to get justice for the trespass ended with a legal victory, albeit one of dubious practicality. All the while, her action to recover the money misappropriated by de Valle was grinding on. The court records show that by November 1304, royal officials were active in trying to bring in the debt.[74] In that same month yet another English writ was sent to Wogan ordering him to expedite collection.[75] From May 1305 onwards, the difficulties which the Irish administration faced in doing so begin to emerge into sharper focus. Its dealings with fitzThomas are both typical and instructive. At that time, the sheriff of Kildare reported that he had seized 23 crannocks of corn from John's manor of Rathangan as well as 12 oxen and 4 afers. However, he continued, fitzThomas had taken the corn back, and he could find no buyers for

71 Ibid., 76–8; *Calendar of chancery warrants, 1244–1326*, 253.
72 *Calendar of the justiciary rolls, Ireland , 1305–07*, 236–7, 240–1, 281.
73 Ibid., 393.
74 Ibid., 213.
75 Ibid., 5.

the livestock. Similarly, the sheriff of Limerick reported that 16 afers and 16 oxen had been seized from John's ploughs, but that no-one dared buy them. He also stated that all of John's rents in the region were being levied by Edmund Butler, as part of the dowry of fitzThomas's daughter.[76] Not surprisingly, when this progress report reached Agnes she was not satisfied, and in October 1305 a further English writ was issued.[77] Accordingly, the sheriffs made another report in January of 1306 to the effect that the situation had not changed significantly. But this time, Agnes's attorneys challenged their returns. It transpired that the sheriff and chief serjeant of Limerick had been lying. Not only had they failed to collect several rents which fitzThomas had been receiving, but they had never actually seized any of his livestock either. It was the same story in Kildare, where the sheriff and his chief serjeant were accused of acting falsely in John's favour. They had claimed to have seized corn from John's share of Maynooth manor, but Agnes's attorneys alleged that they had done nothing of the sort, and moreover that they had failed to seize John's available rents, said to be worth 200 marks *per annum*. The two officials could not deny these allegations, but claimed that 'they dared not make other [returns] for fear of John fitzThomas'.[78]

At this stage, both sets of officials were duly penalized and ordered to report back in March. When they did so, the sheriff of Kildare stated that he would be in a position to collect £20 in May. The sheriff of Limerick had a far more dramatic report to make. He said that his serjeant had made an effort to round up some of John's livestock, but that a group of fitzThomas's men with their great following of Irishmen had taken them back by force and had driven them into Kerry. Furthermore, while John did have crops growing which could be seized, no one dared guard them. Lastly, fitzThomas's *betaghs*, or unfree Irish tenants, had fled *en masse* into Thomond before the serjeant could reach them. Notwithstanding this, he was ordered to arrest the livestock rustlers, seize the crops and chattels, and to report back again the following month. When he did, it was to admit total failure: the rustlers could not be found, but were believed to be in either Kerry or Offaly; fitzThomas had assigned the lands and crops away; all of his goods and chattels had been removed from Limerick; and his tenants were still lying low in Thomond. This state of affairs left John Wogan with a major dilemma. On the one hand he had a duty to implement the royal commands, while on the other he could hardly allow such chaos to continue. He opted for stability, and

---

76 *Calendar of the justiciary rolls, Ireland, 1305–07*, 6–8.
77 Ibid., 204–13, for details of the writ and its consequences.
78 Ibid., 211.

ordered that further execution of the writ be ceased. Significantly, Agnes's attorneys agreed that all that could be done had been done at that time. There does not appear to be any evidence for further attempts being made to recover the money during the remaining years left to Agnes. She seems to have realised that in this instance, local connections were more effective than royal ones.

There is little else of relevance recorded about Agnes's involvement in Ireland. She did continue to try and collect the damages awarded to her against the sheriff and serjeant of Limerick.[79] However, if it is possible to argue from silence, it would seem that she and fitzThomas had tacitly agreed to maintain the *status quo*. In any event, it is likely that events outside of Ireland had sapped her enthusiasm for continuing the struggle, for her second son Baldwin had died, rendering all of her efforts in Hainault worthless.[80] Her own end was heralded by letters patent declaring her perfect health in September and December 1309.[81] She was dead by December 31, when writs were issued to hold inquisitions *post mortem* concerning her property.[82] On 28 February 1310, the estates which she had built up in England were delivered to her heir, her brother, Aymer de Valence, earl of Pembroke.[83] And in Ireland? For the third time, as soon as John fitzThomas heard of Agnes's death he occupied all of her estates, elbowing aside both John de Cogan, Juliana's heir, and a royal official, the escheator, in the process.[84] On this occasion, despite the hostilities which ensued between himself and de Cogan, he was allowed to retain possession and so, after a hiatus of over forty years, the Geraldine inheritance was reunited.[85]

Modern historians like Hand and Richardson and Sayles have already made some use of Agnes's experiences in Ireland. In particular, they have employed the court battles between Agnes and John to demonstrate various aspects of the interaction between the Irish administration and its English counterpart.[86] However, there are other issues raised which are worth examining. Most obviously, the difficulties encountered by Agnes in getting justice done are striking. One further example will eliminate the possibility that her problems were exclusively of fitzThomas's making. In

79 *Calendar of the justiciary rolls, Ireland, 1308–14*, 58, 101, 114.
80 *Cal. inq. post mort.*, v, Edward II, no. 203.
81 *Calendar of the patent rolls, 1307–13*, 189, 201.
82 *Cal. inq. post mort.*, v, Edward II, no. 203.
83 *Calendar of the fine rolls, 1307–19*, p. 58.
84 *Red book of the earls of Kildare*, no. 136.
85 *Calendar of the Carew MSS, Miscellaneous.*, 364; Craig, 'Memoranda Roll', ii, 398.
86 Hand, *English law*, 141, 146, 151, 157; Richardson and Sayles, *The Irish parliament*, 249.

March 1305, William son of Richard, sub-serjeant of Tipperary, made a complaint against Sir James Keating. He stated that he had seized 200 of James' sheep, as part of the campaign to recover the de Valle debts, but that James had taken them back. Furthermore, when he next encountered James, the knight had proceeded to insult him and then to beat him. In his defence, James replied that he had understood that the serjeant was driving his sheep in deep snow, and 'because he would not suffer his sheep to perish of hunger and cold', he had taken them home again.[87] He also admitted that he had struck William on the head with his hand, but claimed that it was not malicious. Edmund Butler, who was presiding over the case solemnly declared that the incident was contrary to the dignity of the king, and committed James to gaol to await the king's mercy. But he was out of prison with a full pardon within the month.[88] As this sort of incident was commonplace, one could justify using the late fourteenth century phrase 'sturdy robbers' to describe men like Keating and fitzThomas.[89] When one contrasts the dogged efforts made by Agnes to attain her rights with the poor response she actually achieved, the impression one gets is that for someone without her connections, such an attempt must have been well-nigh impossible. Of course it could be argued that it would be unrealistic to expect a greatly different outcome, given the contemporary context. By way of contrast, it might be more fruitful to view Agnes's career from a different perspective, that of the Geraldines, and of John fitzThomas in particular.

Initially, it is likely that the Geraldines were delighted by Maurice fitzGerald's marriage to King Henry's niece. However Maurice's premature death raises questions as to the wisdom of paying so high a price for her, given the consequent alienation of so much of their property. That it took them so long to react against this state of affairs appears to be largely due to William de Valence's astuteness in neutralizing Gerald fitz-Maurice. Gerald's subsequent ineffectuality leads one to consider the actions of John fitzThomas. Historians have tended to paint a rather negative picture of John's character. For example, Orpen considered him to be 'the most ambitious man in Ireland'; one who could commit an 'excess of Geraldine audacity'.[90] Richardson and Sayles labelled him as 'the most lawless perhaps, of the Irish barons'.[91] Ambitious he certainly was, but it may be that to judge him for his apparent recklessness and lawlessness is to underestimate the complexity of his position. John had grown up in a

---

87 *Cal. justic. rolls Ire., 1305–07*, 45.
88 Ibid., 45.
89 Frame, *English lordship in Ireland*, 38.
90 Orpen, *Ireland under the Normans*, iv, 113, 115.
91 Richardson & Sayles, *The Irish parliament*, 248.

harsh environment which was shaped to a great extent by warfare. If it is true that such societies tend to place great stress upon the importance of lineages and kindred, then his determination to regain the Geraldine patrimony is quite understandable, especially when it is recalled that his predecessor Gerald fitzMaurice had attempted to do the same. FitzThomas's central problem was that neither royal policy, with its innate bias towards Agnes, nor the strict application of law were likely to work in his favour. And so by necessity, and possibly also by predilection, he had to employ tactics which ran counter to what was deemed to be acceptable behaviour – the robberies, the burning of court records and so on. It might be worth noting that his actions of 1294, which have contributed most to his unsavoury reputation, were undertaken against two men, de Vescy and de Burgh, who were not exactly paragons of virtue themselves either. His dealings with Agnes are more problematic. While his motivation for becoming de Valle's guarantor is unclear, and it is possible that he might have genuinely believed in 1294 and 1303 that Agnes had died, it is difficult to rationalize his wanton vandalism when ordered to vacate her manors. And yet his lawlessness was limited, and he did hand the properties back. Unlike a common robber, John's authority as baron of Offaly was ultimately dependent upon the king. Also, his world might have been physically and even psychologically remote from the world in which Agnes spent most of her life, that of the home counties of England, but he and his retainers were just as appreciative of the fruits and trappings that accrued from royal favour as were the English aristocracy. In short, to maintain his position, fitzThomas also needed respectability. Professor Frame has complimented Edward I on his ability to manage men like fitzThomas, which is a valid point, but perhaps it tends to obscure the inverse possibility, that for John to retain the King's goodwill was no mean achievement.[92]

His success in doing so was basically a function of his military usefulness, partially overseas, but to a greater extent at home. It was this facet of his character which proved to be the decisive factor in the curbing of Agnes's rights. In the 1300s her actions against him were well supported, effectively argued and legally sound, but poorly timed. From the mid 1290s onwards, the entire Leinster colony began to come under severe pressure from the Irish of the midlands and of the Leinster mountains. Because of his behaviour in 1294, Professor Lydon has apportioned a share of the responsibility for this phenomenon to fitzThomas.[93] Notwithstanding that, John, in his capacity as lord of Offaly, proved to

92 Frame, *Colonial Ireland*, 66.
93 Cosgrove, *New history*, II, p. 188.

be one of the most effective bulwarks against the depredations of the mid-
land Irish. By 1305, as part of his defensive role, he was actually maintaining a garrison in Agnes's manor of Geashill, in the extremities of the
marches.[94] The situation was so volatile that the hostilities were in fact an
obstacle to holding the court cases between Agnes and fitzThomas. On
one occasion John was forced to rush back to Offaly in the middle of a
hearing, after Piers de Bermingham's notorious murder of twenty leading
O Connor Falys had inflamed the whole region.[95] Given this state of
affairs, it made little sense for the Irish government, or indeed for the
king, to be devoting their time to harassing fitzThomas and his *betaghs*,
on behalf of a distant absentee. And so they took the pragmatic decision
to leave him alone. It might also be worth observing that, with Agnes out
of the way, John became a more respectable figure, founding the Augustinian Black Abbey at Adare, hosting knighting ceremonies for his associ-
ates and remaining loyal to Edward II during the Bruce invasion, an
action which led to his being created the first earl of Kildare in May
1316.[96] On reflection, to view Agnes from his perspective is to see a dangerous meddling irritant, whose possession of such a large portion of his
family's estates was in itself an aberration caused by a chance drowning
forty years previously.

So in conclusion, what insights can be gained from investigating
Agnes's varied, if rather unsettled life? Perhaps on a very basic level, it
shows the manner in which aristocratic women could be regarded as
being both pawns and players in the business of the acquisition of wealth
and status. But from an Irish viewpoint, it might not be too fanciful to
view her fortunes as a kind of litmus test for the state of the lordship. Her
arrival here was a symbol of the self-confidence possessed by an Irish
aristocratic house at the zenith of the colony's prosperity. For the next
two decades she was able to enjoy her properties in Ireland without
undue difficulty. But towards the end of her life, conditions had changed
to the extent that the Irish government was forced into choosing between
her rights, representing law, and its own need to maintain fitzThomas, the
unlikely representative of order, to her detriment. As events in the fourteenth century were to confirm, the lordship of Ireland was becoming a
land where the virtues of sturdy robbers were appreciated, and where
absentee landladies were an unaffordable luxury.

94 *Calendar of justiciary rolls, Ireland, 1305–07*, 8, 270.
95 Ibid., 77–8.
96 *Ann. Clyn*, 11; *Rot. pat. Hib.*, 22b; Phillips, 'John de Hothum', 73; *Red book of
    the earls of Kildare*, no. 142.

THE FITZGERALDS OF OFFALY

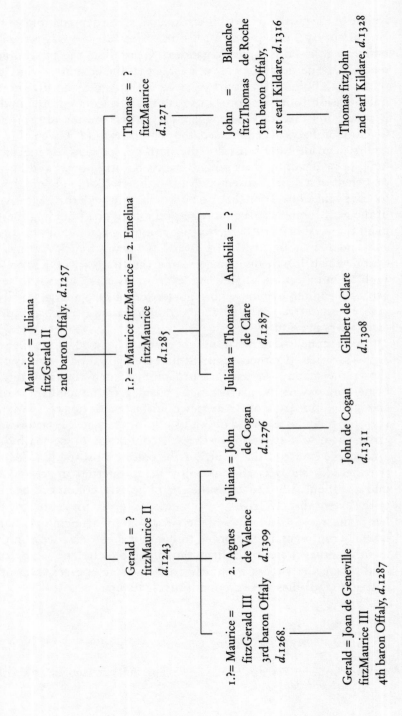

Maurice = Juliana
fitzGerald II
2nd baron Offaly. *d.*1257

Gerald = ?
fitzMaurice II
*d.*1243

Thomas = ?
fitzMaurice
*d.*1271

1.? = Maurice fitzMaurice = 2. Emelina
    fitzMaurice
    *d.*1285

Juliana = John
de Cogan
*d.*1276

Juliana = Thomas
de Clare
*d.*1287

Amabilia = ?

John = Blanche de Roche
fitzThomas
5th baron Offaly,
1st earl Kildare, *d.*1316

1.? = Maurice = 2. Agnes
fitzGerald III   de Valence
3rd baron Offaly   *d.*1309
*d.*1268.

John de Cogan
*d.*1311

Gilbert de Clare
*d.*1308

Thomas fitzJohn
2nd earl Kildare, *d.*1328

Gerald = Joan de Geneville
fitzMaurice III
4th baron Offaly, *d.*1287

The English Noblewoman and Her Family in the Later Middle Ages

Jennifer C. Ward [1]

The description of Philippa, wife of Edmund Mortimer Earl of March, in the Book of Wigmore selected what were regarded as the important things about her from the point of view of the Mortimer family and its abbey of Wigmore.[2] As the only child of Lionel Duke of Clarence, Edward III's second surviving son, she was closely related to the royal family, and provided the Mortimers with their claim to the throne. She was a great heiress, her mother having been in her own right countess of Ulster, and her great-grandmother having inherited one-third of the lands of the Clare earls of Gloucester.[3] Philippa provided a son and heir to the earldom of March, Roger, who died in 1398. Her quasi-royal funeral took place at Wigmore, cementing her identity not with her ancestral lands but with the Mortimer family.

What the writer provided was a stereotype of Philippa, not a description of what she was really like. This type of account was usual in chronicle descriptions of men and women, and much of the difficulty of evaluating the noblewoman's relationships with her family lies in the nature of the evidence and its primary concern with land and money. Marriage settlements were essentially legal documents concerning property. Household accounts were designed to show the accountability of the officials. Legal disputes do not necessarily record both sides of the argument, and it is rare to know the outcome. Much information can be derived from wills, but caution has to be exercised over the language used

---

1 I would like to thank Professor Christine Meek and Dr Katharine Simms for inviting me to give this paper at the Annual Conference of the Irish Association for Research in Women's History at Trinity College, Dublin, in December, 1993. I would also like to thank the participants at the conference for the subsequent stimulating discussion, and Professor Andrew Louth and Dr Paul Fouracre for help with particular parts of this paper.

2 Dugdale, *Monasticon Anglicanum*, VI,1,353. The Book of Wigmore is discussed by M. E. Giffin, 'A Wigmore manuscript', 316–25.

3 Her mother was Elizabeth de Burgh, countess of Ulster (*d*.1363); her great-grandmother was Elizabeth de Burgh (*d*.1360), the youngest daughter of Gilbert de Clare, earl of Gloucester and Hertford (*d*.1295), and coheiress of her brother, Gilbert de Clare, earl of Gloucester and Hertford (*d*.1314).

and its interpretation; expressions of affection may be an interpolation by the clerk, not the words of the testator. Letters can throw much more light on personal relationships, but substantial collections for particular families only survive from the fifteenth century and later. Even in letters, men and women often expressed themselves formally, with little reference to their thoughts, feelings and attitudes. Men and women in the Midddle Ages believed strongly that family relationships had to be placed on a business footing (presumably in case the arrangements later went wrong), and the documents tended to survive in Crown and family archives, simply because they dealt with business matters. Such documents were even drawn up between close relations; the arrangements for the wardship of Hamo Lestrange were the subject of a deed drawn up between his mother and grandmother, as were the provisions for Lady Alice Plumpton's maintenance by her son Robert.[4]

However, it would be a mistake to deduce from the formal and business nature of many of the sources that family relationships were cool and impersonal.[5] The documents provide for the most part a record of actions taken by the family at different stages of its existence. No family had complete freedom of action, as all were subject to the law of the land, to feudal ties and obligations, and to social convention. However, many of the actions taken stemmed from the way in which family members regarded each other. Friendship in the classical and medieval worlds was expected to take a practical and active form, and it is possible to use these actions to assess the nature of family relationships.[6] By combining all the evidence available on particular noble families, it is possible to see great variety in family relationships, as between husband and wife, parents and children, and among the wider kindred group. Family relationships were not necessarily harmonious and should by no means be idealised; dislike was to be found as well as affection.

4 Norfolk Record Office, Le Strange of Hunstanton Collection, no. A7. Stapleton, *Plumpton correspondence*, xxvii–ix.

5 Stone, *The family*, 4–7, sees the characteristic type of family in the sixteenth century and for at least a millenium before as the patriarchal Open Lineage Family where relationships within the family were cool and unemotional, and where there was little to distinguish the relationships between husband, wife and children from those between members of the family, more distant kindred, neighbours and friends. For the early modern period this conclusion has been disputed by, for example, Houlbrooke, *The English family*, 102–5, and Ingram, *Church courts*, 137–44. Both writers cite evidence to show that conjugal love existed in practice.

6 In his treatise, *De amicitia*, Cicero stressed the link between love and friendship, and regarded the mutual giving of gifts and favours as an integral part of friendship; Cicero, *De senectute*, trans. Falconer, 136–44. These points were reiterated by Aelred of Rievaulx in his Book on Spiritual Friendship, finished in 1164; Squire, *Aelred of Rievaulx*, 99–102, 108–9.

The late medieval noble family cannot be dismissed as an impersonal property-running business. Personal factors were often to the fore, and need to be taken into account if the late medieval nobility are to be regarded as human beings rather than cardboard figures. Although much of the evidence emphasises the landed basis of relationships, personal ties appear in letters of the thirteenth and fourteenth centuries as well as in the better known Stonor, Plumpton and Paston correspondence. William Marshal's visit to his sick mother at Chepstow in 1220, and Earl Gilbert de Clare's explanation of his late arrival at court because one of his children was ill provide an unexpected insight into these two men.[7] Gilbert de Clare's insistence that the real reason for his absence should not be publicised also throws light on the way in which feeling for a sick child might well be regarded as unmanly in the late thirteenth century.

Looking at the relationship of the noblewoman and her family, it is important to be aware of the very different setting for relationships from that which we are familiar with in the late twentieth century. Life for noble families was a public rather than a private affair, lived in a household where servants, officials, friends and visitors were always present. Noble society was patriarchal, patriarchy being underpinned by law, but the frequent absence of noble and gentry husbands on war-service and public duties gave the wife a prominent role. Contact with children tended to be occasional after the early years, owing to education away from home and often early marriage. These factors were bound to have an effect on relationships, but did not necessarily preclude affection. The historian has to assess this affection through the practical steps taken to help the child; it is rare, except in a few letters, to find affection expressed in ways which would be familiar at the present day.

When the settlements are examined, the whole business of marriage seems to be a cut and dried arrangement, sorting out dowry and jointure. In 1354 a marriage alliance was projected by Roger Mortimer earl of March and Richard earl of Arundel for their infant offspring; the marriage did not take place, and Roger's son Edmund married Philippa of Clarence. The earl of Arundel agreed to pay £2000 for his daughter's dowry, while Roger Mortimer agreed to settle 200 marks' worth of land and rent on the couple in jointure.[8] The jointure would be held by the couple, and subsequently by the widow if she survived her husband, and only after her death would it revert to her husband's family lands. The

---

7 Public Record Office, London, SC1/4/74; SC1/22/156. Earl Gilbert's letter should be dated to 1291–2; the child referred to may well be his son and heir, born in 1291.

8 *Calendar of the close rolls, 1354–60*, 92–4. The mark was worth 13s. 4d.

size of the jointure varied, and some wives, such as Joan of Acre countess of Gloucester, widowed in 1295, and Alice Chaucer duchess of Suffolk, widowed in 1450, held jointure in all their husband's estates.[9] In addition, for less fortunate wives, the widow was entitled on the death of her husband to one-third of his lands in dower.

Historians have rightly emphasised the prevalence of the arranged marriage and stressed the parental competition for heiresses and advantageous family alliances. Both noblewomen and their husbands were involved in marriage negotiations, and family considerations and a sound economic basis for the marriage were factors which were taken for granted; the agreement for the marriage of Hugh de Courtenay to Margaret de Bohun in 1315 saw Queen Margaret, widow of Edward I, and Earl Humphrey de Bohun and his wife acting for Margaret, and the agreement laid down in detail the financial and property basis for the marriage.[10]

Some arrangements appear particularly cold-blooded, such as that negotiated by Ralph Neville earl of Westmorland and his wife Joan Beaufort for their son William to marry Joan Fauconberg who was an idiot but an heiress.[11] The question however has to be asked as to whether marriage was rather more than the property deal outlined in the settlements. Parents were agreed that romantic love was an inadequate basis for marriage; hence the Pastons' dismay over the marriage of Margery Paston to the bailiff Richard Calle, and her mother's refusal to have her daughter in the house because of the social degradation of the marriage.[12] In this case, as in others, parents had to accept a *fait accompli*. John of Gaunt had to recognise his daughter Elizabeth's marriage to John Holland once Elizabeth was pregnant; it had been arranged that Elizabeth should marry the earl of Pembroke, but John is said to have fallen in love with her at first sight.[13] Similarly an abduction might well result in parents or guardians having to accept a marriage.[14] The practice of a young married

9 *Calendar of the fine rolls, 1272–1307*, 274–5; *Calendar of the patent rolls, 1281–92*, 350–2, 359–60; Edwards, *Littere Wallie*, 177. British Library, London, Harley Charter 54 I 9.

10 Public Record Office, London, DL27/13.

11 Lander, 'Marriage and politics', 121.

12 Davis, *Paston letters*, I, nos. 203, 332. Social degradation is also emphasised in John Paston III's letter when he wrote that he did not wish to see his sister selling candles and mustard in Framlingham market. The Pastons' concern with status and upward mobility is stressed by Richmond, 'The Pastons revisited', 25–36, and *The Paston family ... The first phase*, 116.

13 Hector and Harvey, *The Westminster chronicle, 1381–94*, 192–5.

14 Margaret de Multon's abduction by Ranulf de Dacre in 1314–15, although the marriage was said to have been earlier agreed to by their fathers; Stevenson,

couple living in the household of one of the parents, as envisaged in Edmund Mortimer's projected marriage, probably helped them to build up a relationship before they set up their own household.

There is no evidence that parents consulted their children, but in view of the social contacts among the nobility and gentry it is probable that some children at least knew their marriage partners, and even possible that some parents took their children's friendships into account. The household book of Alice de Bryene of Acton, Suffolk, of 1412–13, points to constant visiting among local gentry families, the husband or wife being sometimes accompanied by son or daughter.[15] John Paston III promised his future mother-in-law not to talk of marriage to Margery Brews until terms were agreed, but Margery was aware of what was going on and pestered her mother to ensure that the marriage actually came about. Yet in sending one of her Valentines to John, she showed that she was aware that without a marriage settlement satisfactory to her father the marriage would never take place.[16] Taking these instances together, the evidence suggests that more lies behind the marriage settlement than the historian can be aware of, but that parents considered that all marriages should be rooted in property.

In looking at the noblewoman's relations with her husband, it is dangerous to assume a lack of affection simply because medieval people only very rarely expressed their feelings. Evidence, principally from letters, points to great variety in marital relations. Husband and wife are seldom seen together; the probability that Bolingbroke (the future Henry IV) played chess with his wife Mary de Bohun indicates that husbands and wives could enjoy recreation together.[17] Husbands and wives went on pilgrimage together, as when Sir Andrew and Elizabeth Luttrell went to Santiago de Compostella in 1361.[18] Many women worked in close partnership with their husbands, and were regarded as friends and companions as well as wives; they were trusted to carry out business and run estates in their husbands' absence. William de Valence entrusted his wife

Chronicon de Lanercost, 223; *Calendar of the patent rolls, 1313–17*, 39; *Calendar of the close rolls, 1313–18*, 504.

15 Redstone and Dale, *The household book of Dame Alice de Bryene*, 7; on Thursday 20 October the guests included Sir John Howard with his wife, daughter, maid, two squires, two yeomen and three grooms. Ibid., 65–6, on Tuesday and Wednesday 23 and 24 May, there was a visit from Sir Richard Waldegrave with his wife, son, maid, squire and six members of his household. Acheson, *A gentry community*, 155–8, points out that most gentry families were acquainted before marriages took place.

16 Davis, *Paston letters*, I, nos. 415–16; II, no. 791.

17 Wylie, *History of England*, III, 325.

18 *Calendar of the close rolls, 1360–4*, 197.

with the overall command of Winchester castle in 1267.[19] His daughter-in-law, Beatrice de Clermont, addressed her husband Aymer de Valence in 1296 as her very dear lord, friend and liege companion; her letter reported on various items of family business.[20] While John Paston I was in London, his wife Margaret remained in Norfolk to bring up the family, supervise the lands, and defend family claims to property; John sent her detailed instructions but she had to make decisions according to local circumstances.[21] There is little sign in the correspondence of a closer relationship but indications of affection appear from time to time.

Love could exist in marriage, as the letters sent by Margery Brews to John Paston III, her 'right worshipful and well-beloved Valentine' show; in one letter she makes it clear that she wanted to join him in London, 'as it is a long while since I lay in your arms'.[22] The letters of Elizabeth Stonor to her husband showed affection and concern for him, as well as relaying London news and discussing business.[23] On the other hand the Plumpton Correspondence makes it clear that there could be deep unhappiness in marriage.[24]

Correspondence provides the best evidence for assessing the relationship of husband and wife. Household accounts can be illuminating if they show husband and wife constantly together, even on journeys and business; such evidence has been used to illuminate the close relationship enjoyed by Margaret Beaufort with her third husband, Henry Stafford.[25] A similar comment may be made about wives who joined their husbands in a war-zone. Elizabeth countess of Hereford was with her husband in Scotland until shortly before the birth of their son Humphrey in 1304;[26] Margaret Holland, wife of Thomas duke of Clarence, joined him in Normandy in 1419.[27]

The evidence of wills is much more ambivalent. The practice of appointing a wife as her husband's executrix points to trust in her business abilities and reflects the likelihood that many husbands and wives worked together during marriage.[28] Other statements in a will are much

19 Shirley, *Royal letters, Henry III*, II, 311.
20 Public Record Office, London, SC1/48/183.
21 Davis, *Paston letters*, I, no. 71.
22 Ibid. I, no. 417.
23 Kingsford, *The Stonor letters*, II, no. 169.
24 Stapleton, *Plumpton correspondence*, xxxix–xl.
25 Jones and Underwood, *The king's mother*, 41, 96.
26 Public Record Office, London, E101/365/20, m. 1.
27 Margaret had previously been married to John Beaufort earl of Somerset, and her Beaufort sons accompanied her to Normandy. Woolgar, *Household accounts*, II, 631–9, 651–5, 670.
28 Archer and Ferme, 'Testamentary procedure', 4–5.

more difficult to interpret with reference to conjugal relations. A limit set on what the wife can claim from the estate may indicate tension within the marriage or a mutual agreement that the children's claims were paramount.[29] The wishes expressed as to place of burial can be interpreted in many ways. The husband's or wife's desire to be buried beside a deceased partner can indicate either affection or compliance with social custom. The decision to be buried elsewhere may point to cool relations between husband and wife, or a predominant concern with one's natal kin, or religious wishes due to changing interests and attitudes during a long widowhood. Marie de St Pol died in 1377 over fifty years after her husband, Aymer de Valence earl of Pembroke; she decided to be buried at the Minoresses' convent at Denny, but provided for requiem masses at Westminster abbey where Aymer had been buried.[30] The evidence of tombs is similarly ambivalent. The portrayal of Sir Ralph Green (*d.*1417) and his wife on their tomb at Lowick in Northamptonshire holding hands may show that they had been in love with each other, or the design may have been copied from the tomb of Richard II.[31] With such evidence, no single interpretation is possible.

Sometimes a woman who had gone through an arranged marriage may well have decided to marry for love on the second or subsequent occasion, although there are instances where she was forced to remarry as a result of parental or royal pressure. This was clearly the case when Elizabeth de Burgh, one of the Clare heiresses, was married to the royal favourite Roger Damory in 1317, and political circumstances explain the king's anger when the year before she had made a runaway match with Theobald de Verdun.[32] It is however noteworthy that many widows chose to please themselves and did not seek the king's consent, as they should have done, to their marriage. Edward I's daughter Joan of Acre was mar-

29 E.g. William de Ferrers of Groby made his will in 1368, shortly after his second marriage to Margaret Percy, widow of Sir Robert de Umfraville. He left her £100 worth of plate and £100 worth of live and dead stock on his manors, but these bequests were to be void if Margaret impeded or molested the executors; Lambeth Palace Library, London, Register of William de Whittlesey, fos. 124v–125r.
30 Jenkinson, 'Mary de Sancto Paulo', 430–4. Marie de St Pol was Aymer de Valence's second wife.
31 Pevsner, *Northamptonshire*, 298; Roskell, Clark and Rawcliffe, *The House of Commons*, III, 229. In 1419 Ralph's executors, including his widow, drew up an indenture with two Derbyshire masons for the erection of the alabaster tomb at Lowick at a cost of £40; the contract specified that husband and wife were to hold hands. I would like to thank Ms Elizabeth Danbury for drawing my attention to this example.
32 Ward, *English noblewomen*, 41–2; *Rotuli parliamentorum*, I, 352–3; *Calendar of the patent rolls, 1313–17*, 644.

ried off in 1290 to Gilbert de Clare earl of Gloucester, then aged nearly fifty, and was left a widow with four young children five years later. While the king was negotiating for her remarriage to Amadeus V of Savoy, she married Ralph de Monthermer, a knight of Earl Gilbert's household, to the fury of her father.[33] In cases like this personal attraction may well have been an important factor, but it is likely that many widows also considered the need for help in looking after their children and estates; second husbands like Ralph de Monthermer and Thomas duke of Clarence found themselves bringing up the children of their wives' first marriages.[34]

At the opposite end of the spectrum from Margery Brews, some noble marriages broke down irretrievably, often because of lack of children and occasionally for political reasons. Some noblemen supported a mistress as well as a wife and brought up their bastard children in their households, as was the case with John of Gaunt and Katherine Swynford.[35] In cases of separation or annulment of the marriage, ecclesiastical records throw some light on relationships, although they have to be carefully assessed, and, especially for the higher nobility, considered in conjunction with information from other sources.[36] John de Warenne, earl of Surrey, and Joan of Bar seem to have been incompatible, and this was possibly accentuated by the difference in their ages. Married in 1306 when John was 19 and Joan 10, John was seeking divorce seven years later and at the same time living with his mistress, Matilda de Nerford. According to a letter of the archbishop of York, the earl alleged that he had only found out that they were related within the prohibited degrees after the marriage; in fact a dispensation had been obtained beforehand. The divorce was never granted, and John seems to have tired of Matilda by about 1325. However there is little sign subsequently of John and Joan living together and certainly there were no children. At the time of his death in 1347 the earl had taken another mistress, Isabel Holland.[37]

Just as there were great differences in the relationships between husbands and wives, so a similar variety emerges over the noblewoman's relations with her children. Again, much of the source material for particular

33 Rymer's *Foedera*, I, 861; Gransden *The Chronicle of Bury St. Edmunds*, 134.
34 The deed drawn up for the upbringing of Isabella Stonor in 1432 makes it clear that the stepfather would not continue to be responsible for her in the event of the death of her mother; Public Record Office, London, C146/1229.
35 Public Record Office, London, DL28/1/2, fos. 21, 24; in 1387, Katherine Swynford and her daughter Joan Beaufort were members of Mary de Bohun's household; Mary was Gaunt's daughter–in–law.
36 E.g. Helmholz, *Marriage litigation*, 96–7.
37 Fairbank, 'The last earl of Warenne', 193–264.

families is concerned with property, finance and business, and relationships have to be assessed on the basis of actions. Such evidence is easier to interpret than the references to children in wills where it is virtually impossible to grade the significance of bequests; moreover in many cases children predeceased their parents. The omission of a surviving child from a will was not necessarily a sign of dislike; the child may well have received the equivalent of a bequest in the testator's lifetime. Taking the evidence overall, it confirms the impression given by contemporary treatises of a concern for the well-being and training of children and of a desire to launch them successfully into their adult lives.[38] Recent work has emphasised that emotional bonds existed between parents and children.[39] The importance of the lineage and the desirablity of the birth of a male heir to secure the continuity of the family were realised throughout noble society. The birth of a child was the occasion for great celebration; according to the Osney annals, both parents were overjoyed when a son was born to Gilbert earl of Gloucester and Joan of Acre in 1291.[40] Often a feast was held when the mother was churched after the birth.[41] The pressure to secure an heir however sometimes resulted in lasting damage to the mother. Mary de Bohun was supposed to remain with her mother after her marriage to Bolingbroke, but her first son was born when she was 12 (he did not survive), and she bore six more children before her death in childbirth in 1394 at the age of 24.[42] Margaret Beaufort was never able to have any more children after the birth of her son by Edmund Tudor, the future Henry VII.[43]

Relatively little is known about the relationship of the noblewoman to her children while they were young. Very occasionally, in saints' lives and letters, there is an insight into the mother's feelings towards her children. Matilda of St Hilary's hysterical reaction to the supposed death of her baby son James may well owe something to the writer who wished to

---

38 Concern for the education of his daughters during his absences from home led the Knight of La Tour Landry to compile his treatise in the later fourteenth century. The medieval grasp of a concept of childhood and the nature of education are discussed by Swanson, 'Childhood', 309–31, and by Orme, *From childhood*, 81–111.

39 Shahar, *Childhood*, 1–7; Ward, *English noblewomen*, 94–101. In contrast, Ariès, *Centuries of childhood*, 368, argues for a distancing between parent and child.

40 Luard, *Annales Monastici*, IV, 328.

41 E.g. Elizabeth countess of Hereford in 1304 after the birth of her son Humphrey; in this case the child died soon after birth. Public Record Office, London, E101/365/20, m. 8.

42 Public Record Office, London, DL28/1/1, fo. 5r. Goodman, *John of Gaunt*, 155; Lodge and Somerville, *John of Gaunt's register*, I, no. 646; II, no. 996; Hector and Harvey, *The Westminster chronicle, 1381–94*, 520–1.

43 Jones and Underwood, *The king's mother*, 39–40.

exaggerate the mother's disbelief that the child was dead. The inclusion of such detail however presupposes a strong contemporary belief that an emotional tie existed between mother and child.[44] Accounts, such as those of Mary de Bohun, record the purchase of clothes and furnishings for the children.[45] About 1252, Eleanor de Montfort was consulted as to whether her son Henry should be placed in the household of Robert Grosseteste, bishop of Lincoln.[46] The accounts of Katherine de la Pole, countess of Suffolk in the early fifteenth century refer to the wet-nurse for her youngest child, the boarding out of her daughters at Bungay priory, and the education of her sons. The children returned home to Wingfield castle at intervals; Alexander was at school at Ipswich from September 1416 to July 1417, and then was fetched home to Wingfield.[47] The practice of sending children away from home at an early age should not automatically be interpreted as meaning lack of affection, but especially with the higher nobility mothers would see relatively little of their children as they grew up. Instead, they became responsible for the training of children from other families who were sent to join their households. In 1380 John of Gaunt arranged for his daughter Katherine to be sent to live with Joan de Mohun.[48]

As children grew up, so tensions could arise in their relationships with their parents. The Paston letters provide the most vivid evidence of strained relationships; Margaret Paston was anxious to foster what she regarded as the well-being and advancement of her children, but often found that they had their own ideas about their future. In 1463 she was clearly annoyed that her eldest son, John Paston II, had passed through Lynn without telling her; she urged him to watch his expenses and pointed out that his grandmother wanted news of him. She was never reconciled to the marriage of her daughter Margery to the bailiff Richard Calle, and left no bequest to her in her will. In 1472, one of the younger sons, John Paston III, wrote that his mother was trying to get him and his brother Edmund out of the house in order to save on their keep; Margaret needed the money for the marriage settlement of her daughter Anne. Margaret was having to decide on her priorities as to whether to support John III and Edmund or to use the money for Anne's marriage, and she

44 Robertson, *Materials*, II, 255–7. In fact the child was revived as a result of a miracle performed by the saint. The episode can be dated soon after 1170 during Matilda's marriage to Roger de Clare earl of Hertford.
45 Public Record Office, London, DL28/1/2, fos. 19r–24v.
46 Brewer, *Monumenta franciscana*, I, 110.
47 British Library, London, Egerton Roll 8776, m. 4, 5.
48 Lodge and Somerville, *John of Gaunt's register*, I, no. 319.

was ready to pay £10 a year to Anne if her marriage to William Yelverton
went ahead. When John III married Margery Brews in 1477, Margaret
was also ready to contribute to the landed settlement for the couple.[49]

Relationships ranging from affection to exasperation are found among
other women and their children. Some letters reflect a calmer relationship, such as the letters sent to Alice de Bryene by her sons-in-law, keeping her up to date with the news of the day, and hoping to hear good news
of her.[50] Where disagreement did occur, land was the most likely cause,
and usually centred on the allocation of dower. Very few mothers permanently alienated land away from their children; the case of Joan de Mohun
selling the Mohun family inheritance of Dunster in Somerset to Elizabeth
Luttrell is exceptional and was unsuccessfully contested after her death.[51]
Many long-lived widows of the fourteenth and fifteenth centuries were
major landholders as a result of their rights to jointure and dower, and as
a result the eldest son might find himself waiting for years for a substantial part of his inheritance; the situation was exacerbated if there was more
than one widow to be supported by the estate. In very few cases did the
mother give up her landed rights. Shortly before her death in 1248,
Matilda Marshal announced that she had given her share of the Marshal
inheritance to her son and heir Roger Bigod earl of Norfolk, but in fact
she was still holding Chepstow castle when she died.[52]

Some mothers seem to have anticipated difficulties with their eldest
sons; the mother of Edmund Earl of March in her will of 1381 tried to
ensure that no dissension arose between Edmund and her executors.[53]
Some sons took legal action to ensure that they received what they
regarded as their rightful inheritance. Gilbert de Clare earl of Gloucester
sued his mother before the royal justices in 1266 for excessive dower and
achieved some reallocation; Henry III had acted wrongly in assigning
some of the earl's principal castles to the widow.[54] Roger Mortimer of
Chirk sued his mother over a grant of land allegedly made to him by his
father; in this case a younger son was concerned over his land.[55]

49 Davis, *Paston Letters*, I, nos. 175, 230, 304, 353, 355, 374–7.
50 Rickert, 'A leaf', 249–55. One of the sons-in-law, John Devereux, wrote in similar
   terms to his wife.
51 Maxwell Lyte, *A History of Dunster*, I, 52–3. Public Record Office, London,
   C66/373, m. 27; CP25/1/200/27, no. 90. Joan's husband had granted the land to
   feoffees with the instruction that Joan should be allowed to do as she pleased with
   the land after his death.
52 Edwards, *Calendar of ancient correspondence*, 29.
53 Nichols, *A collection*, 101–2.
54 Altschul, *A baronial family*, 95–6, 99–100, 117.
55 Public Record Office, London, Just 1/740, m. 48d; British Library, London,
   Additional MS. 31,826, fo. 215v; Horwood, *Year books 20–1 Edward I*, 188–91.

Sons' resentment over their mothers' estates has received greater attention than the practical help given by mothers to all their children, and it
is most unlikely that mothers would have done this without a measure of
affection. Many mothers went out of their way to further the interests of
all their children. William de la Pole, duke of Suffolk, was justified in urging his son to respect his mother. Alice Chaucer acted quickly after her
husband's murder in 1450 to secure his lands; she held the wardship of her
son and arranged his marriage. She proved to be an active administrator
and energetic in the defence of her rights.[56] Mothers made use of their
own inheritance to endow younger sons. Ela countess of Salisbury granted her younger son Nicholas part of her property, and there were plans in
1328, 1335 and 1337 to hand over Joan de Genevill's lordship of Trim to
one of her younger sons, Geoffrey or John Mortimer.[57] On occasion
money was provided by a widowed mother; in the letter, previously cited,
to her husband Aymer de Valence in 1296, Beatrice de Clermont
explained how his mother was making necessary provision to equip him
for campaigning in Scotland.[58] Many widows were active in securing marriages for their children, as Margaret Paston did for her son John III; in
the later thirteenth century Matilda de Lacy countess of Gloucester
played a part in her daughter Rohese's marriage to Roger de Mowbray.[59]
    Moreover, mothers found themselves taking responsibility for their
sons' lands and affairs, as with Hawise de Neville when her son was cru-
sading in the Holy Land in the late 1260s.[60] Hugh de Neville was an
adherent of Simon de Montfort, but was pardoned in 1266 and his lands
partially restored. Writing to him in the Holy Land, his mother went into
detail as to the steps he needed to take in order to ensure the full restoration of his inheritance. She deplored the fact that she could only secure
for him a little of the money raised for the crusade, pointing out that most
of it passed into the hands of the great lords. She wrote that if she could
not see and talk to her son nothing could give her greater pleasure than
receiving good news from him and comforting him with her letters.
    In all these cases, the mother seems to have been taking action as cir-
cumstances dictated; much of the evidence concerns sons, but daughters

56 Archer, '"How ladies"', 153–6.
57 British Library, London, Harley Charter 53 B 12; Frame, *English lordship*, 61. In
    the late thirteenth century, Matilda Mortimer had granted land to her younger son
    William; Public Record Office, London, SC1/19/131.
58 Public Record Office, London, SC1/48/183. Beatrice was living with Aymer's
    mother, Joan de Valence, in 1296–7, and Aymer made frequent visits; Public
    Record Office, London, E101/505/25, 26.
59 Public Record Office, London, C146/6087.
60 Giuseppi, 'On the testament', 359–62.

were not omitted. It is rare to have enough evidence to trace relationships over more than one generation, but the survival of Elizabeth de Burgh's household accounts shows that she was actively helping all her children during her widowhood (1322–60). Before her son William returned to Ireland in 1328 as earl of Ulster, she made careful inquiries as to the state of affairs in Ireland, and she equipped him for his journey. The frequent visits made to her by her two daughters indicate a close relationship, and Elizabeth provided practical help for Isabella in 1343 on the death of her husband, Henry de Ferrers of Groby, and ensured that she secured her jointure, dower and inheritance. Elizabeth was close to her grandchildren as well. The only tension is seen with her daughter-in-law who considered that Elizabeth's jointure from her marriage to John de Burgh was excessive.[61]

The prevalence of death in the later Middle Ages meant that remarriage was common,[62] and the question arises as to whether this caused problems in family relationships. Favouritism certainly did occur, but was by no means universal. Elizabeth de Burgh had one child by each of her three marriages, and there is no sign of partiality on her part in the surviving records. A stepfather who survived the death of his wife was entitled by the custom of curtesy of England to hold his wife's land for life if a child had been born of the marriage, and there was potential for tension here.[63] Relationships between half-brothers and sisters could be cordial, as seen in the family of Margaret Beaufort.[64]

The most serious problem which might arise was the favouring of the chidren of a second marriage at the expense of the first. It is said that Gilbert Pecche was so much in love with his second wife that his eldest son lost out on his inheritance.[65] The creation of conditional fees in the later Middle Ages and the use of feoffees enabled a father to divert land away from his eldest son in favour of other children or relatives. The provision for the children of Ralph Neville earl of Westmorland and his second wife Joan Beaufort meant that the earl's heir, the eldest grandson descended from his first marriage, succeeded to a diminished inheritance,

61 Public Record Office, London, C81/217/8173; E30/1536; E101/91/12, m. 1, 3; E101/91/17, m. 2; E101/92/2, m. 12d–13d; E101/92/24, m. 1d, 4, 7; E101/93/12, m. 1d, 2, 2d, 4. Nichols, *A collection*, 34–7.
62 Rosenthal, 'Aristocratic Marriage', 181.
63 E.g. Robert Sherard of Leicestershire protected his life interest in his wife's property in 1446 by issuing a declaration of which 35 men were said to be the authors that his wife Elizabeth had given birth to a daughter Joan who lived for two hours; Acheson, *A gentry community*, 89–90.
64 Jones and Underwood, *The king's mother*, 31–4.
65 Clark, *Liber memorandorum*, 50.

and fought unsuccessfully to recover what he regarded as his rightful estates.[66]

In considering the noblewoman's relations with her husbands and children, attention has been focussed on the nuclear family, a family which however often contained half-brothers and sisters. These relationships were usually more important to the noblewoman than those with the wider kindred group. There is no doubt that the nobility were well aware of their kindred and made use of them in business if required. This is apparent in the increasing number of entails in the fourteenth and fifteenth centuries to ensure the succession of a male member of the family and to exclude daughters,[67] although there still remained many instances of inheritances passing to one or more heiresses. How daughters felt about exclusion is rarely known, but there are instances of bitterness and hostility towards the fortunate male kinsman. Elizabeth Berkeley and her husband Richard Beauchamp earl of Warwick refused to accept the succession of her cousin James Berkeley to what they regarded as her own inheritance; the earl seized Berkeley castle in 1419, and two years later Elizabeth appeared before the king's council to defend her rights.[68]

As far as personal relations were concerned, the noblewoman's close relationships were more likely to be with her own kin than with her husband's. Some siblings were certainly close. Joan of Acre enjoyed a close relationship with her brother, the future Edward II, offering him practical help when he quarrelled with his father in 1305.[69] The Arundel family appears to have been close in the late fourteenth century; the political alliance of Richard earl of Arundel and his brother Thomas, ultimately Archbishop of Canterbury is well known; Thomas was on very good terms with his sister Joan de Bohun, countess of Hereford, and Joan was close to her son-in-law Henry IV and to her grandchildren. Little is known of her relationship with her daughters, Eleanor and Mary de Bohun, who were on friendly terms with each other, exchanging visits and gifts.[70] Brothers and sisters tended not to be automatically included in wills, and it is likely that such an inclusion indicated a close relation-

66 Lander, 'Marriage and politics', 123, 137; *Calendar of the close rolls, 1441–7*, 150–1, 195–9.
67 E.g. Public Record Office, London, CP25/1/287/41, no. 334, the creation of an entail by Thomas Beauchamp earl of Warwick and his eldest son Guy in 1344.
68 Nicolas, *Proceedings and ordinances*, II, 287, 289, 295–6.
69 Johnstone, *Letters of Edward*, 60, 74.
70 Public Record Office, London, DL28/1/2, fos. 21r, 25v; Legge, *Anglo-Norman letters*, nos. 38, 334; Aston, *Thomas Arundel*, 172–3, 181–91, 194–200.

ship; William de Ferrers of Groby included bequests of plate to both his sisters, and made one of them a supervisor of the will.[71]

Relationships between siblings might equally well be hostile. Elizabeth de Burgh lost her lordship of Usk to her brother-in-law Hugh le Despenser the younger, and expressed her hostility towards him in her secret protest of 1326;[72] she may well also have harboured resentment towards her sister, Eleanor la Despenser. In contrast she looked after her half-brother, Edward de Monthermer, at the end of his life, and provided him with an elaborate funeral and tomb.[73] Clearly, there is great variety in this type of family relationship. Evidence of visits, bequests, and the appointment of executors can be taken as a sign of trust and probably liking. Yet because of the partial survival of such material as wills and household accounts it is only possible to work out relationships for a relatively small number of families.

The concentration on the nuclear family did not however mean that the noblewoman failed to have a strong sense of the importance of lineage and ancestry, and it is important to see how far she identified with her husband's family rather than with her own. Noblewomen's seals with the depiction of the arms of husbands, father, and sometimes other relations indicate the significance to them of all the families with whom they were related. On the seal she was using in 1345, Marie de St Pol, countess of Pembroke, stood under a canopy with small niches on either side containing the arms of her husband Aymer de Valence, and those of her father, Guy de Chastillon.[74] Elizabeth de Burgh's seal included the arms of her three husbands, the arms of Clare (representing her natal family), the leopards of the English royal house, and the emblems of the Crown of Castile and Leon, emphasising her connections through her mother with Edward I and Eleanor of Castile and their descendants.[75]

The concern for family in the widest sense of the term emerges from bequests in noblewomen's wills and from their choice of place of burial. Although it is unknown how much independence they had in deciding these matters, and how much they were swayed by social convention and family tradition, there does appear to be an element of individual choice. Matilda de Vere countess of Oxford, who died in 1366, provided for her burial in the de Vere priory at Colne, Essex, and left bequests to all the de

71 Lambeth Palace Library, London, Register of William de Whittlesey, fos. 124v–125r.
72 Holmes, 'A protest', 207–12.
73 Public Record Office, London, E101/92/12, m. 7–10; E101/93/12, m. 3d.
74 Hunter Blair, 'Armorials', 21.
75 Lloyd and Stenton, *Sir Christopher Hatton's book*, no. 74; British Library, Harley Charter 47 E 39.

Vere religious foundations as well as to friars in Essex, Suffolk and Cambridge.[76] Slightly later, Philippa countess of March (the mother-in-law of the Philippa mentioned at the beginning of this essay) chose to be buried at Bisham abbey; she was a member of the Montagu family, the abbey had been founded by her father, William earl of Salisbury, and she clearly decided that she wanted to remain with her own kin.[77]

Often it was heiresses, the last of their own line, and women who were bringing their inheritance to a new family, who had the strongest sense of lineage, and were concerned in their wills to ensure the continuity of their own ancestral connections. The male line of the de Bohun family came to an end in 1373 and the estates were subsequently divided between the sisters Eleanor and Mary. Eleanor married Edward III's youngest son, Thomas of Woodstock, and her eldest son was named Humphrey, the usual Bohun name for the heir. In her will of 1399 Eleanor emphasised her Bohun ancestry, passing on to Humphrey her family heirlooms. These included a French poem of the history of the knight of the swan (the swan was the Bohun badge), and an illuminated psalter with the arms of her father on the clasps. She bequeathed to him his father's coat of mail which had a cross of latten set over the wearer's heart. She also left her son her gold cross as the possession which she loved best.[78]

In other cases the ancestral link was underlined through bequests to religious houses. Elizabeth de Burgh left money to all the religious houses associated with the Clare family in England and Wales, but showed her individuality by making her principal bequests to the convent of the Minoresses outside Aldgate in London, where she chose to be buried, and to Clare Hall in Cambridge.[79] Anne Stafford, the daughter of Thomas of Woodstock and Eleanor de Bohun, emphasised her Bohun ancestry by arranging for her burial in Llanthony priory, and her connection with her father through her commemoration in his college at Pleshey Castle in Essex.[8] Isabel Despenser, again the last of her line, chose to be buried in the abbey of Tewkesbury with its Clare and Despenser connections, rather than with one or other of her husbands.[81]

Noblewomen were conscious and proud of their ancestry and lineage, but their relationships during their lifetimes concentrated on their immediate family. This family can be described as nuclear rather than extended, even though it often included step-children. The parameters of family

76 Benton, 'Essex wills', 263–5.
77 Nichols, A collection, 98–100.
78 Ibid., 177–86.
79 Ibid., 30–4.
80 Ibid., 278–81.
81 Furnivall, The fifty earliest English wills, 116–17.

relations were set by custom and law, but within these women could and did have considerable influence and responsibility. The nature of many of the surviving sources makes family relations appear formal, cool and authoritarian. Yet judging from noblewomen's actions and from wills and letters, the surface formality concealed a considerable range of feeling, and relations between husbands and wives, and wives and children displayed great variety and certainly an emotional content. The humanity of the English noblewoman and her family needs to be stressed, alongside the concerns for property and power.

Women, Dowries and the Family in Late Medieval Italian Cities

Christine E. Meek

The sources for the legal and social position of women in late medieval Italy are many and varied. Communal statutes regularly include provisions regarding women, and many cities have records of civil, criminal and ecclesiastical courts, showing these legal provisions in operation. Wills, notarial cartularies and other 'documents of practice' preserve many contracts concerning the position and rights of women and show that women were active in the defence of these rights. There are also family memoirs and private letters, which, although usually written by men, show something of the real relationship between women and their families, and make possible comparisons with the relationship set out in prescriptive works, such as treatises on family life, and in works of fiction. These rich sources have attracted a number of scholars in the last twenty-five years, resulting in a picture of the role of women in Italian society that is illuminating, varied and nuanced, even if it may be necessary to modify it in the light of future research.[1]

Italian social organisation was in many ways unfavourable to women. Among the nobility and the urban patriciate family feeling was strong and family groups were a powerful force in local and communal political life. The family might form the basis of commercial and banking associations and kinsmen might own property jointly, especially a family palace or tower, and impose provisions to prevent ownership ever passing out of the hands of family members. A man who founded a chapel or oratory was likely to leave patronage rights over it to his kinsmen. What the family or kin meant in such circumstances was the paternal kin or lineage, some or all of those sharing a common surname. Maternal relatives and in-laws were not without significance, and valuable support and assistance could be expected from even quite distant marital connections.[2] Marriages with powerful lineages shed reflected glory on the kinsmen of

---

1 For a guide to the sources and to recent work on them, Herlihy, 'Women and the sources' and Stuard, 'Sources on medieval women'. For reasons of convenience secondary works cited in this article are confined to those available in English.
2 For the networks of expectations and obligations summed up by the word *parentado*, Gregory, 'Daughters, dowries and the family', 224–31.

those who made such alliances and marriages with women of undistinguished families might be something of an embarrassment, but maternal relatives were not members of a man's family, which was essentially patrilinear.[3]

It was difficult for women to share such feelings. While a man remained a member of the same lineage all his life, a woman left her own family to join that of her husband on marriage and her sons would belong to a different lineage from her father and brothers. If she married more than once, which was not uncommon, she would be likely to return to her natal family after the death of her first husband, leave it again for another family on remarriage and might easily have children by two or more husbands, children who would thus be members of different families. All this must have rendered difficult the development of the kind of family feeling common among men, although there are examples of women, like Alessandra Macinghi Strozzi in mid-fifteenth century Florence, who centred their lives on one family, in her case that of her sons.[4]

The inheritance system also placed women at a disadvantage, although they were not unprovided for or unprotected. There was no primogeniture among male heirs and the normal inheritance system was for all legitimate sons to inherit equally. The property might be held in common at least for some years, or divided equally among the sons or their male descendants. Women were excluded from this. While a man might name his daughters as heirs, if he had no sons, men of the upper classes were more likely to choose a brother or nephews or even cousins. There were few heiresses and one man who did name his daughters as heirs was criticised for having disinherited his greatnephews.[5]

In the later middle ages the normal provision for daughters was the receipt of a dowry on marriage. In many communes a daughter who had not been dowered during her father's lifetime could claim an appropriate dowry from her father's estate, but a daughter who had already received a dowry had no further claim.[6] In earlier centuries a different system had

3 Larner, *Italy in the Age of Dante*, 60–5. For this aspect and its consequences, Chojnacki, 'Dowries and kinsmen', 591–4 and 'Patrician women', 178–85. On legal aspects of the relations of married women, their families of origin and their in-laws, Kuehn, 'Women, marriage and *patria potestas*'. More generally, Heers, *Family clans*.

4 Chojnacki, 'Dowries and kinsmen', 587–90, Hughes, 'Domestic ideals', 137–8, Klapisch-Zuber, 'Cruel mother', 117–20, 130–1. On Alessandra Macinghi Strozzi, Crabb, 'How typical was Alessandra' and Martines, 'A way of looking at women'. Phillips, *The Memoir of Marco Parenti*, which concerns her son-in-law, contains much information about Alessandra Strozzi.

5 Archivio di Stato in Lucca, Archivio Guinigi 29, f. 57r.

6 Chojnacki, 'Dowries and kinsmen', 575 and the authorities cited there. Riemer,

obtained, one which bore more relation to the dower rights of a widow
on her deceased husband's property enjoyed by women in England and
some other parts of Northern Europe. Women had had the right, especially in widowhood to the enjoyment of a quarter of their husband's
property for those living under Lombard law and a third for those living
under Frankish law, and had also been endowed on marriage with a
Morgengabe, a portion of their husband's property over which they
enjoyed fuller rights. There was a somewhat similar system the *donatio
propter nuptias* for those living under Roman law. These various systems,
all of which involved the right of the wife to the enjoyment of a proportion of her husband's property, especially in widowhood, were together
referred to as the wife's right to an *antefactum*.[7]

In the twelfth and thirteenth centuries many communes in Northern
Italy tried to stamp out this practice of the endowment of a wife by her
husband. The first legislation restricting the wife's right to a third of her
husband's property seems to have been in Genoa in 1143, where women
were in future to be allowed only an *antefactum* of a sum that did not
exceed half the value of their dowry or a maximum of £100 genoese as a
counter-dowry from their husband. The *antefactum* had virtually disap-
peared from the customs of Padua, Bologna, Siena and Lucca by 1200 and
from those of Pistoia and Volterra in the early thirteenth century.
Limitations were placed on it in Milan in 1216 and Florence in 1255,
although Ferrara was still legislating against it in 1287 and Brescia in
1298.[8] These changes were certainly seen by contemporaries as unfavourable to women; the twelfth-century *Annals of Genoa*, that record the
measure, contain a marginal drawing of two women bewailing their loss.[9]
However these legal restrictions did not always apply to all kinds of
property and the *antefactum* survived in some places. It persisted especially in Southern Italy, despite some attempts to limit the amount to the
equivalent of what the bride had brought to the marriage, and even in the
North Italian communes where restrictions had first been imposed, the
practice of the husband endowing his wife, or even naming her as his heir
remained strong, especially in the humbler sections of society.

But the general trend, especially in the North of Italy, was to limit a
woman's claims, both with regard to her husband's property and to that

'Women, dowries and capital investment', 62–3, Hughes, 'Brideprice', 278–80. For
an example of the workings of these rules in practice in Florence, Kuehn, 'Some
ambiguities of female inheritance ideology'.

7 Hughes, 'Brideprice', 266–76, also her 'Family structure', 13–14.
8 These changes are discussed in a broad context in Hughes, 'Brideprice', 276–80
and with specific reference to Genoa in 'Family structure', 14–15.
9 Hughes, 'Brideprice', 277.

of her own family. A woman's economic security, especially in widowhood, came to depend more and more on the dowry provided by her own
family at the time of her marriage. It became a principle of canon law that
there should be no marriage without a dowry and the fact that there had
been a marriage could be cited as evidence that there must have been a
dowry.[10] The dowry was often given a cash evaluation, even if part or all
of it was paid in the form of land or goods making up the trousseau.

Marriages for both men and women were largely a matter of family
arrangement. Girls in particular were often married very young and can
have had little real choice of marriage partner, at any rate at their first
marriage. But a girl's father or his heirs had the duty to arrange a suitable
marriage for her, providing a dowry in accordance with his resources. The
dowry that convention required could be very high, both in terms of the
amount of support it would provide for the woman and in terms of the
burden it placed on her family's resources. As early as the beginning of
the fourteenth century Dante speaks of the birth of a daughter striking
fear into her father's heart, knowing that in twelve or fifteen years time he
would have to find a large dowry.[11] Social conventions and the need to
offer a dowry comparable to that of other girls of similar status might
compel hard-pressed parents to make difficult choices, either to pay far
more than their resources permitted,[12] or to accept a marriage below their
social expectations. In 1447 Alessandra Macinghi Strozzi, an upper class
Florentine widow, arranged the marriage of her daughter Caterina to
Marco Parenti, a young silk manufacturer, whose grandfather had been an
artisan. She wrote to her son in Naples, that she had tried to place the girl
in a more noble and politically powerful family, but this would have
required a dowry 400 or 500 florins higher than the 1,000 florins she was

---

10 For the origin of the canon law phrase, Hughes, 'Brideprice', 265, 274. On the
    ubiquity of the dowry, Klapisch-Zuber, 'Griselda complex', 214, Riemer, 'Women,
    dowries and capital investment', 64. For dowries among the lower classes in
    Florence, Cohn, *The laboring classes*, 21. There is one well known case where a
    woman married without a dowry, that of Margherita Datini, Origo, *Merchant of
    Prato*, 48.

11 Contrasting his own time with that of his great great grandfather when:
    'fathers had no cause to fear
    a daughter's birth: the marriageable age
    was not too low, the dowry not too high'
    Purgatorio XV, 103–5, tr. M. Musa.
    On the importance of the girl's age and the practice of subtracting a couple of
    years, if this seemed likely to help the marriage negotiations, Molho, 'Deception
    and marriage strategy'.

12 Queller and Madden, 'Father of the bride' offer interesting evidence of identical
    dowries for daughters of noble families of widely varying resources, although
    stressing other contributors than the father to these dowries.

able to offer and 'this would have meant our ruin'.[13] Alessandra was perhaps more ready than many parents to sacrifice the interests of her daughters to those of her sons, and the Strozzi had particular problems in the
mid-fifteenth century, since Alessandra's sons were in exile as opponents
of the Medici and she was beset by financial difficulties, but it is not difficult to find other examples of families hard put to it to raise the funds
for a daughter's dowry. It was often necesary to borrow money, and
mortgage or sell property in order to raise the amount required.
Sometimes the bridegroom provided a loan of a part of the dowry. In
Lucca the apothecary, Pietro di Giovanni, married his daughter Lena to
Iacobo del Caro in 1378 with a dowry of 350 florins, but borrowed 125
florins from Iacobo the same day, and in 1385 Matteo Mattafelloni lent
100 florins to Marco Manni for a year as part of the 700 florins dowry of
Francesca, Marco's sister and Matteo's bride.[14]

The importance of the dowry and the burden it represented for family resources lies behind the success of the *Monte delle Doti*, or state
dowry bank, in Florence. Founded in 1425 it provided fathers with the
opportunity to pay in cash or convert some of their holdings in the public debt into an investment in the name of an infant daughter, to mature a
maximum of fifteen years later and form part of her dowry. It proved to
be an extremely popular form of investment, and although there began to
be difficulties in paying the accrued dowries as early as the 1450s, citizens
continued to be eager to invest in it.[15] For much the same reasons the provision of dowries for poor girls was a popular form of charity. While a
well-to-do individual might fund a poor girl's dowry during his lifetime,
it was more common to make provision by will, setting aside a certain
sum to provide dowries for poor girls, often specifying the maximum that
any one girl was to receive, but usually leaving the selection of the recipients to the testator's executors.[16]

13 Letter of 24 August 1347, translated in Molho, *Social and economic foundations*,
    202–5. Also Crabb, 'How typical', 52–3. For this and other examples of problems
    in raising dowries, Gregory, 'Daughters, dowries and families', 219–23.
14 Archivio di Stato in Lucca, Archivio de'Notari 195 (unfoliated). It is interesting
    that these transactions were in the form of separate loans, not an agreement to
    defer payment of part of the dowry. The effect of this was certainly to render the
    bride more secure, since a dowry contract guaranteed repayment of the sum the
    bridegroom acknowledged he had received. For payment of dowries in several
    instalments in thirteenth-century Genoa, Epstein, *Wills and wealth*, 105.
15 On the dowry fund, Kirshner, *Pursuing honor while avoiding sin*; Kirshner and
    Molho, 'The dowry fund and the marriage market'; Molho, *Marriage Alliance*.
16 Cohn, *Death and property*, 28–32, 213–14.

For the upper classes the dowry represented a capital sum sufficient to produce an income that would support the woman and her maidservant for the rest of her life. It might be the equivalent of several houses. In Lucca in 1406 ser Pietro Guerci sold three houses for 200 florins, 120 florins and 80 florins respectively in order to raise the necessary cash for the dowry of his daughter Maddalena.[17] The amount needed to dower an upper-class bride may be compared with the sum needed for the endowment of a chapel; the same word 'dos' is used in both cases, but a sum of 300 or 400 florins was regarded as sufficient both to build and equip a chapel or altar and to purchase sufficient lands to support the priest who served it.[18] In Florence in the early fifteenth century branch managers or junior partners in the Medici bank invested sums in the region of 1,000 florins, while the salaries of employees in major enterprises such as the Medici bank or the firm of Francesco di Marco Datini ranged from 15 or 20 florins a year for beginners to 100 florins or more for branch managers.[19] In Venice some daughters were provided with dowries that compared with or exceeded the share of the paternal inheritance that their brothers received,[20] and it was apparently possible for nobles to live on the income of their wives' dowries without engaging in commerce or any other useful activity, something that was a source of anxiety to the Venetian authorities.[21] Even a peasant dowry of 12 to 15 florins represented a valuable accretion of capital at a time when a plough ox could be bought for 8 to 14 florins.[22] Dowries also inflated over time. The average dowry in Siena was £100 in 1201–49, but by 1280–99 this had risen to £205.[23] The average of 650 ducats for patrician dowries in mid-fourteenth century Venice had risen to 1,000 ducats by the end of the fourteenth century. The Senate tried to hold dowry inflation in check by fixing a ceiling of 1,600 ducats on patrician dowries in 1420; an indication of its failure is

---

17 Archivio di Stato in Lucca, Archivio de'Notari 287, ff. 14r–15r, 13 Jan. 1406.
18 Bequest of £1,000 *bona moneta*, (approximately 345 florins) for the foundation of a chapel, Archivio di Stato in Lucca, Testamenti 3, ff. 60r–61v, 88r–89v, 10 Nov. 1350. The testator also provided for dowries of 400 florins plus a suitable *corredo* for each of his daughters. Testamenti 9, ff. 21r–24v, 23 Jan. 1405 included a bequest for a chapel without naming a sum, but it was to purchase sufficient property to provide an income of 40 florins per year.
19 de Roover, *The rise and decline*, 41–50. Only one branch manager of the Medici Bank received as much as 400 florins in 1402.
20 Chojnacki, 'The power of love', 129. Also Hughes, 'Brideprice', 288–9 for dowries that were equal to a full share of the inheritance.
21 Chojnacki, The power of love', 130
22 These are typical figures for Lucca in the late fourteenth and early fifteenth centuries.
23 Riemer, 'Women, dowries and capital investment', 66.

that the measure was repeated in 1515, but with 3,000 ducats as the maximum.[24]

The fate of such large sums of money was a matter of considerable importance. The dowry was paid to the husband on marriage, not to the wife, but it was regarded as the wife's property and might have to be repaid in certain circumstances. A dowry contract was drawn up in which the bridegroom, perhaps in association with his father or brothers, acknowledged receipt of a specified sum of cash or landed property, and formally bound himself and his heirs to restitution should any of the recognised occasions for this arise. These contracts survive in their hundreds in notarial cartularies in Italian archives. The dowry normally remained under the husband's control for the duration of the marriage and was intended in the Roman law phrase, 'to support the burdens of matrimony'. The profits or income of the dowry went to the husband and if it became necessary to restore the dowry, what was repaid was the bare amount received, without any allowance for interest or profits, however long the marriage had lasted.[25] It is not always clear what happened to the dowry during the marriage. Christiane Klapisch-Zuber has stressed the lavish expenditure that honour and custom required of the bridegroom, who was expected to furnish the bridal chamber for the couple's use and also to provide luxurious ceremonial garments for his bride to wear when she left her father's house for her new home. The expenditure involved might go a long way towards counterbalancing the amount received as the bride's dowry.[26] But the dowry also seems to have supplied capital for the husband's business ventures and there are references to the purchase of land as a safe investment for dowry funds.[27]

The statutes or customs of each commune laid down what happened to the dowry when the marriage came to an end through the death of husband or wife, with or without children. These customs varied from place to place, but if the wife predeceased her husband leaving no children, at least a proportion of the dowry usually had to be restored to her kinsmen. This was a third in Lucca, Siena and Pavia, a half in Pisa, Arezzo and

24 Chojnacki, 'Dowries and kinsmen', 571–5. As Chojnacki makes clear, general price movements need to be taken into consideration, but it seems clear that the burden represented by dowries increased.

25 In some places the *antefactum* represented a form of profit on the dowry, Epstein, *Wills and wealth*, 103–5.

26 Klapisch-Zuber, 'Griselda complex', esp. 218–31. However these gifts remained the husband's property. He could repossess them at will and the bride might hold them for only a very short period.

27 Riemer, 'Women, dowries and capital investment', pp. 64–5, Chojnacki, 'Patrician women', 190–1.

Modena and the whole of the dowry in Bologna, although in Brescia and Piacenza the husband retained the dowry.[28] If there were children of the marriage, they, rather than their father, inherited their mother's dowry, although their father would have the right to administer it on the children's behalf during their minority and might have rights of usufruct even after they came of age. But a wife who survived her husband was entitled to the restitution of her dowry in full, even if there were children of the marriage. If she were to remarry, she would take the same dowry, recovered from her late husband's heirs, to her new marriage. If she preferred to leave her late husband's household, whether to return to her own family or to live independently, she was entitled to take her dowry with her. One of the fundamental facts about the dowry was that it belonged to the woman and moved with her, if she left one household for another. A woman had an unquestioned right to the restitution of her dowry on widowhood, often within a very limited period of time, such as within a month of her requesting repayment.[29]

Sometimes dowries were repaid without serious difficulty, but in other cases the husband's heirs were unable or unwilling to pay. Provisions in wills which name the amount of the dowry of the testator's wife and instruct that it should be repaid to her without difficulty are an indication that prompt repayment could not be taken for granted. So from another point of view are provisions that a widowed daughter should receive a second dowry from her father's estate, should it prove impossible to recover her first dowry from her husband's heirs. Women are found insisting on their rights to the restitution of their dowry, and would have the support both of their own families and of the courts in doing so. Women could and did take their husband's heirs to court and force them to pay or to assign lands or houses in lieu. They could also transfer their rights to third parties or sell lands assigned to them for their dowry rights so that the heirs might find themselves dealing with powerful outsiders or losing family property permanently to third parties. The husband's heirs might be his sons by a previous marriage, or collaterals, or indeed a church or a hospital, but some women were quite prepared to undertake legal proceedings against their own children, even children who were minors or infants, in pursuit of their dowry rights. The courts were very favourable to women's dowry and other claims, often granting them spe-

28 A half in Siena after 1283, Riemer, 'Women, dowries and capital investment', 74–5. Larner, *Italy*, p. 68. For Genoa, Hughes, 'Family structure', 15, 'Brideprice', 282–3.
29 Archivio di Stato in Lucca, Statuti 6 (1372), Lib. IV, capp. cxxxiii, cxxxv. Two months in Siena, Riemer, 'Women, dowries and capital investment', 63.

cial summary procedures to protect them from excessive costs or delay-
ing tactics.[30]

One interesting aspect of the relations of women and the families into
which they married, which has only recently begun to be explored, is that
women could in certain cases take legal action against their husbands to
secure their dowry rights. Roman law had allowed such proceedings
where a husband began to misuse his resources and verge on insolvency,
and these rights were confirmed and extended in the legal practice of
many Italian communes. Where it began to look as though a husband
would not have sufficient resources to cover his wife's dowry, she could
demand immediate restitution or the assignment of sufficient lands to
meet her claims. This applied not merely where the husband had taken to
drink or gambling, but also to cases where he had suffered business losses, which came into the category of misfortune rather than negligence. A
wife might also be able to reclaim her dowry, if her husband had been
banished or fined or found himself in any other position that put her
dowry at risk.[31]

Legal proceedings of this sort were common in Florence, Lucca and
Siena and were applicable to all levels of society,[32] but there are also many
documents in which men voluntarily recognise that they are in such
financial difficulties as to be verging on insolvency and therefore make
provision for the security of their wives' dowries. A husband was not
necessarily reluctant to repay his wife's dowry or transfer property to her
in such circumstances. He might do so in order to protect her future and
ensure that she got her due, but he might also be trying to save something
from the ruin that faced him. It could reasonably be assumed that the wife
would use the dowry funds thus recovered for the support of the family;
indeed Roman law required that she did. The wife was treated as her husband's first creditor and her claims were given preference over those of all
other creditors. In some cases the couple may have been in collusion to
defraud the husband's other creditors, an indication of confidence
between husband and wife, if nothing else. The communal authorities

30 Riemer, 'Women, dowries and capital investment', 63, 68. Chabot, 'Widowhood
    and poverty', 295, 298–9.
31 See the fundamental study of Julius Kirshner, 'Wives' claims against insolvent hus-
    bands' esp. 275–8. For similar rights in thirteenth-century Siena, Riemer, 'Women,
    dowries and capital investment', 68–9, and for efforts to protect women's dowries
    in Venice, Chojnacki, 'Dowries and kinsmen', 586–7.
32 There were 460 cases in Florence in which wives were awarded their dowries on
    the grounds of their husband's insolvency 1435–1535 and in 90 cases the wives of
    rebels or exiles reclaimed their dowries successfully 1375–1431, Kirshner, 'Wives'
    claims', 278, 299.

were suspicious of wives' claims to *augmentum dotis*, that is to an additional sum paid after the original dowry, unless the woman could prove that such a sum had really been paid, and there are documents that show that these suspicions were sometimes justified; one man declared that his wife's dowry had been 500 florins and if he had named a higher sum in other documents, this had only been done to deceive his creditors.[33]

Since the whole of a man's property was liable in law for the repayment of his wife's dowry, a woman could make claims against property that her husband had owned at the time of their marriage, even if he had subsequently alienated it.[34] In consequence the purchaser of property might require that the seller's wife consent to the sale and renounce any dowry or other claims to it. She was required to give this consent in proper legal form, and in many communes could only do so with the consent of her own nearest kinsman (as well as that of her husband, which in the circumstances would presumably be forthcoming). The notary who drew up the contract might also be required to inform her of the legal rights that she was about to renounce and question her to ensure that she was acting voluntarily. Obviously no system would be proof against collusion by these various parties, but the requirement for a woman's nearest male relative to give his consent probably did offer good protection to women's property rights. It would prevent a husband from persuading his wife into a semi-secret transaction to her disadvantage and a woman's own kin were unlikely to consent to anything damaging to her interests, if only because it might impair their own prospects of perhaps inheriting from her or risk leaving her dependent on them.[35]

One matter that was of considerable importance to all parties was the

---

33 Archivio di Stato in Lucca, Archivio Guinigi 1, f. 243r, 7 Aug. 1439. Kirshner, 'Wives' claims', 272, 296–9. For fraudulent use of women's dowry rights, Kuehn, 'Women, marriage and *patria potestas*', 208–9 and 'Legal guardianship', 228.
34 This did not apply to merchandise, Kirshner, 'Wives' claims', 288.
35 Riemer, 'Women, dowries and capital investment, p. 63. For the natal kin's interest in a woman's dowry and its protection, including the requirement that the husband deposit with public officials sufficient resources for its repayment, Chojnacki, 'Patrician women', 191–3. The situation was somewhat different in Florence, where a woman required the consent of a *mundualdo*, selected by herself with the approval of a notary. The *mundualdo* did not have to be the woman's kinsman and could be her husband. While a husband could not act as *mundualdo* for a contract from which he stood to gain, some Florentine husbands did manage to persuade their wives to renounce their dowry rights, leaving them dependent on their natal kin, Kuehn 'Legal guardianship', 217–26. But the consent of the *mundualdo* could be a formality, which left a woman free to make her own decisions, Crabb, 'How typical', 51, and there are examples of women acting without a *mundualdo*, Rosenthal, 'The position of women', 377–8.

question of the remarriage of widows. Theoretically a widow had several
choices. A husband, making his will, often in the face of imminent death,
normally stipulated that his wife should have her dowry repaid, if she
chose to leave his house, or she could stay with his heirs, in which case
she would have her keep, including clothing and the usufruct of such of
his goods as she would need for her honourable maintenance, or even the
usufruct of all his goods, provided that she remained a widow and did not
ask for the restitution of her dowry.[36] A father, making his will, usually
stipulated that any daughter could return to his house in case of widowhood, and be provided with lodging, though not always with board or
clothing, since she would after all bring her dowry with her.[37] A widow
could, therefore, either stay on in her late husband's house or return to
that of her father, either temporarily until she remarried, or permanently.
She might even live in an establishment of her own.[38]

     Theoretically and legally the choice was hers, but the degree of free-
dom she enjoyed in reality would depend on a number of factors, her
own age, whether or not she had children, and the views and ambitions of
her late husband's heirs and her own relatives. A widow who was still
young and had no children would be likely to remarry, and her late husband and his heirs were probably resigned to this, even though it meant
the loss of her dowry. Her own family would be eager for her to remarry. They would be able to use her to make a new matrimonial alliance
without having to produce another dowry, and they would probably be
anxious to get her safely settled into another marriage, since it was not felt
that a young woman could be relied upon to live as a respectable widow
without threatening the family's honour.[39]

     More problems arose in the case of women with children. When a
father provided that a widowed daughter could return to his house, this
did not include her children, who in any case belonged to her late husband's family, not to hers. So if a widow returned to her father's house or
remarried, she had to leave her children behind. Where the children were
minors, the husband had probably hoped that she would stay with the

36 Riemer, 'Women, dowries and capital investment', 64, Epstein, *Wills and wealth*,
   106–9.
37 Klapisch-Zuber, 'Cruel mother', p. 122. In Florence the *tornata*, or return of a
   widow to her father's house, was guaranteed by statute, although this was not
   always observed, Chabot, 'Widowhood and poverty', 297.
38 For women exercising these various choices, including that of living separately,
   Rosenthal, 'Position of women', 369–70.
39 Klapisch-Zuber, 'Cruel mother', 119–24. On the fragility of women's reputations
   and care for the honour of women of the family, Gregory, 'Daughters, dowries
   and families', 233–4.

family, looking after them and also not depriving them of her dowry. He might therefore try to influence her choice by leaving her legacies and usufructs on his property, conditional on her remaining in his house as a widow, indeed usually as a chaste widow, since he too was concerned for family honour.[40] A widow would usually still have only the same dowry as she had had at her first marriage; she would not have any share in her late husband's property comparable to the dower system in Northern Europe and any legacies and usufructs were likely to be conditional on continued widowhood. She was therefore not likely to be more attractive to a potential husband than she had been at her first marriage, and there was probably a fairly low upper age limit at which it would be possible to find a second husband and few women seem to have married more than twice.[41] But second marriages for women seem to have been quite common. One factor that encouraged this was the fact that girls married very young, often in their early or mid-teens, while men married at a much later age. There might well be a ten or fifteen year age difference between husband and wife, so that widowhood was quite likely, and a woman who had married for the first time at anything from twelve to eighteen years of age might still not be too old to find a second husband after fifteen or even twenty years of marriage. Even widows with young children quite frequently remarried. It is difficult to ascertain how willingly such women left their children with their late husband's relatives in order to

---

40 Klapisch-Zuber, 'Cruel mother', 121–5. Riemer, 'Women, dowries and capital investment', 64. Chojnacki, 'Patrician women', 183 n. 21, 199, but see his 'Power of love', 136–7, for examples of cases where such legacies were unconditional.

41 Klapisch-Zuber, 'Cruel mother', 120–1 on the prospects of remarriage for women, arguing that these declined sharply with age and that few widows over forty had much chance of remarriage. In Lucca a father providing in his will for a second dowry for his daughters, should their first prove irrecoverable, limited this to daughters under thirty, Testamenti 12, ff. 34v–37v, 17 June 1456. There are some late sixteenth-century examples of the remarriage of older widows. A widower of fiftyseven, after weighing up the pros and cons of remarriage, chose a widow of fortyeight, who was exceptionally pious, virtuous, home-loving and sensible. He also recommended remarriage to his widowed son, suggesting that he look for a woman of about forty, preferably without children and not bother too much about the size of her dowry, Lucca, Biblioteca Statale, *Libro di ricordi di Antonio Minutoli*, ff. 155r, 176v–177r. Giovanna Lazzari found a second husband when not far off fifty in 1426, Archivio di Stato in Lucca, Archivio Guinigi, Pergamene *121, 18 Jan. 1434. Her new husband acknowledged the receipt of a large dowry, although no dowry was paid. The marriage was apparently an attempt on his part to put part of his resources beyond the reach of his creditors, a fact of which Giovanna was well aware. Her agreement to a marriage in such circumstances itself suggests interesting reflections on the role of women and their freedom of choice.

embark on a second marriage. Leaving their children in this way did not, of course, mean that they never saw them again; there are indications of continued contacts in some cases, though there are also examples of children who later complained of having been abandoned in this way. It is difficult to discover what the women themselves really wanted. They would certainly have to consent to a second marriage, as indeed to a first, and to leave their late husband's house to return to their father's. It is also reasonable to suppose that they would have been more capable of making a choice and getting their own way than when first married. They would have more experience and would have legal control of their own dowry, but they must also have been subject to conflicting pressures and persuasion, and perhaps even bullying.[42]

Evidence can occasionally be found that does indicate women's ideas and preferences, and interestingly their choices differ significantly from those of men. In Venice women were in an unusually favourable position, because they had the right to decide the destiny of the whole of their dowries after their deaths by testamentary dispositions. Since dowries were exceptionally high in Venice, women could thus have considerable sums of money at their disposal. A study by the American scholar Stanley Chojnacki of 305 surviving wills of members of the large Morosini clan between 1300 and 1450, including 140 wills of women who had married into the Morosini family, found evidence of a particular concern on the part of women for the welfare of other women, and especially a consciousness of the importance to a girl's marriage prospects of an adequate dowry. While married women with children not unnaturally made them their principal beneficiaries, they not only did not favour sons over daughters, as men usually did, but they often favoured daughters over sons. Both men and women sometimes made contributions to the dowries of nieces or granddaughters, but while men gave preference to girls who were members of their own lineage, that is the daughters of their own sons or brothers, women left dowry contributions also to the daughters of their own daughters or sisters, which meant that they were assisting lineages which were neither the one they had been born in nor the one into which they had married.[43] Chojnacki argued that this was an indication that lineage meant less to them and ties of affection more and

42 Klapisch-Zuber, 'Cruel mother', 126–8. Rosenthal, 'Position of women', 375–6 for concrete examples and also for a more positive view of women's possibility of making a choice. Trexler, 'In search of a father'. For women's consent to marriage, Meek, 'Women, the Church and the law'.
43 Chojnacki, 'Dowries and kinsmen', 580–600, 'Patrician women', 184–5, and 195–6, where he argues that women's contributions to dowries had a significant effect on dowry inflation. See also, Queller and Madden, 'Father of the bride'. For

that there were special links among women. He has also detected 'a higher regard for women and a deepening of husband-wife affection' in fifteenth-century Venice, which he connects with the increasing resources women had at their disposal, which could even have the result of attracting further legacies to them, in the hope of retaining their benevolence towards both their natal or marital kin.[44]

Most of what has been said so far applies primarily to upper class women. Those of peasant and artisan status are more difficult to study because they were less likely to preserve collections of family papers or keep memoirs, and family relationships are more difficult to follow because they often used patronymics, that varied from generation to generation, rather than fixed surnames.[45] But peasants and artisans, male and female, made wills, had contracts drawn up and engaged in litigation, thus providing valuable information, including material on the position and rights of women.

The importance of the dowry and the laws regarding its safeguard and restitution apply equally to artisan and peasant women. The effect cannot have been the same, however, because an upper or middle class woman could live quite comfortably on the income from her dowry, especially if she was also entitled to free lodging in her father's house, whereas a poor girl's dowry of 12 or 15 florins was not a capital sum sufficient to provide even a modest income. Studies of lower class women, especially in Genoa and Venice, suggest that, while the law was the same for them as for upper and middle class women, actual practice was different and indicate that the bond between husband and wife was relatively more important and their relationship with their respective relatives less important than in the upper classes. Artisans would often be immigrants or the descendants of immigrants, so that they would have fewer kinsmen living in the same area on whom to rely and a man would need the contribution a wife could make in order to support a household.[46]

In Genoa artisan marriage settlements for the twelfth century show that the *antefactum* not only survived, but equalled or exceeded the wife's

bequests to women by women in Florence, Rosenthal, 'Position of women', 373–4.
44 'The power of love', 128–32, 135–7. More limited evidence for late thirteenth-century Siena also suggests a preference by women testators for female beneficiaries and a tendency to put affection before considerations of lineage, Riemer, 'Women, dowries and capital investment', 71–4. For Genoa 1150–1250 any preference for daughters over sons by female testators was very slight, Epstein, *Wills and wealth*, 82–3, 120–2.
45 Hughes, 'Domestic ideals', 117–18.
46 For patricians, Hughes, 'Domestic ideals', 118–24, for artisans, 124–9.

dowry in nearly 50 per cent of the cases, and was over half the dowry in 70 per cent. In the second half of the thirteenth century nearly 80 per cent of artisans gave their brides an *antefactum* that equalled or exceeded the dowry, despite laws fixing the maximum *antefactum* at half the value of the dowry.[47] Artisans also frequently named their wife as heir, even where the couple had children. The wife was already entitled to her dowry back on widowhood, plus the *antefactum* her husband had granted her on marriage. Artisan wives probably normally engaged in some trade or occupation to supplement their husband's earnings, and could be expected to continue to do so as widows. The husband presumably felt that she could be relied upon to look after the children, and artisans frequently named their wife as guardian of the children in their wills. With their dowry, their *antefactum* and perhaps their husband's entire inheritance, artisan widows frequently remarried. In contrast to the upper classes where the children belonged to the husband's lineage, artisan widows did not have to leave their children on remarriage. A widow might make special conditions for the support of the children of her first marriage when she remarried, but the arrangements often seem to have been informal, although the second husband did not become his step-children's guardian. Artisan widows who remarried presumably did so out of choice or for economic considerations, since it took the earnings and resources of both man and wife in order to maintain a household at a reasonable level.[48]

Similar factors produced similar results in Venice in the fourteenth century. Artisans were often of relatively recent immigrant origin and their families were usually small, so that they would have fewer relatives on whom to rely and less sense of lineage than the upper classes. Marriages might be arranged, but it often seems to have been on the basis of shared participation in a particular trade or the need to pool resources and earnings in order to survive. Women needed a dowry, but also contributed to the household by working, usually at relatively unskilled occupations in the textile industry, food processing or retailing, or as servants or wetnurses. Artisan husbands named their wife as heir less frequently in Venice than in Genoa, and more frequently tried to influence their wives against remarriage by making legacies to them conditional on continued widowhood, especially where there were children, presumably out of fear of the children's inheritance falling into the hands of stepfathers. But artisan men often showed considerable trust in both the capa-

---

47 Hughes, 'Domestic ideals', 129–30, 'Family structure', 23–4.
48 Hughes, 'Domestic ideals', 139–40, 'Family structure', 24–6. Epstein, *Wills and wealth*, 108–9.

bilities and the good intentions of their wives, granting them power of attorney to receive money or handle business affairs on their husband's behalf, and especially in naming them executor or one of the executors of their wills. Despite their late husband's attempts to discourage remarriage, Venetian artisan widows often did remarry, presumably for much the same reasons as in Genoa, that is that a widow's dowry and her own earnings were not enough to support a household adequately; that took two incomes. But a widow with her dowry, her own earning capacity, perhaps a legacy from her first husband or the use of her children's inheritance until they came of age, was an attractive prospect for marriage with a second artisan, who also needed a wife's contribution for economic security.[49]

Peasant women and artisan women elsewhere have not been studied as intensively as in Genoa and Venice,[50] but it seems likely that the same considerations apply. Somewhat unsystematic observations in Lucca indicate that there too the lineage was of much less significance among artisans and peasants than it was among the upper and middle classes, and that the marriage bond was correspondingly more important. There too artisans and peasants frequently named their wives as guardians and executors, and not infrequently as heirs, especially where there were no children, and artisan and peasant widows frequently remarried.

Since the law on such questions as marriages, wills and inheritance, dowries and the protection of women's rights were essentially the same for all classes, the differences that have been observed between the upper classes and artisans were a matter of practice rather than of law. The differences appear to stem from the importance of the lineage among the upper classes, with the consequent need to protect the inheritance rights of males, especially with regard to land, by limiting the inheritance rights of women, who would leave the lineage to marry into another, taking their property rights with them. Family honour and practical considerations required that women were not left unprovided for and their property rights, especially with regard to their dowries, were given extensive legal protection. The dowry system acquired its own momentum, with a constant tendency for dowries to inflate, due to social pressures, not least from women themselves, with the result that, especially as widows, women sometimes came to control significant amounts of wealth and the

---

49 Romano, *Patricians and popolani*, 56–64.
50 See however, Klapisch-Zuber and Demonet, 'A uno pane e uno vino' and Klapisch-Zuber and Herlihy, *Florentines and their families*, for much relevant information on all classes, although neither is concerned primarily with women. Chabot tackles some of these problems with regard to widows, 'Widowhood and poverty', 301–4.

influence that went with it. While complaints about the burden represented by dowries are common, the system continued because many could hope to benefit from it. One man's daughter was another man's wife and another man's mother. It was normally only necessary to provide a daughter's dowry once, while a man who married more than once would receive a new dowry with each wife, and there are examples of families calculating the balance of dowries paid against dowries received. The dowry might have to be repaid to a woman on widowhood, and she might have the right to dispose of all or part of it by will, but it would eventually return to her heirs, who were likely to be her relatives, whether these were her own children, or the family into which she had been born or that into which she had married.

The Lady in the Tower

THE SOCIAL AND POLITICAL ROLE OF WOMEN IN TOWER HOUSES

Mary McAuliffe

Tower houses are perhaps the most distinctive and numerous stone ruins on the Irish landscape. These buildings, as well as being defensive strongholds or safe havens in time of war, were also family homes. It is in these tower houses that many of the chiefs and nobles of medieval Ireland lived with their wives and families. The smooth running of the tower house as a home, and as a social centre was within the sphere of the woman of the house.

Because of the continuing need for fortification the architecture of a tower house had some disadvantages when it came to providing comfort for its inhabitants. For example, most tower houses would have had little natural light or ventilation, as narrow loops usually performed (badly) the function of letting in air and light. Many of the foreign travel writers of the sixteenth and seventeenth century were dismissive of the aesthetic and comfortable aspects of the tower house. For example, M. de la Boullaye le Gouz, a seventeenth-century French traveller wrote 'the castles of the nobility consist of four walls, extremely high, but they are nothing but square towers, without windows, or at least having such small apertures as to give no more light than is in a prison'.[1] Other writers said that these buildings were 'old, high, narrow and inconvenient ... [the] chambers being narrow and steep'.[2]

These and many other comments from foreign travellers paint a picture of dark, damp, gloomy, uncomfortable buildings, and it is in these houses that many of the wives of Anglo-Irish nobles and Gaelic chiefs had to provide good, comfortable lodging, and entertainment for their families, relatives, dependants, servants and guests. The numerous ruins to be found in Ireland today show that most tower houses were thick-walled buildings between three and six storeys high, with between one and three vaults. Each storey was divided into one or two big chambers; in addition there could be small chambers built into the thickness of the

---

1 Maxwell, *Contemporary sources* (Le Gouz), 62.
2 Falkiner, *Illustrations* (Brereton), 389.

walls or vaults, although these could be 'confined and gloomy rooms'.[3]

However, these buildings may not have been as uncomfortable as the medieval travel writers say. While medieval women were hampered by the very architecture of the tower houses from providing houses with natural light and ventilation, there is evidence that the homes of the nobility were warm and comfortable. The ground floor was usually the storage area, where all the equipment for farming, and cultivation was kept. It is also possible that the kitchen was on the ground floor.[4] However, usually the lady of the house did not actively participate in the activities of the kitchen, and it is on the upper floors that she would be more at home.

The upper storeys of the tower house normally contained the living quarters of the resident family. Most descriptions of the interior of tower houses are usually concerned with what were, to the visitors, the two most important areas, the lord's dining room and the bed chambers. It is in the main hall, which was commonly on the second or third floor, that the lord and lady of the house spent the greater part of their indoor life. It was from these chambers that the lady ruled the activities of the household. The providing of food, the storing of provisions for winter, or (in case of war) for siege, was the responsibility of the lady of the tower. This was a huge undertaking because in addition to her immediate family, the lady of the house was also answerable for dealing with the many servants, soldiers, labourers, workmen and inevitable guests who all had to be housed and fed. Most tower houses were probably self-sufficient in the basic foods.

Stanihurst mentions that he received several types of meats in the homes of the nobility including 'beef, pork and fish'.[5] Other staples include milk, which Moryson said the Irish drink 'like nectar', and 'esteem for a great dainty sour curds, vulgarly called ... Bonaclabbe'.[6]

Many contemporary writers were struck by the fertility of the soil. Payne mentions that the yields included 'Wheate, Rye, Barly, Peason, Beanes, Oates, Woade, Mather, Rape, Hoppes, Hempe, Flaxes, and all other graines and fruites that England anywise doth yeelde'.[7] He also mentions 'a great sort of Swanes, Cranes, Pheasants, Partiges, Heathcocks, Plovers, Curlew, Quailles [as well as] Oysters, Muscles, Cockles and Samphiere'.[8]

3 Crofton-Croker, *Researches*, 265.
4 MacLysaght, *Irish life*, 94.
5 Lennon, *Stanihurst*, 146–50.
6 Falkiner, *Illustrations* (Moryson), 229–30.
7 Smith (ed.), 'A brief description' (Payne), 6.
8 Ibid., 7.

These were some of the foods indigenous to Ireland which the ladies of the tower houses could provide for their table. They also had access to imported luxury foods such as fruits and spices as well as Spanish and French wines. In fact one thing served at the tables of the nobility which pleased the foreign writers was the amount of drink, which included wine, beer, mead, ale and usquebagh (whiskey), which Moryson held was 'the best in the world'.[9] As these examples show, the lady of the tower could provide a varied and interesting diet for the inhabitants of the tower house. The meats would be provided by the herds of cattle and sheep held by the lord, while the grain was provided by the demesne lands, as well as grain paid by tenants in lieu of rent.

It is also probable that some vegetables and perhaps herbs were culti-vated in the vicinity of the tower house, perhaps in the bawn area. For example, in a description of one of the Earl of Desmond's main strong-holds at Newcastle West, Co. Limerick, it is stated that 'within the walls [of the bawn are] ... One garden, and in the same, two fishponds. And outside the walls and near there are divers orchards and gardens'.[10] There is also evidence that some tower houses would have had their own mills to grind grain as at Pallis, the stronghold of MacCarthy Mór in Co. Kerry.[11]

As well as providing for the day-to-day needs of the inhabitants of the tower house, the noblewomen of medieval Ireland also took part in a tra-dition of hospitality. Many contemporary sources have commented on the generosity of Irish chiefs and Anglo-Irish nobles towards guests. As Tadhg Rody wrote in 1683, 'the inhabitants ... are very much addicted to hospitality, freely inviting and receiving all men into their houses and giv-ing them the best fare they have'.[12] Stanihurst wrote that 'they [the lords] are men of great hospitality and you cannot gratify them more than by visiting their homes frequently or by extending invitations to them.'[13]

The owners of the tower houses had kept up the practices which had prevailed in this regard in pre-Norman Ireland. Most particularly lords, and their ladies, were anxious to feed the wandering bards and poets who would provide entertainment in return for food, or conversely who could destroy a lord's reputation with a satire, or sarcastic poem, if turned away.

Although the sources, for example the Irish annals, mainly refer to the hospitality of the lords and chiefs, the great tables they maintained, the entertainment to be had at their houses, there is also some mention of the

9 Falkiner, *Illustrations*, 227.
10 Maxwell, *Contemporary sources*, 63.
11 MacLysaght, *Kenmare manuscripts*, 144.
12 MacLysaght, *Irish life*, 18.
13 Lennon, *Stanihurst*, 147–50.

fact that noblewomen were also providers of hospitality. For example the Annals of Connacht under the year 1327 mention in the obit of Gormlaith, wife of Fearghal O'Hara, that she was 'the best woman of her race for good report and bounteous bestowing of gifts'.[14] Later the annals mention in the obit of the Countess of Desmond under the year 1392 that she was a 'charitable, hospitable woman'.[15]

The Irish poets and bards who wandered the countryside depended on the hospitality of the nobles and chiefs for food and lodging and in return provided the families with recitations of their histories, pedigrees, genealogies and, of course, told their own tales and poems. Many of the bards, rhymers and poets were grateful to the civilisation and hospitality of Ireland's women. For example a poem ascribed to Earl Gerald the Rhymer, reads 'They do no murder nor treachery, woe to him who speaks ill of women'.[16] Some of the poems address noblewomen as protectors, as able as any chief or lord to provide hospitality and patronage.

Again the annals speak of several women who were protectors of poets. In the Annals of Connacht under the year 1481 there is mention of Sláine, wife of MacWilliam 'a universal protector of the poets of Ireland'.[17] In 1513 the obit of Margaret, wife of O'Rourke, mentions the fact that she was a woman of 'great wealth, hearth of hospitality and maintenance, humanity and charitable entertainment for scholars and ollavs, the weak and the wretched and all, whether mighty or outcast, who stood in need ... one who never as long as she lived denied any man craving a boon'.[18]

The same annals also mention Mór, wife of O'Hanly, 'the best woman who ever lived in Cenel Dobtha, foster mother to the poets and exiles of Ireland ... the greatest bestower of alms'.[19] Other women of great hospitable repute mentioned include Gormlaith wife of Aodh O'Neill 'a most bounteous and hospitable woman who has bestowed many gifts upon ... the literary men and ollaves'[20] and Mór wife of Donnchadh O'Brien 'a woman who kept a house of open hospitality'.[21]

There is evidence in the sources for the type of hospitality provided by the lords, the chiefs, and their ladies. Luke Gernon gives a description of the treatment he received when visiting a 'castle' in the southwest in 1620: 'The lady of the house meets you with her train ... salutation past, you shall be presented with all the drinks in the house, first beer, then aquavitae, then sack, then old ale ... the lady tastes it. You must not refuse it'.[22] In addition to a feast, the owners of the house also provided the

14 *Ann. Conn.*, s.a. 1327:3
15 *Ann. Conn.*, s. a. 1392:4
16 Jackson, *A Celtic miscellany*, 101.
17 *Ann. Conn.*, s.a. 1481:6.
18 Ibid., s.a. 1513:2.

19 Ibid., s.a. 1527:20.
20 *A.F.M.* , s.a. 1524.
21 Ibid., s.a. 1524.
22 Quinn, *The Elizabethans*, 74–5;
   Falkiner, *Illustrations* (Gernon), 360.

guests with many entertainments including poets, bards, genealogists, harpers, dancers and card players. As well as music, poetry and song Moryson writes that the Irish delighted in playing at cards and dice.[23] Luke Gernon writes of the great 'jollity' to be found at these feasts.[24] The company feast sumptuously while they may lack delicacies in their cuisine.

In addition to providing food, entertainment and hospitality, the lady of the house also had to see to the comforts of the occupants and guests of the tower house. While some of the foreign writers give the impression that the tower houses were very uncomfortable we know from other sources that these buildings might contain the furnishings and trappings needed for a relatively comfortable lifestyle. In an inventory of Castleisland, Co. Kerry, a stronghold of the Earl of Desmond taken in 1590 when the castle had been granted to Sir William Herbert after the Desmond Rebellion we have a complete list of the contents of a stronghold.

Contrary to the grievances of writers like Moryson, who stated that the Irish nobility slept on rushes strewn on the floor, we find that Castleisland[25] contained enough linen to dress several beds, including sheets of many different types – 'holland', 'dowles', 'color sheets' and so forth; and by way of bedding, featherbeds with bolsters, pillows, blankets, canopies and 'curtaynes' of different materials and colours. Other furnishings show that the walls and floors at Castleisland and perhaps other tower houses were not bare. There are eight pieces of tapestry, carpets, window carpets and so on mentioned. Other pieces of furniture include stools, leather chairs, long boards, square boards, and there were spoons, ladles, knives, silver spoons, silver cups and several different types of bowls.

The inventory also mentions many of the items needed in the kitchen, on the farm and in the garden, including spades, shovels, saws, harrows, baskets and so on. Perhaps the most surprising items on the list, in addition to the armour and munitions stored at Castleisland, are the 'one hundred books of sundry sort, great and little', and of course 'the bible and a book of common prayer'.

Therefore, as we can see, the ladies of the tower houses were not trying, hopelessly, to provide shelter and comfort for their families and guests in grim, damp, dark, thick-walled strongholds. As well as having access to food which was provided by the family's own land, the noble-

---

23 Falkiner, *Illustrations* (Moryson), 248.
24 Falkiner, *Illustrations* (Gernon), 361.
25 O'Shea, 'Castleisland inventory', 37–46.

women of medieval Ireland could also furnish their homes to a high standard. There may not have been much natural light or ventilation, but with candles, fires and rich tapestries the ladies could provide a warm, comfortable atmosphere in which to live, eat, entertain and sleep. Apart from being responsible for the smooth running of the household, there is very little evidence as to what type of work the lady of the house actually did. As well as supervising the servants and overseeing the entertainment of guests, she probably also indulged in the more ladylike domestic pursuits such as sewing, making preserves and so forth.

However, women were also involved in other aspects of medieval life. Most historians until recently would have concentrated totally on the history of men in relation to war, politics, or economics. Women, if they were mentioned at all, were either mentioned in relation to men or in relation to social or family life. Of course historians always mentioned the few isolated examples of women, such as Grace O'Malley or Iníon Dubh O'Donnell, who were involved in the male preserve of politics. However, these women were seen as extraordinary and somewhat abnormal. In fact, it was thought that if women were to be involved in war and politics it was as pawns, hostages or victims, such as Dearbhforgaill (Dervorgilla) wife of O'Rourke, whose abduction by Diarmait MacMurrough eventually led to the Norman invasion of Ireland. Similarly Diarmait's daughter Aoife was the pawn whom Strongbow used (and married) to legitimize his claim to the kingdom of Leinster. Most of the aristocratic marriages in medieval Ireland were dynastic, in that the bride was usually bestowed on the groom as part of a treaty between families. The value of women as brides/pawns can be seen in the fact that women who outlived their husbands were married off again and again. One example of a woman married for political power was Gormlaith who, in the late tenth and early eleventh century was married at various times to Olaf, King of Dublin, and the high-kings Brian Boruma, and Maelsechlainn II.[26] In 1395 the obit of Cobhlach Mór mentions the fact that she was married several times, being the wife of Niall O'Donnell, Lord of Tirconnell, of Aodh O'Rourke, Lord of Breifne, and of Cathal, son of Aodh Breifneach O'Connor 'royal heir' (*ríoghdhamhna*) of Connacht.[27]

However, more recent research has shown that medieval women were more actively involved in the politics of the era than previously thought. Women could be wealthy, powerful and important in their own right. Anglo-Irish women, if widowed, were entitled to a life-interest in one-third of their husband's lands, and to certain dower lands. The wives of Irish lords could retain the goods they brought to their marriage, and

26 *A.F.M.*, s.a. 1030.   27 Ibid., s.a. 1395.

some were entitled to receive revenues from their husband's lands for their own use. For example the wife of MacCarthy Mór could collect a rent from his lands known as the *Cáin bheag*, or 'little tax'.[28] Therefore many noble women would have some wealth and power, independent of that of their father, husband, brothers or other kinsmen.

There are many examples in the annals of noblewomen partaking in the politics of medieval Ireland, and for much of the time, being involved in medieval Irish politics, meant taking an active part in warfare. For example, it is commonly thought that the murder of the Earl of Ulster in 1333 was instigated by one Gyle de Burgh whose brother had been killed by the Earl. In 1315 it is said that Aodh O'Donnell, King of Tirconnell, ravaged Carbury after 'being advised thereto by his wife ... She herself, with all her gallowglasses and men of the Clan Murtagh that she could obtain, marched against the churches of Drumcliff and plundered many of its clergy'.[29] Then in 1316 when Ruaidhri O'Connor of Carbury surrendered to the above-mentioned Aodh, Aodh's wife, Dearbhfhorgaill, unwilling to abandon a longstanding feud, 'hired a band of gallowglasses and gave them a reward for killing Ruaidri ... so by them he was killed, in violation of oaths sworn to him previously on the relics of Tirconnell.'[30]

These examples show that Gráinne (or Grace) O'Malley was not the only warlike woman to emerge from medieval Ireland. It was a warlike time and the women of those days partook of the motives and ideas of the men. They shared their husbands' politics and sometimes his fate. It is true that many women were caught up as innocent victims in the continuous petty wars that plagued medieval Ireland. Tower houses, as well as being the homes of these medieval noble ladies, were also fortified strongholds directly in the front line of many of the wars of that period. The architecture of the tower house shows the importance of its military role. It was used to protect its owner and family from the ravages of robber bands and thieves. While it could be taken in sieges, usually a siege before the age of cannons was too costly in manpower and time to undertake, so a tower house could be defended very easily.

However with the development of the cannon it was easier to besiege and take a tower house, putting the occupants of these tower houses more at risk. Even in earlier times many women were caught up in the ravages of war. For example in 1254 Sadhbh O'Brien and her husband Séafraidh (Geoffrey) O'Donoghue 'were killed and burned ... in [their] own house' at Gortalassa, near Killarney by Finghin MacCarthy.[31] In 1367 Dearbhail

28 Nicholls, 'Irishwomen and
    property', 21.
29 *Ann. Conn.*, s.a. 1315:20.

30 Ibid., s.a. 1316:2.
31 'MacCarthaigh's book', s.a, 1254.

wife of Ualgharg O'Rourke 'was killed by the Clann-Murtough'.[32] In 1415 Lochlainn O'Hanly's daughter was killed in the house of her foster-father Tomaltach O'Beirne when it was attacked and burned[33] and in 1471, during an attack launched by MacCostello against his own kins-men, Elec, the daughter of Fearghal Óg O'Higgin was killed 'in her own house ... most unhappily'.[34]

Later in the tumultuous times of the later 16th century, especially dur-ing the Desmond Rebellions, many women, both active participants and innocent victims, were caught up in the warfare. For example Eleanor, wife of the last Earl of Desmond, had tried to persuade her husband to bow to the demands of the government, dispense with his huge band of armed followers and behave more like a loyal English noble rather than an independent Gaelic king. After her efforts failed and the rebellion had begun she remained with the earl until his death in 1584. However, Eleanor survived the destruction of the earldom and continued to petition London unceasingly to have her son restored to his rightful position. She continued in her political role when she married O'Connor Sligo in 1596 and this time was more successful as an intermediary between her hus-band and the government, and the lands of O'Connor Sligo remained intact through the disruptive decades of the late 16th century.[35]

Most of Ireland was involved in war in the late sixteenth century from the time of the Desmond rebellions through the rebellion of Hugh O'Neill, right up to the defeat at Kinsale. However, the nature of warfare had changed and women were now more likely to be caught up in it. Previously tower houses were taken by an enemy, only to be returned later when peace negotiations were concluded. Also the more innocent people in the tower house, that is, the women and other non-combatants were usually not injured or killed. With the coming of cannon and the determination of the government to reduce the intransigent Irish chiefs and Anglo-Irish nobles there was a change in the type of warfare prac-tised. In the campaigns in Munster and Connacht in the sixteenth centu-ry by Englishmen like Sir Humphrey Gilbert and Sir Richard Bingham when tower houses were taken all occupants were put to the sword. For example, after Carrigafoyle, the seat of O'Connor Kerry, fell to the English, all the occupants, soldiers, servants, women and children, were killed.

Women were not always the innocent victims of war. As already men-tioned many of the noblewomen of medieval Ireland were as bloodthirsty and warlike as their men. Also because some women were landowners

32 *A.F.M.*, s.a. 1367.   34 Ibid., s.a. 1471:26
33 *Ann.Conn.*, s.a. 1415:12.   35 Chambers, *As wicked a woman.*

and wealthy in their own right, they were as legitimate targets of violence as the men. Again the annals show that women were attacked and deprived of their property in the same manner as medieval noblemen. For example in 1495 Conn O'Donnell 'marched to MacEoin of the Glens and made himself master ... but he afterwards made full restitution to MacEoin's wife of all such property as was hers.'[36] In 1536 O'Donnell and his army invaded north Connacht 'and they captured the daughter of Walter Burke ... as well as her cattle'.[37] In fact, as with their male contemporaries, many medieval women built tower houses themselves to protect their own interests.

Usually it is very difficult to state who actually built a particular tower house. Most builders leave no record and in the case of most tower houses it is impossible even to date the construction of the building. However, normally the builders of tower houses were men. One of the functions of the tower house was to establish the strength of the landowner and provide a base from which he could control and protect his lands and family. From the tower house the lord or chief could launch his cattle raids or defend his lands from similar raids launched by his enemies.

Although there are many tower house ruins on the Irish landscape, these buildings could only be afforded by men (or women) of power and wealth. The tower house, although cheaper than the great castle, still cost the builder a lot of money, and since men controlled the economy of medieval Ireland it follows that the builders of the tower houses were predominantly men.

However there is evidence that there were a few women who had enough power and wealth to build these strongholds. Many references in the annals refer to women 'in their own house'. Of course one cannot surmise from these vague references that the women built these houses. It is possible that like the Dowager Countess of Desmond they were widows who had been granted a life interest in a tower house, or that these houses came as part of their dowry. There are a few references which suggest that women did built tower houses and/or strongholds for themselves

For example in 1507 the Four Masters tell us that 'Catherine, daughter of the Earl of Desmond ... Lady of Hy-Carbury ... died. It was by her that Beann-dubh and Dún-na-mbeann were erected'.[38] Beann-dubh turns out to be Castle Salem, Ross Carbery, Co. Cork, seat of MacCarthy Reagh, the lord of Hy-Carbury, and Dún-na-mbeann is Dunmanway which afterwards belonged to MacCarthy of Gleann-a-Chruim who held it until 1690. Both these strongholds must have been built in the fifteenth

36 *A.F.M.*, s.a. 1495.
37 *Ann. Conn.*, s.a. 1536:18.
38 *A.F.M.*, s.a. 1507

century, which was the height of tower house construction. Other examples of tower houses built by women are few and far between but the lack of examples does not mean that women were not building, or causing these strongholds to be built. For example the tower house of Castle Cove in south Kerry is said to have been built by the wife of O'Sullivan Mór in the sixteenth century, while he was absent on campaigns, in order to protect their lands.

The fact that women were involved in tower house construction shows that some women, especially those more actively involved in medieval politics and warfare, recognised, like their male counterparts, the need to provide themselves with a fortified stronghold. From these strongholds the women could hold and protect their land and property. As further research shows more and more the involvement of medieval women, especially women of the upper echelons of society, in all aspects of medieval life social, political, economic and military, perhaps more in-depth study into the lives of these women will show the importance of their contribution, independently from that of men, to the history of the era. Whether providing for the needs of family, dependants or guests, or involved in politics or war, the history of the 'lady of the tower' is as important as that of the men who lived in these strongholds.

Was There a Political Role for Women in Medieval Ireland?

LADY MARGARET BUTLER
AND LADY ELEANOR MACCARTHY

Elizabeth McKenna

It is often argued that the role of European women of the landed classes during the later Middle Ages was a somewhat restricted one. Royalty apart, their energies and abilities were officially relegated to the domestic arena. They were excluded from the realm of public affairs and indeed women and their fortunes were effectively at the disposal of parents, brothers or husbands, and in the case of orphaned heiresses, either of the king or a guardian appointed by him.[1] However, one widespread practice of the day – that of the political marriage – could and did present some women with the opportunity of involvement in state affairs.

In Ireland women were also allocated a subordinate place in the order of things. Evidence presented by the Kilkenny Jury as late as 1537 states that two members of the jury, Walter Clery and Fraunceis Drome, accompanied by female members of their families, were attacked by thieves:

> who made assaulte on the same Walter, and hym did bete and wounde and 46s. 8d. in money from the saide Walter did feloniously stele and bere awaye and revisshed the sister of the said Walter and doughter of the said Fraunceis.[2]

No doubt these offences were presented in order of importance, and as such are indicative of the position of women during this period. In Ireland also, the contemporary perception of the judiciously arranged marriage as a means whereby families consolidated and improved their social, financial and political status led to abuses. Many such marriages were forced, and women were beaten in order to coerce them into marriages of their guardians' choice. During the hearing of a divorce case in the Armagh diocese in 1434, witnesses testified that Catherine MacKesky

1 *Cal. pat. rolls Ire. Hen. VIII–Eliz.*, no.72.
2 Hore and Graves, *The Social state*, 122.

'was compelled by her parents and in the betrothal she was lamenting'[3] and further that ' her mother beat her grievously with a bedoke and broke the bedoke ... and afterwards her father beat her to the ground'[4]. The political implications of such carefully arranged alliances were recognised and exploited throughout the medieval period and are clearly expressed in the words of Donough O'Brien to his brother-in-law, James, Lord Butler, some hundred years later, 'I have marryd your syster; and for becawys that I have marryd your syster, I have forsakyn my father, myn unkyll and all my frendes and my countrye to cume to you to helpe to doo the King servys.'[5]

This perception of the political role of marriage is further underlined by Ap Parry's report to Cromwell when he describes James Butler as the man most capable of serving the king, 'by reason he ys so calyd by the maryge of hys systers and by my lady hys wyffe that other by fere ore by love, he ys lyke to do thee servys, and put the Kyng to less charge than any alyve'.[6]

Obviously therefore, marriage alliance between the leading families was regarded as a basic element in the political process and one, moreover, which could be used to allow women of spirit and intelligence the opportunity of becoming involved in official political affairs, and as will be seen there was no shortage of women capable of influencing events far outside the domestic sphere in Ireland at this time.

Contemporary evidence supports the belief that a number of women were lettered if not actually literary, many of them like Margaret O'Reilly, 'a woman that was learned in Latin and in English and in Irish',[7] or the daughter of O'Connor Faly who, in 1553 travelled to England

> relying on the number of her friends and relatives there and on her knowledge of the English language to request Queen Mary to restore her father to her, and on her appealing to her mercy, she obtained her father and brought him home.[8]

On a relatively minor level, Dame Genet Sarsfield, in an attempt to gain the upper hand in a financial dispute with her son-in-law, ransacked his father's house and as he reported to the Council in Dublin 'She stripped

3 Chart, *Register of John Swayne*, 165.
4 Ibid.
5 *S.P. Hen. VIII*, II, pt iii, 282–6.
6 Ibid., 286.
7 *A.U.*, s.a. 1490
8 *A.F.M.*, s.a. 1553.

the house', including 'portals, chests and glass windowes'[9] and he 'was fain to compound with her for the boards of the hall'[10]. Margaret O'Carroll of Ely in 1433 is given full personal credit for holding two extremely expensive banquets for the poets of Ireland[11] and a few years later she negotiated the release of hostages with the Anglo-Irish 'and that unadvised to Calwagh' (her husband, An Calbhach O'Connor Faly).[12]. A century later, in 1553, the annals report that

> a hosting was made by MagUidhir and by the daughter of Macnamighi, namely by the wife of O'Domnaill and they went to aid the Saxons and the deputy of the King, namely, William Skeffington.[13]

At a most crucial political level, Lady Janet Eustace, wife of Sir Walter Delahide, was regarded by no less than John Alen as having a prime role in the Kildare Rebellion. In a letter to Cromwell in 1535, he describes her as 'the Earl of Kildare's aunt, and most of secrets with him and by all probable conjecture, she was the chief councillor and stirrer of this inordinate rebellion'.[14]

The almost complete absence of women in general accounts of this period could lead to the assumption that they were quite irrelevant to the political and public life of the country – excepting the political dimension of marriage, in which in many cases they were simply pawns. There is for instance, no indication that the wives of English officials who accompanied their husbands to Dublin tried to assist the process of anglicisation on their own account. The references to women in public records or state papers are very infrequent, so it is therefore important to examine them when they do occur. A closer look at the lives of two of the most remarkable women of this period proves how influential women could be even within such a restricted sphere.

Margaret Fitzgerald, wife of Sir Piers Ruadh Butler and daughter of the Great Earl of Kildare was one of these women. Brought up in the household of one of the most powerful men in Ireland at that time, Margaret's early life, in the absence of any evidence to the contrary, probably followed the same pattern as that of her peers. There is no doubt but

---

9 Gallwey, 'The Cusack Family', 674.
10 Ibid.
11 *Ann. Conn.*, s.a. 1433.
12 *Ann. MacFirbis*, 212. (Quoted in Simms, 'The legal position', 109.)
13 *A.U.*, s.a. 1535.
14 *S.P. Hen. VIII*, II, Part iii, 228.

that she was fully aware of the traditional rivalry between her family, the Fitzgeralds of Kildare and Desmond, and the Butlers of Ormond, to which family Piers belonged. This ongoing bitterness which occasionally erupted into open enmity and war had been somewhat alleviated by the Yorkist success in the English Wars of the Roses. Butler fortunes were closely linked to the House of Lancaster, and this, together with Acts of Attainder passed against them, sufficed to force the Earls of Ormond into the role of absentee landlord and more or less out of direct conflict with the Yorkist Fitzgeralds. Their place in Ireland was taken by a deputy appointed by them, Sir James MacRichard Butler, father of Piers Ruadh. Unfortunately, the untimely deaths of Edward IV and Richard III and the consequent accession of the Lancastrian Henry VII tipped the balance in favour of the absentee Earl and his Irish cousins, and in an attempt to redress this setback for the Fitzgeralds, resorting to a normal political expedient of the time, a marriage was arranged between Margaret Fitzgerald and Piers Ruadh Butler.

According to the Book of Howth, this marriage took place in 1485 'so that by menes and polissy the Erle of Wormond was so occupied in his own countrey he could not attend to do any damage to the Erle of Kildare.'[15] Although the 'Earl of Ormond' in this case appears to refer to James Butler, otherwise engagingly known as the Black Bastard (who had not yet in fact arrived in Ireland and of whom more below) rather than the actual Earl of Ormond, the principle remained firmly the same. The marriage was most likely a response to the improvement in the fortunes of the Butlers in general (as a result of the Lancastrian accession and the subsequent appeal of the Act of Attainder in November 1485) and the improvement in the fortunes of Piers in particular. His father, Sir James, in 1487 bequeathed to him (quite illegally) the office of Irish deputy to the Earl of Ormond. The Earl's subsequent confirmation of the office gave Piers not only control of the MacRichard Butler estates (his personal inheritance), but also of the earl's demesne manors in Kilkenny and Tipperary, including Kilkenny Castle itself. His position was still sufficiently precarious (internal rivalries amongst branches of the Butler family in Ireland were costly, divisive and probably exacerbated by an alliance with their traditional enemy, the Fitzgeralds) to render him an effective ally, but not a threat. Piers, however, had just acquired his greatest asset, Margaret, described by Thomas Carte as 'a person of great wisdom and courage uncommon in her sex.'[16]

15 *Cal. Carew MSS: Book of Howth*, 176–7.
16 Carte, *Life of James, duke of Ormonde*, I, 50.

Together they set about transforming Ormond. She was regarded as the 'meane at those days whereby hir husbande's countrey was reclaymed from the sluttish and uncleane Irish custome, to Englishe bedding, house-keeping and civilitie.'[17] Doubtless also, Margaret played some part in per-suading Piers to accept the office of Sheriff of Kilkenny under the seal of the Dublin-crowned 'King Edward' (the Yorkist pretender Lambert Simnel) thus, tacitly at least, to move even further away from the tradi-tional Butler commitment to the House of Lancaster. The fact that Henry VII later confirmed him in this office was more indicative of Henry's dif-ficulties at the time, than that Piers' defection had gone unnoticed either by him or by Earl Thomas. The arrival in Ireland of Perkin Warbeck forced Henry to take action against the Earl of Kildare and his friends. Retribution arrived in the person of Sir James Butler, illegitimate nephew of Earl Thomas, and with strong Gaelic connections through his mother, Raghnailt (or 'Reynalda') O'Brien. It was intended that with the help of a force provided by the King he should become the focus of anti-Kildare/Yorkist sympathy, but the biggest blow to Piers' ambitions was James' appointment as deputy to Earl Thomas. That James Butler proved a most effective thorn in Kildare's side is a matter of record – for his daughter Margaret the effect was little short of catastrophic.

James' illegitimacy barred him from inheriting the title, thus posing no threat to Earl Thomas' Irish kinsmen, so he had no difficulty in enlisting their support. Piers, dispossessed, was hunted and driven through his own territory 'forced to houer and lurke in woodes and forrestes'.[18] Margaret was left in dangerous and straitened circumstances. Piers, writ-ing to Earl Thomas in 1497 explains:

> He (James) without any cause or occasion on my side, kept me from all myne own landes and duties, and over this took and kept me in prison by such a long season ... and over that took goods and cattle from such as he knew were towards me, as far forth as he might to their great hurt and impoverishing and to the utter undo-ing of some of them forever.[19]

Margaret's position was certainly not an enviable one. She had small children to protect, her husband's life was in constant danger, even her father's position was threatened and 'great and manifolde were the mis-

---

17 *Holinshed's Irish chronicle*, 256
18 Ibid., 326.
19 Graves and Prim, *History architecture & antiquities*, 193–4.

eries the Lady Margaret sustayned'[20]. Nevertheless she cared for her children and did her best to contain the damage arising from her husband's position. The murder of Sir James by her husband in 1497 no doubt eased the situation somewhat, but both rival Butlers and hostile O'Briens and their allies continued to plague Piers and in 1499, the O'Briens inflicted a severe defeat on him in which 'the Sovereign of Kilkenny and many others were killed.'[21] Her father's attitude was no help either – he had hoped to obtain the farm of the Butler lands for himself during the height of Margaret's troubles, although he certainly supported Piers' claim at a later date.[22] Possibly this ambivalence on the part of Kildare was responsible for her decision to give her husband's affairs priority until she became 'in heart and soul a Butler and instigated him to give vigorous opposition to her own kinsmen'.[23]

The long period out of favour with Earl Thomas lasted until 1505, when 'for the singular love and affection and cousynage that he hath to the saide Sir Piers'[24] the Earl of Ormond granted him the deputyship of Ormond, having just appointed him to the office of Seneschal of Tipperary. To some degree this signalled the end of the wilderness years, and 'Lady Margaret began to take hearte, hir naturall stouteness floted'.[25] Not that her troubles were by any means over. Favour from Earl Thomas merely activated opposition from the Butler kin, and the following years saw a spate of activity on her part designed to strengthen her husband's position in Ormond and his claim to the earldom in the event of the Earl of Ormond's failure to provide a male heir. She came 'in person into the chancel of the Cathedral of the Holy Trinity Dublin' and in the presence of the notary and witnesses,' she produced 'one John Becket a merchant of Dublin'[26] to give evidence regarding the entail of the Ormond lands and title. Later, according to Bagwell, (who unfortunately does not quote his sources) Piers was summoned to appear before his brother-in-law Kildare and the Irish Council in connection with the vexed question of the entail. Piers, claiming he was busy fighting, sent his wife instead who not only procured an adjournment, but also a stipulation that no rents should be paid in the meantime.[27] Certainly in 1517 the fine hand of

20 *Holinshed's Irish chronicle*, 326.
21 *A.U.*, s.a.1499.
22 Conway, *Henry VII's relations*, 239–41.
23 Graves and Prim, *History Architecture & Antiquities*, 211.
24 *Ormond deeds*, iv, 335, no.74.
25 *Holinshed's Irish chronicle*, 326.
26 *Ormond deeds*, iv, 23.
27 Bagwell, *Ireland under the Tudors*, i, 126.

Margaret can be discerned in the presence of an old servant of her father's giving conclusive evidence in support of Piers' claim[28] and, incidentally, adding weight to the view that Margaret considered that her position was best served by supporting the interests of the Butlers rather than those of her own family. The information gathered by this servant was gained on a mission to London as late as 1500 on behalf of Gerald of Kildare to discuss a possible marriage between another daughter, Eleanor, and George Saintleger, one of the Ormond heirs general, a move calculated to strengthen his own position but undermining Margaret's at the same time. The death of Earl Thomas in 1515 without a son had undoubtedly brought the question of succession firmly to the fore. Piers' claim appears to have been generally recognised in Ireland – certainly within the Butler family itself.[29] Unfortunately, complications arose in the shape of Henry VIII's involvement with the Boleyn family. His infatuation with Anne Boleyn, granddaughter of the late Earl, led to a conflict of interest in which Piers was inevitably the temporary loser. However he graciously accepted the title of Earl of Ossory in tail male, together with the seneschalship of the royal manor of Dungarvan and relinquished the title of Earl of Ormond, thus allowing Henry to grant the title of Ormond and Wiltshire to Sir Thomas Boleyn, father of Anne, in December 1529. While the final prize had eluded Piers for the moment, he certainly did not come away empty-handed. He had total effective control of the Irish lands, and was in possession of the psychological high ground. The Boleyn position was fundamentally weak, given Henry's fickleness, and their ultimate fall from favour resulted in the restoration of Piers to the earldom of Ormond on the 22 February 1538. The management of this affair does not at all accord with the picture of the rather simple, straightforward, soldierly Piers as presented by Stanihurst, but carries the hallmark of a much more subtle mind, one which fits Margaret admirably.

That Margaret was involved in her husband's political career is not in question. In a series of articles against Piers Butler, Gerald, ninth Earl of Kildare, refers to the 'said Erle (Piers) or my Lady, his wif, by whome he is only ruled'.[30] At what point she decided, or even if she consciously decided, that her husband's success would be at her brother's expense is impossible to tell. As early as 1513, she witnessed an indenture between her husband and her brother-in-law, Donal MacCarthy Reagh, binding them to support each other against all foes 'except the most illustrious Lord Gerald Earl of Kildare against whom neither of them shall aid the

---

28 *Ormond deeds*, iv, 27.
29 *Ormond deeds*, iv, 43
30 *S.P. Hen. VIII*, II, pt iii, 123.

other or rise up against him by colour of any excuse.'[31] There is no mention of Kildare's heirs in the document. The murder of Sir Robert Talbot, a trusted friend of the Ossorys by one of her brothers, Sir James Fitzgerald, was reported to have caused such a furore, that:

> both sides broke out into open enmity and especially the Countesse of Ossorie, Kildare's sister, a rare woman and able for wisdome to rule a realme ... Here began informations of newe treasons passing to and fro with complaintes and replies.[32]

Certainly by 1525, Kildare in correspondence with the King is trying to explain away a possibly incriminating letter written by him to the Earl of Desmond and forwarded to the King simply to cause trouble 'which letter his sister the Lady of Ormond caused to bee taken from oon of his servantes then lodged in her owne house'.[33] Margaret's own actions lead to a perception of her role which can only be underpinned by an almost contemporary view of Piers Butler as Lord Deputy of Ireland

> in which office being himself (save only in feates of armes) a simple gentle-man, he bare out his honour and the charges of government very worthely, through the singular wisdome of his countesse; a lady of such porte that all estates of the Realme couched unto hir, so politique that nothing was thought substancially debated without hir advice.[34]

During all this time Margaret did not neglect the other aspects of her role – she bore her husband six daughters and three sons, one of whom, Thomas, was murdered with the probable connivance of the Fitzgeralds. Meantime she helped

> plante great civility in ye countyes of Tipperary and Kilkenny & to give good example to ye people of that country brought out of Flanders and other countreys diverse Artificiers, who were daily kept at worke by them in theyr Castle of Kilkenny where they wrought and made diaper, Tapistry, Turkey-carpetts, Cushions and other like workes.[35]

31 *Ormond deeds*, iv, no.16, 11.
32 *Holinshed's Irish chronicle*, 328.
33 *S.P. Hen. VIII*, II, pt iii, 124.
34 *Holinshed's Irish chronicle*, 256.
35 Graves and Prim, *History architecture & antiquities*, 248.

Only someone who was extremely familiar with her husband's affairs would remember a few short months after his death to send to Henry VIII two goshawks as a gift 'since luke as my lord my husband whose sowle Jhesu rest, at tymes delytetd to provide such pleasures in this lande as sholde be acceptable to your Majestie'.[36] Her continuing importance in her own right even three years after her husband's death is attested to by

> a bond of Margaret Fitzgerald, widow Countess Ormond to James Butler Earl of Ormond in sum of 1000 to abide by the award of Sir Gerald Aylmer, Chief Justice of the King's Bench, Sir Thomas Luttrell Knight, Chief Justice of the Common Pleas and one Thomas Howth, secondary justice of the said Bench, concerning the possession of Bellaragged, Donaghmore, the Fenans and Ballynrahan.[37]

Although the precise reasons for this bond are not known as yet, her son James obviously felt sufficiently threatened by her to justify such a pledge. After the death of her husband Margaret's capabilities were officially recognised when an order was made 'whereby the rule of the counties of Kilkenny and Tipperary were committed to the government of the Ladie Dowager of Ormond, Sir Richard Butler, her second son and others'.[38]

Should any doubts regarding the possible political role open to women in the later medieval period still linger, the activities of Margaret Fitzgerald's sister Eleanor can only serve as a further example of the opportunities open to those women who were capable of availing themselves of them. Eleanor managed to get her first husband Donal McCarthy Reagh to sign a pact with her agreeing, amongst other items, that 'she shall have a full half of the whole lordship of the same Donal prince of Carbery'.[39] She is described as

> always knowne and accounted of eche man, that was acquainted of hir conversation of life for a paragon of liberalitie and kindness, in all hir actions vertuous and godly, also in a good quarrel rather stoute than stiffe.[40]

36 *S.P. Henry VIII*, II, pt iii, 222.
37 *Ormond deeds*, iv, 216.
38 Index to Council Book, British Museum, Add. Ms. 4790 (quoted in Hore and Graves, *The social state*, 80).
39 *Ormond deeds*, iv, 13.
40 *Holinshed's Irish chronicle*, 286.

In 1535, herself then a widow, she was offered marriage by Maghnus (or Manus) O'Donnell of Tir Conaill, whose wife, her cousin Joan had just died. Maghnus, dismissed by Lord Ossory as 'a naughtie lewde person',[41] and too far away from Dublin to cause any real trouble, was at first quite unacceptable to Eleanor. However the aftermath of the Kildare rebellion and the need to protect her nephew, Gerald, forced her to change her mind. Obliged to flee from the Pale and hunted by the government, young Gerald had, after a year of wandering through Munster, sought refuge with Eleanor in Carbery. Here,

> considering the distress of hir young nephew, how hee was forced to wander Pilgrimwise from house to house, eschewing the punishment that others deeserved, smarted in his tender years with adversitie, before he was of discretion to enjoy any prosperitie ... [42]

she eventually decided to accept O'Donnell 'with this caveat or promise that he shoulde safely shield and protect the sayde young Gentleman in this his calamitie'.[43] This decision to marry O'Donnell unleashed a flood of official correspondence. Her journey from Carbery to Donegal was the cause of agitated comment, and her arrival in Donegal with her nephew, safely delivered from the clutches of the English caused such alarm in Dublin that the Council wrote to Cromwell 'so as the combination of O'Neill being nere of kin to the said Alianor and Gerald with O'Donylle and them unto whom the Irisshe Scots oft tymes resortithe and in a maner are at their draght and pleasure is moche to be doubted'.[44] The political acumen which led her to negotiate her own alliance with O'Donnell in order to save her nephew, led her a year later to repudiate this alliance when she suspected O'Donnell of treachery. She succeeded by her own initiative in spiriting young Gerald away to the continent

> had hir nephew disguised storing him like a liberall and bountifull Aunt, with seven score Porteguises not only in valoure but also in coyne, incontinently shipped him secretely in a Brytons vessel of Saint Malouse, betaking him to God, and to their charge that accompanied him.[45]

Not content with simply organizing her nephew's safe removal from

41 *S.P. Henry VIII*, II, pt iii, 299.
42 *Holinshed's Irish chronicle*, 286.
43 Ibid., 287.
44 *S.P. Henry VIII*, II, pt iii, 299.
45 *Holinshed's Irish chronicle*, 287.

Ireland, Eleanor next decided to deal with Maghnus O'Donnell and his perceived failure to honour their marriage agreement. Reminding him fairly sharply that the only reason she agreed to marry him was to gain protection for her helpless nephew and that O'Donnell

> should well vnderstande, that as the feare of his daunger mooued hir to annere to such a clownish Curmudgen, so the assuraunce of his safetie should cause hir to sequester hirselfe from so butcherly a cutthrote, that would be like a pelting mercenarie patche hyred, to sell or betray the innocent bloud ... [46]

of their young relative. Having delivered herself of this masterly indictment of O'Donnell's character, Eleanor 'trussing vp bag and baggage, she forsooke Odoneyle and returned to hir countrey'.[47] Despite this provocative political behaviour, in 1545 she successfully petitioned for a royal pardon, having received a safe conduct from the government 'in respect of the tyme, to allure her from any practyse in the southe parties, wheare greate brute ys of the arryvall of the Frenchmen'.[48] Whatever the details of Eleanor's relationship with O'Donnell, and her success in getting her nephew safely to the continent, the fact that she herself was regarded as a serious threat to Anglo-Irish relations is perfectly clear.

> By the pestiferous working of this O'Donnylle's wife (Eleanor) the Erle of Kildare's sister they whoos auncesters were ever at discencyon bee made oon ... so that there never was seen in Ireland so great a hoost of Irishmen and Scottes both of the outer Yles and of the Mayne land of Scotland.[49]

With the inclusion of the Earl of Desmond and his allies, Eleanor's achievement can only be described as unique.

To some degree, Margaret's efforts with regard to acquiring the earldom of Ormond for her husband could be construed as family business and well within her preserve as his wife and mother of his sons, and would probably be regarded by contemporaries as part of the networking indulged in by other women of her calibre and status, as indeed would Eleanor's involvement on behalf of her nephew. The correspondence of Lady Honor de Lisle, wife of the Governor of Calais[50] gives a very clear insight into what was obviously regarded as the role of the wife of a polit-

---

46 Ibid., 287.
47 Ibid., 287
48 *S.P. Henry VIII*, II, pt iii, 520.

49 *S.P. Henry VIII*, II, pt iii, 415.
50 Byrne, *The Lisle letters*.

ical figure – forced as she was by the accepted standard of the period to operate at a secondary level. However, both Margaret and Eleanor Fitzgerald took this support a stage further. All of the women referred to in this essay were capable and courageous – some of them were highly intelligent. They all operated within a society circumscribed by conventions which on the one hand regarded them as creatures of little account, and on the other, forced them to operate within such restricted fields that the force of their influence, by concentrating it within such narrow boundaries was even more marked. All of them operated within the system as adjuncts of their menfolk. Eleanor Fitzgerald, a widow, was forced to marry again in order to work through her husband. Major factors in the retention of successive Earls of Kildare as chief governor in Ireland, despite regular advice to the contrary, were lack of effective alternative candidates for the job and the control they were seen to exercise through their network of alliances, particularly amongst the Gaelic Irish. These alliances, in the main, had been built up by a carefully planned network of marriages. Marriage was one of the most potent weapons in the battle for family aggrandisement. On the whole the system worked very well, spectacularly well when women were able to make the system work for them. Eleanor Fitzgerald, by negotiating her own marriage contract, not only saved her brother's heir, but caused serious alarm in the Dublin government as well. Margaret, caught within the system, was forced ultimately to choose between her husband and brother. The fact that she rejected the normally-held pattern of working for her own family rather than that of her husband is a tribute to her courage and individuality. The outcome of her decision testifies to her ability despite the fact that

> she sticked not to abuse hir husbande's honor against hir brother's folly, notwithstanding I learne not that she practised his vndoing (which ensewed ...) but that she by indirect meanes lifted hir brother out of credite, to aduance hir husband, the common voyce and the thing it selfe speaketh.[51]

51 *Holinshed's Irish chronicle*, 256.

Bibliography

PRINTED SOURCES

AL = *Ancient laws of Ireland*, ed. W. Hancock et al., 6 vols, Dublin 1865–1901.
Accounts of the Lord High Treasurer of Scotland vol. IV (1507–1513), ed. J. Balfour Paul (Edinburgh, 1902).
Amt, Emilie, ed., *Women's lives in medieval Europe: a sourcebook*, New York and London 1993.

ANNALS

A.L.C. *Annals of Loch Cé, The*, ed. W.M. Hennessy, 2 vols, London 1871.
A.F.M. *Annála Ríoghachta Éireann, Annals of the Kingdom of Ireland by ... the Four Masters.*, ed. J. O'Donovan, 7 vols, Dublin 1851.
A.I. *Annals of Inisfallen*, ed. S. MacAirt, Dublin 1951.
A.U. *Annála Uladh, Annals of Ulster*, ed. W.M. Hennessy and B. MacCarthy, 4 vols, Dublin 1887–1901.
Ann. Conn. *Annála Connacht: The Annals of Connacht (A.D. 1224–1544)*, ed. A. Martin Freeman, Dublin 1944.
Ann. Clonm. *Annals of Clonmacnoise, being annals of Ireland from the earliest period to A.D. 1408, The*, trans. Connell Mageoghagan, ed. Denis Murphy, Dublin 1896.
Ann. Clyn. *Annals of Ireland by Friar John Clyn and Thady Dowling, together with the annals of Ross, The*, ed. Richard Butler, Dublin 1849.
Ann. MacFirbis 'The Annals of Ireland, from the year 1443 to 1468, translated by ... Duald MacFirbis', ed. J. O'Donovan, *Miscellany of the Irish Archaeological Society* I (Dublin 1846), 198–302.
'MacCarthaigh's Book', *Miscellaneous Irish Annals*, ed. S. Ó hInnse, Dublin 1947, 2–115.

Bieler, Ludwig, ed., *The Irish penitentials*. Scriptores Latini Hiberniae V, Dublin 1963.
Binchy, D.A. ed., '*Bretha Crólige*', *Ériu* 12 (1938) 1–77.
——, *Críth Gablach*, Mediaeval and Modern Irish Series vol. XI, Dublin 1941.
——, ed., *Corpus Iuris Hibernici*, 6 vols, Dublin 1978.
Braga, Theophilo, *Contos tradicionaes do Povo Portuguez com uno Estudo Sobre a Novellistica Geral e Notas Comparativas, Historias e Exemplos de Thema Tradicional e Forma Litteraria*, Porto, 1890, vol. II.
Breatnach, Liam, ed., *Uraicecht na Ríar. The poetic grades in early Irish law*, Early Irish Law Series, vol. 2, Dublin 1987.
Brewer, J.S. and Howlett, R., eds, *Monumenta franciscana*, 2 vols, Rolls Series, London, 1858–82.

Burgess, Glyn S. and Busby, Keith, trans., *Lais of Marie de France*, Harmondsworth, 1986.

Byrne, St Clair S., ed., *The Lisle letters*, vols I–VI, Chicago, 1981.

CCH = *Collectio Canonum Hibernensis*, ed. H. Wasserschleben, *Die irische Kanonensammlung*, second ed., Leipzig 1885.

CIH = *Corpus Iuris Hibernici*, ed. D.A. Binchy, 6 vols, Dublin 1978.

CL = '*Cáin Lánamna*: "Die Regelung der Paare"', ed. Rudolf Thurneysen, in *Studies in early Irish law*, ed. D.A. Binchy, Dublin 1936, 1–80.

Calder, George, *Auraicept na nÉces: the scholar's primer*, Edinburgh 1917.

Calendar of chancery warrants ... 1244–1326, London 1927.

Cal. doc. Ire. = *Calendar of documents relating to Ireland ... 1171–[1307]*, eds H.S. Sweetman and G.F. Handcock, 5 vols, London 1875–86.

Cal. inq. post. mort = *Calendars of inquisitions post mortem and other analogous documents ... Henry III – [15 Richard II]*, 16 vols, London 1909–74.

Calendar of patent rolls of Ireland, I: *Hen. VIII – Eliz.*, ed. James Morrin, Dublin 1861.

Calendar of the Carew manuscripts V–Book of Howth and Miscellaneous, eds J.S. Brewer and W. Bullen, London 1871.

Calendar of the Carew manuscripts preserved in the archiepiscopal library at Lambeth, eds J.S. Brewer and W. Bullen, 6 vols, London 1867–73.

Calendar of the close rolls ... 1272–[1509], 47 vols, London 1892–1963.

Calendar of the fine rolls ... 1272–[1509], 22 vols, London 1911–62.

Calendar of the justiciary rolls ... of Ireland ... Edward I [1295–1307], ed. James Mills, 2 vols, Dublin 1905–14.

Calendar of the justiciary rolls of Ireland: I to VII years of Edward II, eds Herbert Wood and A.E. Langman; revised by M.C. Griffith, Dublin [1956].

Calendar of the patent rolls ... 1232–[1509], 53 vols, London 1891–1971.

Carney, James, *Studies in Irish literature and history*, Dublin 1955; repr. 1979.

——, *Medieval Irish lyrics*, Dublin 1967.

——, ed., *The poems of Blathmac son of Cú Brettan together with the Irish Gospel of Thomas*, Dublin 1964.

——, 'Two poems from *Acallam na Senórach*', *Celtic Studies: Essays in memory of Angus Matheson, 1912–1962*, eds J. Carney and D. Greene, London 1968, 22–32.

Carte, Thomas, *An history of the life of James duke of Ormonde*, 3 vols, London 1735–6.

Chart, D.A., ed., *The Register of John Swayne, archbishop of Armagh, 1418–1439*, Belfast 1935.

Chartularies of St Mary's abbey, Dublin; with the register of its house at Dunbrody, and annals of Ireland, ed. J.T. Gilbert, 2 vols, London 1884.

Cicero, trans. W.A. Falconer, *De senectute, De amicitia, De divinatione*, Loeb Classical Library, London and Cambridge, Mass. 1959.

Clark, J.W., ed., *Liber memorandorum ecclesie de Bernewelle*, Cambridge, 1907.

Close rolls of the reign of Henry III ... 1227–[1272], 14 vols, London 1902–38.

Crane, T.F., ed., *The exempla or illustrative stories from the 'Sermones Vulgares' of Jacques de Vitry*, New York 1890.

Davis, N., ed., *Paston letters and papers of the fifteenth century*, 2 vols, Oxford 1971, 1976.

de Beaulieu, Marie Anne Polo, *Edition et étude d'un receuil d'exempla du XIVe siècle: la 'Scala Celi' de Jean Gobi*, doctoral thesis, École des Hautes Études en Sciences Sociales, Paris 1984.

DIL = *Dictionary of the Irish Language: based mainly on Old and Middle Irish materials*, ed. E.G. Quin et al, Royal Irish Academy, Dublin 1913–1976, compact edition 1983.

Dobbs, Margaret E., ed., 'The *Ban-Shenchus*', *Revue Celtique*, XLVII, 1930, 282–339; XLVIII, 1931, 163–234; XLIX, 1932, 437–89.

Drew, Katherine Fisher, ed., *The Lombard laws*, Philadelphia 1973.

Dugdale, W., ed., *Monasticon Anglicanum*, revised J. Caley, H. Ellis and B. Bandinel, 6 vols, London 1817–30.

Edwards, J.G., ed., *Calendar of Ancient Correspondence concerning Wales*, Board of Celtic Studies, University of Wales History and Law Series, II, Cardiff 1935.

——, ed., *Littere Wallie*, Board of Celtic Studies, University of Wales History and Law Series, V, Cardiff 1940.

Falkiner, C. Litton, ed., *Illustrations of Irish history and topography*, London 1904.

Freeman, A.M., *see* Annals.

Furnivall, F.J., ed., *The fifty earliest English wills*, Early English Text Society, original series LXXVIII, London 1882.

Gairdner, J., ed., *Paston letters*, London 1904.

Gransden, A., ed., *The chronicle of Bury St Edmunds, 1212–1301*, Edinburgh 1964.

Greene, David., ed., *Fingal Rónáin and other stories*, Mediaeval and Modern Irish Series vol. XVI, Dublin 1955.

Hancock, W. et al., eds, *Ancient laws of Ireland*, 6 vols, Dublin 1865–1901.

Hanning, R. and Ferrante, J., trans., *The Lais of Marie de France*, Durham, N.C. 1982.

Hart, Mother Columba and Bishop, Jane, trans., *Hildegard of Bingen: Scivias*, New York 1990.

Haureau, B., *Notices et extraits de quelques MSS latins de la BN*, VI, Paris 1890–3 (reprint 1967).

Hector, L.C. and Harvey, B.F., *The Westminster chronicle, 1381–94*, Oxford 1982.

Hennessy, W.M., *see* Annals.

Holinshed, Raphael and Stanyhurst, Richard, *Chronicles of England, Scotlande and Irelande*, London 1577.

Holinshed's Irish chronicle, eds L. Miller and E. Power, Dublin, 1979.

Horwood A.V., ed., *Year Books 20–1 Edward I*, Rolls Series, London 1866.

Hull, Vernam, ed., '*Bretha im Gatta*', *Zeitschrift für celtische Philologie* 25 (1956), 211–25.

——, *Longes Mac nUislenn: the exile of the sons of Uisliu*, New York 1949.

IR = Rudolf Thurneysen, *Irisches Recht* (I *Díre*. Ein altirischer Rechtstext; II Zu den unteren Ständen in Irland). Abhandelungen der preussischen Akademie der Wissenschaften, 1931. Phil.-hist. Klasse 2. (Berlin 1931).

Irish historical documents 1172–1922, eds E. Curtis and R.B. MacDowell, London 1943.

Jackson, K.H., ed., *A celtic miscellany* (revised ed.), Harmondsworth 1971.

Johnstone, H., ed., *Letters of Edward prince of Wales, 1304–5*, Cambridge 1931.

Kibler, William W., trans., *Chretien de Troyes – Arthurian romances*, London 1991.

Kingsford, C.L., ed., *The Stonor letters and papers, 1290–1483*, 2 vols, Camden Society, third series, XXIX, XXX, London 1919.

Legge, M.D., ed., *Anglo-Norman letters and petitions*, Anglo-Norman Text Society, III, Oxford 1941.

Letters & papers illustrative of the reigns of Richard III & Henry VII, I–III, ed. J. Gairdner, London 1861–3.

Letters and papers foreign and domestic Henry VIII, I–XXVIII, eds J. Gairdner and J. Brodie, London 1862–1932.

Lisle letters, I–V, ed. E. Curtis, Dublin 1935.

Little, A.G., ed., *Liber exemplorum ad usum predicantium*, Edinburgh 1898.

LL = *The Book of Leinster (T.C.D. MS no.1339 - H.2.18)*, ed. R.I. Best et al., 6 vols, Dublin 1954–83.

Lloyd, L.C. and Stenton, D.M., eds, *Sir Christopher Hatton's book of seals*, Oxford 1950.

Lodge, E.C. and Somerville, R., eds, *John of Gaunt's register, 1379–83*, 2 vols, Camden Society, third series, LVI, LVII, London 1937.

LU = *Lebor na hUidre, 'The Book of the Dun Cow' (R.I.A. MS no.226 - 234/25)*, ed. R.I. Best and O. Bergin, Dublin, 1929.

Luard, H.R., ed., *Annales monastici*, 5 vols, Rolls Series, London 1864–9.

MacCarthy, B., *see* Annals.

MacLysaght, E., ed., *The Kenmare manuscripts*, Dublin 1942, repr. Shannon 1970.

Maxwell, C., ed., *Irish history from contemporary sources 1509–1610*, London 1925.

Meyer, Kuno, ed., *Cáin Adamnáin: An Old Irish treatise on the law of Adamnan*, Oxford 1905.

——, 'Mitteilungen aus irischen Handschriften', *Zeitschrift für Celtische Philologie* 7 (1909), 297–312.

——, 'Mitteilungen aus irischen Handschriften', *Zeitschrift für Celtische Philologie* 13 (1921), 3–30.

——, ed., *The triads of Ireland*, Todd Lecture Series XIII, Dublin 1906.

Murphy, D., *see* Annals.

Nicolas, N.H., ed., *Proceedings and ordinances of the Privy Council of England*, 7 vols, Record Commission, London 1834–7.

Nichols, J., ed., *A Collection of all the wills of the kings and queens of England*, London 1780.

O'Donoghue, Tadhg, ed., 'Advice to a prince', *Ériu* IX, 1921–3, 43–54.

O'Donovan, J., *see* Annals.

Ó hInnse, S., *see* Annals.

O'Keeffe, J.G., ed., *Buile Shuibhne*, Dublin 1931, repr. 1975.

O'Rahilly, Cecile, ed., *Táin Bó Cúalnge from the Book of Leinster*, Dublin 1967.

O'Rahilly, T.F., ed., *Dánta Grádha: an anthology of Irish love poetry (A.D. 1350–1750)*, revised and expanded edition, Cork 1926.

Ormond deeds, Calendar of, ed. E. Curtis, 6 vols, Irish Manuscripts Commission, Dublin 1932–43.

O'Shea, Rev. K., ed., 'A Castelisland inventory', in *Journal of the Kerry Archaeological and Historical Society* XV–XVI, 1982–3, 37–46.

Parry, J.J., trans., *The art of courtly love: Andreas Capellanus*, New York 1941.

Plummer, Charles, ed., *Vitae sanctorum Hiberniae*, 2 vols, Oxford 1910, repr. 1968.

——, ed., *Bethada Náem nÉrenn: lives of Irish saints*, 2 vols, Oxford 1922, repr. 1968.

Power, E., trans., *The Goodman of Paris*, Folio Society, London 1993.

Quiggin, E.C., *Poems from the book of the Dean of Lismore*, Cambridge, 1937.

Radice, Betty, trans., *The letters of Abelard and Heloise*, Harmondsworth 1974.

Records of the parliament holden at Westminster, A.D. 1305, ed. F.W. Maitland, London 1893.

Red book of the earls of Kildare, The, ed. Gearóid Mac Niocaill, Dublin 1964.

Redstone, V.B., ed., and Dale, M.K., trans., *The Household book of Dame Alice de Bryene of Acton Hall, Suffolk, September 1412–September 1413*, Suffolk Institute of Archaeology and Natural History, Ipswich 1931.

Richardson, H.G. and Sayles, G.O., eds, *Rotuli parliamentorum Anglie hactenus inediti*, MCCLXXIX–MCCCLXXIII, London 1935.

Robertson, J.C., ed., *Materials for the history of Thomas Becket*, 7 vols, Rolls Series, London 1875–85.

Robbins, Harry W., trans., *The romance of the rose by Guillaume de Lorris and Jean de Meun*, New York 1962.

Rot. pat. Hib. = Rotulorum patentium et clausorum cancellarie Hiberniae calendarium [ed. Edward Tresham], Dublin 1828.

Rotuli parliamentorum ... [1278–1503], 7 vols [London 1783–1832].

Rotulorum patentium et clausorum cancellarie Hiberniae calendarium [ed. Edward Tresham], Dublin 1828.

Rutebeuf, *La Complainte d'Outre Mer*, in *Oeuvres Completes de Rutebeuf*, E. Faral et J. Bastin, eds, Paris 1969.

Rymer's foedera, 1066–1383, eds A. Clarke, J. Caley, J. Bayley, F. Holbrooke and J.W. Clarke, 4 vols, Record Commission, London 1816–69.

Shirley, W.W., ed., *Royal letters, Henry III*, 2 vols, Rolls Series, London 1862–6.

Smith, A., ed., 'A brief description of Ireland: 1590', *Tracts relating to Ireland published by the Irish Archaeological Society* I, Dublin 1841 (separately paginated).

Stapleton, T., ed., *Plumpton correspondence*, Camden Society, old series, IV, London 1839.

State Papers, Henry VIII: Correspondence, vol. II, parts iii & iv, London 1834.

Stevenson, J., ed., *Chronicon de Lanercost*, Bannatyne Club, LXV, Edinburgh 1839.

Stokes, W., ed., *Cóir Anmann, Irische Texte*, eds W. Stokes and E. Windisch, 3.2 (1897), 285–444.

—— and Strachan, J., eds, *Thesaurus palaeohibernicus*, 2 vols, Dublin 1901–3.

—— and Windisch, E., eds, *Irische Texte* 3.2, Leipzig 1897.

——, ed., *Félire Oengusso Céli Dé: the martrytrology of Oengus the Culdee*, London, 1905, reprinted Dublin 1984.

Strachan, John, 'Two monastic rules', *Ériu* II, 1905, 227–9.

Thiébaux, Marcelle, *The writings of medieval women*, New York and London 1987.

Thompson, Stith, *Motif-index of folk literature*, 6 vols, Bloomington, Indiana, 1932–36.

Thorpe, Lewis trans., *Gerald of Wales: The journey through Wales and the description of Wales*, Harmondsworth 1978.

Virgoe, Roger, ed., *Illustrated letters of the Paston family*, London 1989.

Ward, Jennifer, ed. and trans., *Women of the English nobility and gentry 1066–1500*, Manchester 1995.

Woolgar, C.M., ed., *Household accounts from medieval England*, 2 vols, British Academy Records of Social and Economic History, new series, XVII, XVIII, Oxford 1992–3.

SECONDARY WORKS

Acheson, E., *A gentry community: Leicestershire in the fifteenth century, c.1422–c.1485*, Cambridge 1992.

Allen, P.L., *The art of love. Amatory fiction from Ovid to the romance of the rose*, Philadelphia 1992.

Altschul, M., *A baronial family in medieval England: the Clares, 1217–1314*, Baltimore 1965.

Anderson, B.S. and Zinsser, J.P., *A history of their own*, London 1988.

Archer, R.E., '"How ladies ... who live on their manors ought to manage their households and estates": women as landholders and administrators in the later Middle Ages', *Woman is a worthy wight: women in English society c.1200–1500*, ed. P.J.P. Goldberg, Stroud 1992, 149–81.

—— and Ferme, B.E., 'Testamentary procedure with special reference to the executrix', *Medieval women in southern England*, Reading Medieval Studies, XV, 1989, 3–34

Aries, P., trans. Baldick, R., *Centuries of childhood*, London 1962.

——, *L'homme devant la mort*, Paris, 1977: translated as *The hour of our death* by Helen Weaver, London, 1981.

——, 'The indissoluble marriage', *Western sexuality: practice and precept in past and present times*, eds Philippe Ariès and André Béjin, trans. Anthony Forster, Oxford 1985, 140–57.

Aston, M., *Thomas Arundel*, Oxford 1967.

Bagwell, R., *Ireland under the Tudors*, I, London 1885.

Baldwin, John W., 'Five discourses on desire: sexuality and gender in Northern France around 1200', *Speculum* LXVI, 1991, 797–819.

——, *The language of sex: five voices from northern France around 1200*, Chicago 1994.

Bartlett, Robert, *Gerald of Wales 1146–1223*, Oxford 1982.

Bateman, Meg, 'The Gaelic tradition', *An anthology of Scottish women poets*, ed. C. Kerrigan, Edinburgh 1991, 12–113, 336–43.

Baumgarten, R., ' "*Cr(a)ide hé* ... " and the early Irish copulà sentence', *Ériu* 45 (1994), 121–6.

Bauml, Franz, 'Transformations of the heroine: from epic heard to epic read', *The role of women in the Middle Ages*, ed. Rosemarie Morewedge, New York 1975, 23–40.

Belanoff, Patricia A., 'Women's songs, women's language: *Wulf and Eadwacer* and *The wife's lament*', *New readings*, eds Damico and Olsen, 193–203.

Bennett, H.S., *The Pastons and their England*, Cambridge 1990.

Benton, G.M., 'Essex wills at Canterbury', *Transactions of the Essex Archaeological Society*, new series, XXI, 1933–7, 234–69.

Benton, John F., 'Clio and Venus: an historical view of medieval love', *The meaning of courtly love*, ed. F.X. Newman, New York 1973, 19–42.

——, 'The court of Champagne as a literary center', *Speculum* XXXVI, 1961, 551–91.

Bernard, J.H., and Atkinson, R., *The Irish liber hymnorum*, 2 vols, London 1897.

Best, R. I. and Bergin, O., eds, '*Tochmarc Etaíne*', *Ériu* XII, 1938, 137–96.

Binchy, D.A., ed., *Studies in early Irish law*, Dublin 1936.

——, 'The legal capacity of women in regard to contracts', *Studies in early Irish law*, ed. D.A. Binchy, Dublin 1936, 207–34.

Bitel, Lisa, 'Women's donations to the churches in early Ireland', *Journal of the Royal Society of Antiquaries of Ireland* CXIV, 1984, 5–23.

——, 'Women's monastic enclosures in early Ireland: a study of female spirituality and male monastic mentalities', *Journal of Medieval History* XII, 1986, 15–36.

Blair, C.H. Hunter, 'Armorials on English seals from the twelfth to the sixteenth centuries', *Archaeologia*, LXXXIX, 1943, 1–26.

Bloch, R.H., *Medieval misogyny and the invention of western romantic love*, Chicago and London 1991.

Blumenthal, Uta-Renate, ed., *Carolingian essays: Andrew W. Mellon lectures in early Christian studies*, Washington 1983.

Boase, R., *The origin and meaning of courtly love*, Manchester 1977.

Bogdanow, F., 'The love theme in Chrétien de Troyes' *Chavelier de la charette*', *Modern Language Review*, LXVII, 1972, 50–61.

Bradshaw, B., 'Cromwellian reform and the origins of the Kildare rebellion 1533–1534', *Transactions of the Royal Historical Society*, 5th Series, XXVII, 1978,

——, *Irish constitutional revolution of the sixteenth century*, Cambridge 1979.

Bragg, Lois, *The lyric speakers of Old English poetry*, London/Toronto 1991.

Brémond, C., Le Goff, J., and Schmitt J.-Cl., *L'Exemplum*, La Typologie des Sources du Moyen Age Occidental vol. XL, dir. L. Génicot and R. Bultot, Tournhout 1982.

Brooke, C., 'Aspects of marriage law in the eleventh and twelfth centuries', *Proceedings of the 5th International Congress of Medieval Canon Law*, Salamanca 1976, publ. Vatican city, 1980, 333–44.

——, *The medieval idea of marriage*, Oxford 1989.

Brooks, E. St J., 'The family of Marisco', *Journal of the Royal Society of Antiquaries of Ireland*, LXII, 1932, 50–74.

——, 'The de Ridelesfords', *Journal of the Royal Society of Antiquaries of Ireland*, LXXXII, 1952, 45–61.

Bruckner, Matilda Tomaryn, 'Fictions of the female voice: the women troubadours', *Speculum* LXVII, 1992, 865–91.

Brundage, James A., 'Concubinage and marriage in medieval canon law', *Journal of Medieval History* I, 1975, 1–17.

——, *Law, sex, and Christian society in medieval Europe*, Chicago and London 1987.

Burgess, Glyn, S., *The Lais of Marie de France. Text and context*, Georgia 1987.

——, *Marie de France: an analytical bibliography*, London 1977.

Bryan, D., *Gerald Fitzgerald, The Great Earl of Kildare*. Dublin, 1935.

Burns, E. Jane, *Bodytalk: When women speak in Old French literature*, Philadelphia 1993.

Bynum, Caroline Walker, 'The female body and religious practice in the later middle ages', *Fragments for a history of the human body, part one* ed. M. Feher et al., New York 1989, 160–219.

Carney, James, 'The so-called "Lament of Créidhe"', *Éigse* XIII, 1969–70, 227–42.

Chabod, I., 'Widowhood and poverty in late medieval Florence', *Continuity and Change* III, 1988, 291–311.

Chambers, Anne, *As wicked a woman: the biography of Eleanor, Countess of Desmond*, Dublin 1986.

Charles-Edwards, Thomas M., 'Review article: the *Corpus Iuris Hibernici*', *Studia Hibernica* XX, 1980, 141–62.

——, *Early Irish and Welsh kinship*, Oxford 1993.

——, Owen, M.E. and Walters, D.B., eds, *Lawyers and laymen: studies in the history of law presented to professor Dafydd Jenkins*, Cardiff 1986.

Chojnacki, S., 'Dowries and kinsmen in early Renaissance Venice', *Journal of Interdisciplinary History* V, 1975, 571–600.

——, 'Patrician women in Renaissance Venice', *Studies in the Renaissance* XXI, 1974, 176–203.

——, 'The power of love: wives and husbands in late medieval Venice', *Women and power in the Middle Ages*, eds M. Erler and M. Kowaleski, Athens, Ga. and London 1988, 126–48.

Clanchy, Michael., *England and her rulers*, London 1983.

Clancy, Thomas Owen, 'Saint and fool: the image and function of Cummíne Fota and Comgán Mac Da Cherda in early Irish literature', unpublished Ph.D. thesis, University of Edinburgh, 1991.

——, 'Fools and adultery in some early Irish texts', *Ériu* XLIV, 1993, 105–24.

Classen, Albrecht, ed., *Women as protagonists and poets in the German middle ages: an anthology of feminist approaches to Middle High German literature*, Göppingen 1991.

Cohn, S., *The laboring classes in Renaissance Florence*, New York 1980.
——, *Death and property in Siena, 1205–1800: strategies for the afterlife*, Baltimore and London 1988.
Conway, A., *Henry VII's relations with Scotland and Ireland 1485–1498*, Cambridge 1932.
Cormier, R., 'The maddening rain: a comparison of the Irish and Provençal versions', *Éigse* XI, 1966, 247–51.
Cosgrove, A., ed., *New History of Ireland*, vol. II, Dublin 1987.
——, ed., *Marriage in Ireland*, Dublin 1985.
Crabb, A.M., 'How typical was Alessandra Macinghi Strozzi of fifteenth-century Florentine widows?', *Upon my husband's death: widows in the history and literature of medieval Europe*, ed. L. Mirrer, Ann Arbor 1992, 47–68.
Craig, D.V., 'The memoranda roll of the Irish exchequer for 3 Edward II', 2 vols, Ph.D. thesis, University of Dublin, 1984.
Croker, T. Crofton, *Researches in the south of Ireland*, London 1824.
Cross, T. Peete, *Motif index of early Irish literature*, Bloomington, Indiana [1952], reprint Kraus 1969.
Crossland, J., *Medieval French literature*, Oxford 1956.
Cunningham, Bernadette, 'Women and Gaelic literature, 1500–1800', *Women in early modern Ireland*, eds Margaret MacCurtain and Mary O'Dowd, Dublin 1991, 147–59.
Curtis, E., *History of medieval Ireland 1086–1513*, 2nd ed., London 1938.
——, ed., *Ormond deeds*, I–V, Dublin, 1935, 1985.
Damico, Helen and Olsen, Alexandra Hennessey, eds, *New readings on women in Old English literature*, Indiana 1990.
Damon, S.F., 'Marie de France, psychologist of courtly love', *Publications of the Modern Language Association of America* XLIV (1929), 968–96.
Davies, Wendy, 'Celtic women in the early Middle Ages', in *Images of women in antiquity*, eds Averil Cameron and Amélie Kuhrt, London, 1983, 145–66.
Davis, Natalie Zemon, *Society and culture in early modern France*, Stanford 1965.
——, *The return of Martin Guerre*, Cambridge, Mass. and London 1983.
Delumeau, Jean, *La peur en occident (XIVè–XVIIIè siècles)*, Paris 1978.
de Paor, Liam, *St Patrick's world: the Christian culture of Ireland's apostolic age*, Dublin 1993.
de Roover, R., *The rise and decline of the Medici bank 1397–1494*, Cambridge, Mass., 1963.
Desmond, Marilynn, 'The voice of exile: feminist literary history and the anonymous Anglo-Saxon elegy', *Critical Inquiry* XVI (1990), 572–90.
Dillon, Myles, 'The relationship of mother and son, of father and daughter, and the law of inheritance with regard to women', *Studies in early Irish law*, ed. D.A. Binchy, Dublin 1936, 129–79.
Donahue, Charles Jr., 'The policy of Alexander the Third's consent theory of marriage', *Proceedings of the Fourth International Congress of Medieval Canon Law Toronto, 21–25 August 1972*, ed. Stephen Kuttner, Vatican 1976, 251–81.
——, 'The canon law on the formation of marriage and social practice in the later Middle Ages', *Journal of Family History* VIII, 1983, 144–89.

Dronke, P., *The medieval lyric*, 2nd ed., London 1978.

——, *Women writers of the Middle Ages*, Cambridge 1984.

Duby, Georges, *Love and marriage in the Middle Ages*, trans. Jane Dunnett, Chicago 1994.

——, *Medieval marriage – Two models from twelfth century France*, trans. Elborg Forster, Baltimore 1991.

——, *Le chevalier, la femme et le prêtre*, Paris 1981: translated as *The knight, the lady and the priest; the making of modern marriage in medieval France* by Barbara Bray, London 1984.

Duggan, Charles, 'Equity and compassion in papal marriage decretals to England', *Love and marriage in the twelfth century*, Mediaevalia Lovaniensia Ser I/ Studia VIII, Leuven 1981, 59–87.

Ellis, S., *Tudor Ireland*, London 1985.

——, 'Tudor policy and the Kildare ascendancy', *Irish Historical Studies*, XX, 1977, 235–71.

Elton, G.R., *England under the Tudors*, London 1977.

Empey, C.A., 'The settlement of the kingdom of Limerick', *England and Ireland in the later middle ages*, ed. J.F. Lydon, Dublin 1981, 1–25.

Epstein, S., *Wills and wealth in medieval Genoa 1150–1250*, Cambridge, Mass. and London 1984.

Erler, M. & Kowaleski, M., eds, *Women and power in the Middle Ages*, London 1988.

Fairbank, F.R., 'The last earl of Warenne and Surrey and the distribution of his possessions', *Yorkshire Archaeological Journal*, XIX, 1907, 193–264.

Fell, Christine, *Women in Anglo-Saxon England*, London 1984.

Ferrante, J., *Women as image in medieval literature*, New York 1975.

——, 'The education of women in the Middle Ages in theory, fact and fancy', *Beyond their Sex: learned women of the European past*, ed. P. Labalme, New York and London 1980, 9–42.

Flower, R., 'A Franciscan bard', *Dublin Review* CLXVIII, 1921, 221–8.

——, *Catalogue of Irish Manuscripts in the British Museum* vol. II, London, 1926.

Frame, R. F., *Colonial Ireland, 1169–1369*, Dublin 1981.

——, *English lordship in Ireland, 1318–61*, Oxford 1982.

——, 'Ireland and the barons' war' *Thirteenth-century England*, eds P.R. Ross and S.D. Lloyd, Woodbridge 1986, 158–67.

Frater, A., 'Scottish Gaelic women's poetry up to 1750' unpublished Ph.D. thesis, University of Glasgow, 1994.

G. E. C., *Peerage, see* Gibbs, Vicary et al., *Cokayne's Complete Peerage*.

Gallwey, H., 'The Cusack family of cos. Meath and Dublin', *The Irish Genealogist*, V, 1974–8.

Gibbs, Vicary et al., *Cokayne's complete peerage of England, Scotland, Ireland, Great Britain and the United Kingdom*, 13 vols, London 1910–59.

Gies, Frances, and Gies, Joseph, *Marriage and the family in the Middle Ages*, New York 1978.

Giffin, M.E., 'A Wigmore manuscript at the University of Chicago', *National Library of Wales Journal* VII, 1951–2, 316–25.

Gillies, William, 'Courtly and satiric poems in the Book of the Dean of Lismore', *Scottish Studies* XXI, 1977, 35–53.

——, 'Gaelic poems of Sir Duncan Campbell of Glenorchy (III)', *Scottish Gaelic Studies* XIV, 1983, 59–82.

Giuseppi, M.S., 'On the testament of Sir Hugh de Nevill, written at Acre, 1267', *Archaeologia* LVI, part 2, 1899, 351–70.

Glover, Helen and Gibson, Margaret, eds, *The letters of Lanfranc, archbishop of Canterbury*, Oxford 1979.

Gold, Penny Schine, *The lady and the Virgin: image, attitude and experience in twelfth-century France*, Chicago 1985.

Goodman, A., *John of Gaunt: The exercise of princely power in fourteenth-century Europe*, London 1992.

Goody, Jack, *The development of the family and marriage in Europe*, Cambridge 1983.

Gravdal, Kathryn, *Ravishing maidens writing rape in medieval French literature and law*, Philadelphia 1991.

Graves, J. and Prim, J.G.A., *The history, architecture and antiquities of the cathedral church of St Canice*, Dublin 1857.

Green, D.H., *Irony in the medieval romance*, Cambridge 1979.

Greene, David, 'St Brigid's Alefeast', *Celtica* II, 1954, 150–3.

—— and O'Connor, Frank, *A golden treasury of Irish poetry, AD 600–1200*, London 1967.

Gregory, H., 'Daughters, dowries and the family in fifteenth-century Florence', *Rinascimento* XXVII, 1987, 215–37.

Gwynn, A. and Hadcock, R.N., *Medieval religious houses: Ireland*, London 1970.

Hallam, Elizabeth, *Capetian France, 987–1328*, London 1980.

Hand, G.J., *English law in Ireland, 1290–1324*, Cambridge 1967.

Hanning, R.W., *The individual in twelfth-century romance*, London 1977.

Heers, J., *Family clans in the middle ages*, Amsterdam 1977.

Heist, W.W., *Vita Sanctorum Hiberniae, ex codice olim Salamanticensi nunc Bruxellensi*, Brussels 1965.

Helmholz, R.H., *Marriage litigation in medieval England*, Cambridge 1974.

Henry, P.L., *Dánta Ban: poems of Irish women, early and modern*, Cork 1991.

Herlihy, D., 'Women and the sources of medieval history: the town of Northern Italy', *Medieval women and the sources of medieval history*, ed. J.T. Rosenthal, Athens, Ga, 1990, 133–54.

—— and Klapisch-Zuber, C., *Tuscans and their families: a study of the Florentine catasto of 1427*, New Haven and London 1985.

Holmes, G.A., 'A protest against the Despensers, 1326', *Speculum*, XXX, 1955, 207–12.

Hore, H.J. and Graves, J., *The social state of the southern and eastern counties of Ireland in the sixteenth century*, 3 vols, Dublin 1870.

Horner, Shari, 'En/Closed subjects: the *Wife's lament* and the culture of early medieval female monasticism', *Æstel* II, 1994, 45–62.

——, 'Spiritual truth and sexual violence: the Old English *Juliana*, Anglo-Saxon nuns and the discourse of female enclosure', *Signs* XIX, 1994, 658–75.

Houlbrooke, R.A., *The English family 1450–1700*, London 1984.

Hughes, Diane Owen, 'Domestic ideals and social behavior: evidence from medieval Genoa', *The family in history* ed. C.E. Rosenberg, Philadelphia 1975, 115–43.

——, 'From brideprice to dowry in Mediterranean Europe', *Journal of Family History* III, 1978, 262–96.

——, 'Urban growth and family structure in medieval Genoa', *Past and Present* LXVI, 1975, 3–28.

Hughes, Kathleen, *Early Christian Ireland: introduction to the sources*, Ithaca, NY 1972.

Hull, Veman P., 'The Milesian invasion of Ireland', *Zeitschrzft fü Celtische Philologie* 19 (1932), 155–60.

Ingram, M., *Church courts, sex and marriage in England 1570–1640*, Cambridge 1987.

Jackson, W.T.H., 'The *De Amore* of Andreas Capellanus and the practice of love at court', *Romanis Review* XLIX, 1958, 243–51.

Jaeger, C. Stephen, *The origins of courtliness – civilizing trends and the formation of the courtly ideals – 939–1210*, Philadelphia 1991.

Jenkinson, H., 'Mary de Sancto Paulo, foundress of Pembroke College, Cambridge', *Archaeologia* LXXXVI, 1915, 401–46.

Jones, M., ed., *Gentry and lesser nobility in late medieval Europe*, Gloucester 1987.

Jones M.K. and Underwood, M.G., *The King's Mother: Lady Margaret Beaufort, Countess of Richmond and Derby*, Cambridge 1992.

Kelly, Amy, 'Eleanor of Aquitaine and her Courts of Love', *Speculum* XII, 1937, 3–19.

Kelly, Fergus, *A Guide to early Irish law*, Early Irish Law Series III, Dublin 1988.

Kelly, Patricia, 'The *Táin* as literature', *Aspects of the* Táin, ed. J.P. Mallory, Belfast 1992, 69–102.

King, P.D., *Law and society in the Visigothic kingdom*, Cambridge 1972.

Kirshner, J., *Pursuing honor while avoiding sin: the monte delle doti of Florence*, Milan 1978.

——, 'Wives' claims against insolvent husbands in late medieval Italy', *Women of the medieval world*, eds J. Kirshner and S.F. Wemple, Oxford 1985, 256–303.

—— and Molho, A., 'The dowry fund and the marriage market in early Quattrocento Florence', *Journal of Modern History* L, 1978, 403–38.

—— and Wemple, S.F., *Women of the medieval world*, Oxford 1985.

Klapisch-Zuber, C., 'The "cruel mother": maternity, widowhood and dowry in Florence in the fourteenth and fifteenth centuries', *Women, family and ritual in Renaissance Italy*, 117–31.

——, 'The Griselda complex: dowry and marriage gifts in the Quattrocento', *Women, family and ritual in Renaissance Italy*, 213–46.

——, *Women, family and ritual in Renaissance Italy*, trans. Lydia G. Cochrane, Chicago and London, 1985.

—— and Demonet, M., '"A uno pane e uno vino": the rural Tuscan family at the beginning of the fifteenth century', *Women, family and ritual in Renaissance Italy,* 36–67.

Knoch, August, 'Die Ehescheidung in alten irischen Recht' *Studies in early Irish law,* ed. D.A. Binchy, Dublin 1936, 235–68.

Knott, Eleanor, ed., *Togail Bruidne Da Derga,* Mediaeval and Modern Irish Series VIII, Dublin 1936.

Kuehn, T., '"Cum consensu mundualdi": legal guardianship of women in Quattrocento Florence', *Viator* XIII, 1982, 309–33, reprinted in his *Law, family and women,* 212–37.

——, *Law, family and women: toward a legal anthropology of Renaissance Italy,* Chicago and London 1991.

——, 'Some ambiguities of female inheritance ideology', *Continuity and Change* II, 1987, 11–36, reprinted in his *Law, family and women,* 238–57.

——, 'Women, marriage and *patria potestas* in late medieval Florence', *Tijdschrift voor Rechtsgeschiedenis* XLIX, 1981, 127–47, reprinted in his *Law, family and women,* 197–211.

Lander, J.R., *Government and community: England 1430–1509,* London 1980.

——, 'Marriage and politics in the fifteenth century: the Nevilles and the Wydevilles', *Bulletin of the Institute of Historical Research* XXXVI, 1963, 119–52.

Lapidge, Michael, 'A seventh-century insular Latin debate poem on divorce', *Cambridge Medieval Celtic Studies* X, 1985, 1–23.

Larner, J., *Italy in the age of Dante and Petrarch,* London 1980.

Lehmann, Ruth P.M., 'Woman's songs in Irish, 800–1500, *Vox feminae: studies in medieval woman's song,* ed. John F. Plummer, Kalamazoo, 1981, 111–34.

Lennon, C., *Richard Stanihurst the Dubliner, 1547–1618,* Dublin 1981.

Logan, J., 'Historical introduction', in MacKenzie, *Sar–Obair nam bard Gaelach,* Glasgow 1841.

Löwe, Heinrich, ed., *Die Iren und Europa im frühen Mittelalter,* 2 vols, Tübingen 1982.

Lucas, Angela M., *Women in the Middle Ages. Religion, marriage and letters,* Brighton 1983.

Lydon, J.F., *Ireland in the later Middle Ages,* Dublin 1973.

——, *The lordship of Ireland in the Middle Ages,* Dublin 1972.

——, 'The expansion and consolidation of the colony, 1215–54', *A new history of Ireland* II, ed. Art Cosgrove, Oxford 1987, 156–78.

——, 'The years of crisis, 1254–1315', *A new history of Ireland* II, ed. Art Cosgrove, Oxford 1987, 179–204.

Mac Cormack, Geoffry, 'Inheritance and wergeld in early Germanic law', *Irish Jurist* VIII, 1973, 143–63, IX, 1974, 166–83.

MacCurtain, M. and Ó Corráin, D., eds, *Women in Irish society, the historical dimension,* Dublin 1978.

—— and O'Dowd, M., eds, *Women in early modern Ireland,* Dublin, 1991.

MacLysaght, E., *Irish life in the seventeenth century,* 4th ed., Dublin 1979.

Mac Niocaill, Gearóid, 'Christian influence in early Irish law', *Irland und Europa: Die Kirche in Frühmittelalter,* eds P. Ní Chatháin and M. Richter, Tübingen 1984, 151–6.

Mallory, J.P., ed., *Aspects of the Táin*, Belfast 1992.

Martin, Francis Xavier, 'Ireland in the time of St Bernard, St Malachy, St Laurence O'Toole', *Seanchas Ard Mhacha* XV, 1992, 1–35.

McCone, Kim, 'Dubthach Maccu Lugair and a matter of life and death in the pseudo-historical prologue to the *Senchas Már*', *Peritia* V, 1986, 1–35.

——, *Pagan past and Christian present in early Irish literature*, Maynooth Monographs III, Maynooth 1991.

Mac Craith, M., 'Cioth na Baoise', *Béaloideas* LI, 1983, 31–53.

MacDonald, D., 'Proverbs, sententiae, and exempla in Chaucer's comic tales: the function of comic misapplication', *Speculum* XLI, 1966, 453–65.

MacEoin, Gearóid, 'The life of Cuimine Fota', *Béaloideas* XXXIX–XL, 1971–3, 192–205.

MacKenzie, John, *Sar-obair nam bard Gaelach*, Glasgow 1841.

McKitterick, Rosamund, 'Frauen und Schriftlichkeit im Frühmittelalter', *Weibliche Lebensgestaltung im frühen Mittelalter* ed. H.W. Goetz, Cologne-Weimar 1991, 65–118.

Mac Gill-eain, Somhairle, *Ris a' Bhruthaich: The criticism and prose writings of Sorley MacLean*, ed. W. Gillies, Stornoway 1985.

McLeod, Neil, *Early Irish contract law*, Sydney Series in Celtic Studies I, Sydney 1993.

Márkus, Gilbert, 'Early Irish "feminism"', *New Blackfriars* LXXIII (1992) 375–88.

Martines, L., 'A way of looking at women in Renaissance Florence', *Journal of Medieval and Renaissance Studies* IV, 1974, 15–28.

H.C. Maxwell Lyte, *A history of Dunster*, 2 vols, London, 1909.

Meale, C., *Women and literature in Britain 1150–1500*, Cambridge 1993.

Meek, C.E. , 'Women, the Church and the law: matrimonial litigation in Lucca under bishop Nicolao Guinigi (1394–1435)' in *Chattel, servant or citizen; women's status in state and society*, M. O'Dowd and S. Wichert, eds, Institute of Irish Studies, Belfast, 1995, 82–90.

Meek, Dohmnall E., *Màiri Mhór nan Òran*, Glasgow 1977.

Meyer, Kuno, *Comrac Líadaine ocus Cuirithir: The meeting of Líadain and Cuirithir*, London 1902.

Mickel, E.J., 'A reconsideration of the *Lais* of Marie de France', *Speculum* XLVI, 1971, 39–65.

Molho, A., 'Deception and marriage strategy in Renaissance Florence: the case of women's ages', *Renaissance Quarterly* XLI, 1988, 193–218.

——, *Marriage alliance in late medieval Florence*, Cambridge, Mass. and London 1994.

——, *Social and economic foundations of the Italian Renaissance*, London, New York 1969.

Moody, T.W., ed., *Nationality and the pursuit of national independence*, Belfast 1978.

Moore, J., 'Love in twelfth-century France', *Traditio* XXIV, 1968, 429–42.

Mosher, J.A., *The exemplum in the early religious and didactic literature of England*, New York 1911.

Muir, L.R., *Literature and society in medieval France: the mirror and the image 1100–1500*, London 1985.

Murphy, Gerard, 'The Lament of the Old Woman of Beare', *Proceedings of the Royal Irish Academy* LV, 1953, C, 83–109.

——, *Early Irish lyrics*, Oxford 1956.

Nelson, Janet, 'Perceptions du pouvoir chez les historiennes du Haut Moyen Age', *Les femmes au Moyen Age*, ed. M. Rouche, Paris 1990, 77–85.

——, 'Gender and Genre in women historians of the early middle ages', *L'historiographie médiévale en Europe*, Paris 1991, 149–63.

Neville, G., 'Fox eats heron in learned Irish love poetry', *Mythes, croyances et religions dans le monde Anglo-Saxon*, Université d'Avignon X, 1992, 83–96.

Ní Annracháin, Máire, '"Ait liom bean a bheith ina file"', *Léachtaí Cholm Cille* XII: *na mná sa litríocht*, Maynooth 1982, 145–82.

Ní Chatháin, P. and Richter, M., eds, *Irland und Europa: Die Kirche in Frühmittelalter*, Tübingen 1984.

—— and Richter, M., eds, *Irland und die Christenheit. Bibelstudien und Mission: Ireland and Christendom, the Bible and the missions*, Stuttgart 1987.

Nicholls, K., *Gaelic and gaelicised Ireland in the Middle Ages*, Dublin 1972.

——, 'Irishwomen and property in the sixteenth century', *Women in early modern Ireland*, eds M. MacCurtain and M. O'Dowd, Edinburgh 1992, 1–31.

Ní Dhonnchadha, Máirin, 'The guarantor list of *Cáin Adomnáin*', *Peritia* I, 1982, 178–215.

——, 'The *Lex innocentium*: Adomnan's law for women, clerics and youths, 697 A.D.' in *Chattel, servant or citizen*, O'Dowd and Wichert, eds, 58–69.

——, 'Two female lovers', *Ériu* XLV, 1994, 113–20

Noble, P., *Love and marriage in Chrétien de Troyes*, Cardiff 1982.

Noonan, John T., 'Power to choose', *Viator* IV, 1973, 419–34.

Ó Baoill, Colm, *Bàrdachd Sìlis na Ceapaich c.1660–c.1729*, Edinburgh 1972.

—— and Bateman, Meg, *Gàir nan clàrsach: The harps' cry: an anthology of 17th century Gaelic poetry*, Edinburgh, 1994.

Ó Caithnia, L., *Apalóga na bhFilí, 1200–1645*, Dublin 1984.

O'Connor, Frank, *A short history of Irish literature: a backward look*, New York 1967 [English edition, *The backward look: a survey of Irish literature*, London 1967].

Ó Corráin, Donnchadh, 'Irish law and canon law', *Irland und Europa*, eds Ní Chatháin and Richter, Tübingen 1984, 157–66.

——, 'Irish vernacular law and the Old Testamant', *Irland und die Christenheit*, eds Ní Chatháin and Richter, Stuttgart 1987, 284–307.

——, 'Marriage in early Ireland', *Marriage in Ireland*, ed. Cosgrove, Dublin 1985, 5–24.

——, 'Nationality and kingship in pre-Norman Ireland', *Nationality*, ed. Moody, Belfast 1978, 1–35.

——, 'Women and the Law in Early Ireland' in *Chattel, Servant or Citizen: Women's Status in Church, State and Society*, eds M. O'Dowd and S. Wichert, Belfast 1995, 45–57.

——, 'Women in early Irish society', *Women in Irish society: the historical dimension*, eds M. MacCurtain and D. Ó Corráin, Dublin 1978, 1–13.

——, Breatnach, Liam and Breen, Aidan, 'The laws of the Irish', *Peritia* III, 1984, 382–438.

——, Breatnach, Liam and McCone, Kim, eds, *Sages, saints and storytellers: Celtic studies in honour of Professor James Carney*, Maynooth 1989.

O'Donoghue, B., *The courtly love tradition*, Manchester 1982.

O'Dowd, M. and Wichert, S., eds, *Chattel, servant or citizen: women's status in church, state and society*, Belfast 1995.

Ó hAodha, Donncha, 'The lament of the Old Woman of Beare', *Sages, saints and storytellers*, ed. D. Ó Corráin, et al., Maynooth 1989, 308–31.

O'Leary, Philip, 'The honour of women in early Irish literature', *Ériu* XXXVIII, 1987, 27–44.

Origo, I., *The merchant of Prato*, Harmondsworth 1963.

Orme, N., *From childhood to chivalry: the education of the English kings and aristocracy 1066–1530*, London 1984.

Orpen, G.H., *Ireland under the Normans, 1169–1333*, 4 vols, Oxford 1911–20.

Orpen, G.H., 'The Fitzgeralds, barons of Offaly' in *Journal of the Royal Society of Antiquaries of Ireland*, XLIV, 1914, 99–113.

Ó Súilleabháin, Seán, *Irish wake amusements*, Cork 1967.

Ó Túama, Seán, *Caoineadh Airt Uí Laoghaire*, Dublin 1961.

Owst, G.R., *Literature and pulpit in medieval England*, Oxford 1961.

Paden, William D., *The voice of the trobairitz: perspectives on the women troubadours*, Philadelphia 1989.

Painter, Sidney, 'To whom were dedicated the *Fables* of Marie de France?', *Modern Language Notes* XLVIII, 1933, 367–9.

Partner, Nancy, ed., *Studying medieval women* = *Speculum* LXVIII, 1993, 305ff.

Pevsner, N., *Northamptonshire*, Harmondsworth 1973.

Phillips, J.R.S., 'The mission of John de Hothum to Ireland, 1315–1316', *England and Ireland in the later middle ages*, ed. J.F. Lydon, Dublin 1981, 62–85.

Phillips, M., *The memoir of Marco Parenti: a life in Medici Florence*, Princeton and Guildford 1987.

Plummer, John F., ed., *Vox feminae: studies in medieval woman's song*, Kalamazoo, 1981.

Pollard, M., ed., *Property and Politics: essays in later medieval English history*, Gloucester 1984.

Powell, W. R., ed., *A history of the county of Essex*, IV, Oxford 1956.

Power, E., *Medieval women*, ed. M.M. Postan, Cambridge 1975.

Power, Nancy, 'Classes of women described in the Senchas Már', *Studies in early Irish law*, ed. Binchy, Dublin 1936, 81–108.

Powicke, F.M., *The thirteenth century*, Oxford 1953.

Pratt, R.A., 'Chaucer and the hand that fed him', *Speculum* XLI, 1966, 619–42.

Pryce, Huw, 'Early Irish canons and medieval Welsh law', *Peritia* V, 1986, 107–27.

Queller, D.E. and Madden, T.F., 'Father of the bride: fathers, daughters and dowries in late medieval and early Renaissance Venice', *Renaissance Quarterly* XLVI, 1993, 685–711.

Quin, E.G., 'The early Irish poem *Ísucán*', *Cambridge Medieval Celtic Studies* I, 1981, 39–53.

Quinn, D.B., 'Henry VIII and Ireland 1509–1534', *Irish Historical Studies* XII, 1960–1.

——, *The Elizabethans and the Irish*, Ithaca 1966.

Ramsey, Lee C., *Chivalric romances*, Bloomington 1983.

Reynolds, Roger E., 'Unity and diversity in Carolingian canon law: the case of the *Collectio Hibernensis*', *Carolingian essays: Andrew W. Mellon lectures in early Christian studies*, ed. Uta-Renate Blumenthal, Washington 1983, 99–135.

Richardson, H.G. and Sayles, G.O., *The Irish parliament in the middle ages*, Pennsylvania and London, 2nd ed., 1964.

Richmond, C., *The Paston family in the fifteenth century: The first phase*, Cambridge 1990.

——, 'The Pastons revisited: marriage and the family in fifteenth-century England', *Bulletin of the Institute of Historical Research*, LVIII, 1985, 25–36.

Rickert, E., 'A leaf from a fourteenth-century letter book', *Modern Philology*, XXV, 1927–8, 249–55.

Riemer, S., 'Women, dowries and capital investment in thirteenth-century Siena', *The marriage bargain: women and dowries in European history*, ed. M.A. Kaplan, *Women and History* X, 1985, 59–79.

Robertson, D.W., 'The concept of courtly love as an impediment to the understanding of medieval texts', *The meaning of courtly love*, ed. F.X. Newman, New York 1973, 1–18.

Robinson, Fred C., 'Old English poetry: the question of authorship', *The tomb of Beowulf and other essays on Old English*, Oxford 1993, 164–9.

Romano, D., *Patricians and popolani: the social foundations of the Venetian Renaissance state*, Baltimore and London, 1987.

Rosenthal, E.G., 'The position of women in Renaissance Florence: neither autonomy nor subjection', *Florence and Italy: renaissance studies in honour of Nicolai Rubinstein*, eds P. Denley and C. Elam, London 1988, 369–81.

Rosenthal, J.T., ed., *Medieval women and the sources of medieval history*, Athens, Ga. 1990.

——, 'Aristocratic marriage and the English peerage, 1350–1500: social institution and personal bond', *Journal of Medieval History*, X, 1984, 181–94.

Roskell, J.S., Clark, L. and Rawcliffe, C., *The House of Commons 1386–1421*, 4 vols, History of Parliament Trust, Stroud, 1992.

Ross, Margaret Clunies, 'Concubinage in Anglo-Saxon England', *Past and Present* CVIII, 1985, 3–34.

Ryan, John, 'The *Cáin Adomnáin*', *Studies in early Irish law*, ed. D.A. Binchy, Dublin 1936, 269–76.

Sankovitch, Tilde A., *French women writers and the book*, Syracuse 1988.

Sawyer, 'Roger, *we are but women': women in Ireland's history*, London 1993.

Schmitt, J.-Cl., *Prêcheurs d'exemples: ecrits de prédicateurs du Moyen Age*, Paris 1985.

Shahar, S., *Childhood in the Middle Ages*, London 1990.

Sheehan, Michael M., 'Choice of marriage partner in the Middle Ages: development and mode of application of a theory of marriage', *Studies in Medieval and Renaissance History* I (old ser. vol. XI), 1978, 3–33.

Sheehy, Maurice P., 'The *Collectio Canonum Hibernensis*, a Celtic phenomenon', *Die Iren und Europa*, ed. H. Löwe, Tübingen 1982, 525–35.

——, 'The Bible and the *Collectio Canonum Hibernensis*', *Irland und die Christenheit*, eds P. Ní Chathain and M. Richter, Stuttgart 1987, 277–83.

Showalter, Elaine, 'Feminist criticism in the wilderness', *The New Feminist Criticism*, ed. E. Showalter, London 1986, 243–70.

Sims-Williams, Patrick, *Religion and literature in Western England, 600–800*, Cambridge 1990.

Simms, Katharine, 'The legal position of Irishwomen in the later Middle Ages', *Irish Jurist* X, 1975, 96–111.

——, 'The poet as chieftain's widow: bardic elegies', *Sages, saints and story-tellers*, ed. D. Ó Corráin et al., Maynooth 1989, 400–11.

——, 'Women in Anglo-Norman Ireland', *Women in Irish society*, eds M. Mac Curtain and D. Ó Corráin, Dublin 1978, 15–25.

——, 'Women in Gaelic society during the age of transition', *Women in early modern Ireland*, eds M. MacCurtain and M. O'Dowd, Dublin 1991, 32–42.

Smith, Roland M., ed., 'The alphabet of Cuigne mac Emoin', *Zeitschrift für celtische Philologie* XVII, 1928, 45–72.

——, ed., 'The *Senbríathra Fíthail* and related texts', *Revue Celtique* XLV, 1928, 1–92.

Squire, A., *Aelred of Rievaulx: a study*, London 1969.

Stacey, Robin, ed., '*Berrad Airechta*: an Old Irish tract on suretyship' in *Lawyers and laymen*, eds T. Charles-Edwards, M.E. Owen and D.B. Walters, Cardiff 1986, 210–33.

Stone, L., *The family, sex and marriage in England 1500–1800*, London 1977.

Strubel, A., 'Exemple, fable, parabole: le récit bref figuré au moyen age', *Le Moyen Age* XCIV, pts 3–4, 341–61.

Stuard, Susan Mosher, 'Sources on medieval women in Mediterranean archives', *Medieval women and the sources of medieval history*, ed. J.T. Rosenthal, Athens, Ga. 1990, 342–58.

Swanson, J., 'Childhood and childrearing in *ad status* sermons by later thirteenth century friars', *Journal of Medieval History*, XVI, 1990, 309–31.

Thomson, Derick, *An introduction to Gaelic poetry*, Edinburgh 1990.

——, ed., *The companion to Gaelic Scotland*, rev. ed. Glasgow 1994.

Thurneysen, Rudolf, ed., 'Aus dem irischen Recht i: 1. Das Unfrei-Lehen', *Zeitschrift für celtische Philologie* XIV, 1923, 335–94.

——, ed., 'Aus dem irischen Recht iii: 4. Die falschen Urteilssprüche Caratnia's; 5. Zur Überlieferung und zur Ausgabe der Texte über das Unfrei-Lehen und das Frei-Lehen', *Zeitschrift für celtische Philologie* XV, 1925, 302–76.

——, ed., *Cóic Conara Fugill. Die fünf Wege zum Urteil*. Abhandlungen der preussischen Akademie der Wissenschaften. Jahrgang 1925. Phil.-Hist. Klasse Nr. 7. Berlin 1927.

——, ed., 'Aus dem irischen Recht iv: 6. Zu den bisherigen Ausgaben der Irischen Rechtstexte', *Zeitschrift für celtische Philologie* XVI, 1927, 167–230.

——, ed., *Die Bürgschaft im irischen Recht*. Abhandlungen der preussischen Akademie der Wissenschaften. Jahrgang 1928. Phil.-Hist. Klasse Nr. 2. Berlin 1928.

——, ed., 'Aus dem irischen Recht v: 7. Zu *Gúbretha Caratniad*; 8. Zur der

Etymologie von irisch *ráth* 'Bürgschaft' und zu der irischen Kanonensammlung und den Triaden; 10 Nachträge zur Bürgschaft', *Zeitschrift für celtische Philologie* XVIII, 1930, 353–408.

——, ed., *Irisches Recht* (I *Díre*. Ein altirischer Rechtstext; II Zu den unteren Ständen in Irland). Abhandelungen der preussischen Akademie der Wissenschaften, 1931. Phil.-hist. Klasse 2. Berlin 1931.

——, ed., '*Cáin Lánamna*: "Die Regelung der Paare"', *Studies in early Irish law*, ed. D.A. Binchy, Dublin 1936, 1–80.

——, ed., 'Heirat', *Studies in early Irish law*, ed. D.A. Binchy, Dublin 1936, 109–28.

——, 'Mittelirische Verslehren', *Irische texte* III.1, eds W. Stokes and E. Windisch, 1891, 1–182.

Tobin, Rosemary Barton, 'Vincent of Beauvais on the education of women', *Journal of the History of Ideas*, XXXV, 1974, 485–489.

Topsfield, L.T., '*Fin'amors* in Marcabru, Bernart de Ventadorn and the *Lancelot* of Chrétien de Troyes', in *Love and marriage in the twelfth century*, *Mediaevalia Lovaniensia* Ser 1/ Studia VIII, Leuven 1981, 236–49.

Trexler, R.C., 'In search of a father: the experience of abandonment in the recollections of Giovanni di Pagolo Morelli', *History of Childhood Quarterly* III, 1975, 225–52.

Tubach, F.C., *Index exemplorum: A handbook of medieval religious tales*, Helsinki, Suomalainen Tiedeakatemia Akademia Scientiarum Fennica, 1969.

van Houts, Elisabeth, 'Women and the writing of history in the early Middle Ages: the case of abbess Matilda of Essen and Aethelweard', *Early Medieval Europe* I, 1992, 53–68.

——, 'The state of research: women in medieval history and literature', *Journal of Medieval History* XX, 1994, 277–92.

Van Vleck, Amelia E., '*Tost me troubaretz fenida*: Reicrocating composition in the songs of Castelloza', *The voice of the trobaritz: perspectives on the women troubadours*, ed. William D. Paden, Philadelphia 1989, 95–111.

Vinaver, E., *The rise of romance*, 1969.

Wagner, H., 'Zu *Gúbretha Caratniad* §39', *Ériu* XX, 1966, 66.

Walsh, P. and Ó Fiannachta, P., *Catalogue of Irish Manuscripts in Maynooth College Library: Clár Láimhscríbhinní Gaeilge Choláiste Phádraig Má Nuadh*, 8 vols, Maynooth 1943–73.

Walters, D.B., *The comparative legal method: marriage, divorce and the spouse's property rights in early medieval European law and Cyfraith Hywel* (Pamphlets on Welsh law), Aberystwyth 1982.

——, 'The European legal context of the Welsh law of matrimonial property" in *The Welsh law of women*, D.Jenkins and M.E. Owen eds, Cardiff 1980, 115–31.

Ward, Jennifer, *English noblewomen in the later Middle Ages*, London 1992.

Wasserschleben. H., ed., *Die irische Kanonensammlung*, 2nd ed., Leipzig 1885.

Watson, J. Carmichael, ed., *The Gaelic songs of Mary MacLeod*, London/ Glasgow 1934.

Watson, W.J., *Scottish verse from the Book of the Dean of Lismore*, Edinburgh 1937.

Weisweiler, Josepf, 'Die Stellung der Frau bei den Kelten und das Problem des "keltischen Mutterrechts"', *Zeitschrift für celtische Philologie* XXI, 1940, 205–79.

Welter, J.T, *L'exemplum dans la littérature religieuse et didactique du moyen age*, Paris/Toulouse 1927, reprinted Geneva 1973.

Wemple, Suzanne Fonay, *Women in Frankish society: marriage and the cloister, 500 to 900*, Philadelphia 1981.

Wilson, Katharina M., ed., *Medieval women writers*, Athens, Ga. 1984.

Wood, Ian, 'Pagans and holy men, 600–800', *Irland und die Christenheit. Bibelstudien und Mission*, eds Próinseas Ní Chatháin and Michael Richter, Stuttgart, 1987, 347–61.

Woulfe, Patrick, *Sloinnte Gaedheal is Gall: Irish names and surnames*, Dublin 1923.

Wright, A.P., ed., *A history of the county of Cambridgeshire and the isle of Ely*, VIII, Oxford 1982.

Wylie, J.H., *History of England under Henry the Fourth*, 4 vols, London, 1884–98.

List of Contributors

THOMAS OWEN CLANCY obtained his Ph.D. at University of Edinburgh for a thesis 'The Saga of Liadán and Cuirither' and now teaches in the Department of Celtic Studies, University of Glasgow.

BART JASKI is a history graduate of Utrecht, with an M.Phil. from University College, Cork. He obtained his Ph.D. at Trinity College, Dublin in 1995, for a thesis on 'Irish Regnal Succession 900–1200 A.D.'

MARY MC AULIFFE obtained her Ph.D. at Trinity College, Dublin in 1992 for a thesis 'The Tower Houses of Co. Kerry' and, after teaching in Canada, is now researching in Dublin.

ELIZABETH MC KENNA obtained her B.A. in history and history of art at Trinity College, Dublin and is now doing post-graduate work on patronage in medieval Ireland.

CHRISTINE MEEK is Associate Professor in Department of Medieval History at Trinity College, Dublin. She has written three books on Italian history and several articles on medieval Italian women and is at present working on Women in the Commune of Lucca.

GRACE NEVILLE is a member of the Department of French, University College, Cork. She is the author of numerous articles on the relationship between French and Irish literature.

CORMAC Ó CLEIRIGH is a Ph.D. student at Trinity College, Dublin and is currently preparing thesis on John FitzThomas, 1st earl of Kildare.

KATHARINE SIMMS is a Senior Lecturer in the Department of Medieval History at Trinity College, Dublin, and is concerned with the social history and literature of Gaelic Ireland, especially bardic poetry. She is the author of *Irish warlords: the changing political structure of Gaelic Ireland in the later Middle Ages* (Boydell Press, 1987).

JENNIFER WARD is Senior Lecturer at Goldsmiths' College, University of London and is the author of two recent books, *English noblewomen in the later Middle Ages* (Longman, 1992) and *Women of the English nobil-*

ity and gentry 1066–1500 (Manchester, 1995). She is now developing this work in new directions.

BERNADETTE WILLIAMS is a graduate of Trinity College, Dublin who obtained her Ph.D. in 1991 for a thesis on Irish Franciscan Chronicles. She teaches an evening course on medieval women at Trinity and has a special interest in literature.

DAVID BERESFORD compiled the index.

Index

Modern authors are placed in italics